Exam Schools

● ● ● ● ● ● ● ● ●

Exam Schools

Inside America's Most Selective Public High Schools

Chester E. Finn, Jr., and **Jessica A. Hockett**

Princeton University Press

Princeton and Oxford

Published by Princeton University Press, 41 William Street, Princeton, New Jersey 08540
In the United Kingdom: Princeton University Press, 6 Oxford Street, Woodstock, Oxford-
    shire OX20 1TW

press.princeton.edu

Library of Congress Cataloging-in-Publication Data
Finn, Chester E., 1944- author.
    Exam schools : inside America's most selective public high schools / Chester E. Finn, Jr.,
and Jessica A. Hockett.
        pages cm
    Includes bibliographical references and index.
    ISBN 978-0-691-15667-5 (hardcover : alk. paper)
        1. High schools—United States—Case studies.   2. Public schools—United States—
Case studies.   3. College preparation programs—United States—Case studies.
I. Hockett, Jessica A., author.   II. Title.
    LB1620.F46 2012
    373.22'40973—dc23   2012015184

British Library Cataloging-in-Publication Data is available

This book has been composed in Verdigris MVB Pro Text

Printed on acid-free paper. ∞

Printed in the United States of America

10 9 8 7 6 5 4 3 2 1

For our children and grandchildren—
Emma, Alexandra, *and* Isabel Finn, Mason *and* Harley Hockett:
May they be both well schooled and well educated.

Contents

• • • • • •

Introduction

• • • • • •

Selective public high schools that serve motivated kids and high achievers, many of them also very smart, have been a tiny but important part of the U.S. secondary-education landscape for generations. Some are world famous and boast celebrated alumni/ae. Others may be virtually unknown beyond their immediate communities, but there they often play distinctive and highly valued roles.

Yet nowhere can one learn much about this galaxy within the American secondary-schooling universe. There's no orderly list of these schools, nor any trade association to which they all belong—and that hires lobbyists and publicists to advance their interests. Many have low profiles, perhaps intentionally so. They don't hold great interest for contemporary education reformers, philanthropists, or elected officials, most of whom concentrate on the challenges of *low*-achieving and disadvantaged youngsters. They've also been largely ignored by scholars and analysts. If they appear at all in the media, it's usually because of some diversity- or fairness-related ruckus involving their admissions practices. And practically nobody except those directly involved seems to know what actually goes on inside them.

Our purpose in this book is to explore this obscure yet consequential corner of the public-education cosmos, mindful that these schools intersect in important ways with four urgent policy challenges facing American education.

First, is the United States providing *all* of its young people the education that they need in order to make the most of their capacities, both for their own sake and for that of the larger society?

Second, have we neglected to raise the ceiling while we've struggled to lift the floor? As the country strives to toughen its academic standards, close its wide achievement gaps, repair its bad schools, and "leave no child behind," is it also challenging its high-achieving and highly motivated students—and those who may not yet be high achievers but can learn substantially more than the minimum?[1] Are we as determined to build more great schools as to repair those that have collapsed?

Third, is America making wise investments in its own future prosperity and security by ensuring that its high-potential children are well prepared to break new ground and assume leadership roles on multiple fronts?

Finally, at a time when we're creating new school choices and individual learning opportunities of many kinds, as well as the means for many more families to avail themselves of those options, are we paying sufficient attention to *this* kind of choice: the academically selective high school, and the learning opportunities it offers to youngsters with the capacity and inclination to benefit from them?

All are serious, complicated issues that bear on America's future, and we don't promise to settle them here. We do, however, promise to escort readers into a fascinating sector within public education that illustrates the larger challenges while offering at least a partial response to them.

The book is organized into three sections. In part I, we explain how we defined and identified the "academically selective public high schools" that belong on our list (which can be found in appendix I.) We also supply considerable information about the schools as a group and how they compare with public high schools in general.

Part II features profiles of eleven schools that we visited in nine states and the District of Columbia. Each illustrates unique approaches to finding, selecting, and educating eager and talented students beyond the traditional high school environment. Following these profiles, we reflect on trends, patterns, and differences that we observed among them.

In part III, we discuss some of the issues, challenges, and policy choices that these schools pose and offer our own thoughts regarding the role of schools like these in addressing the great challenges of American education.

Appendix I explains our school identification and selection methods in greater detail and names the 165 schools that made it through our filters.

Appendix II reproduces the survey that we sent to principals or senior administrators at all those schools.

This project was a joint undertaking of the Thomas B. Fordham Institute and the Task Force on K–12 Education of Stanford University's Hoover Institution. It has been supported by both of those organizations as well as the Kern Family Foundation, for whose assistance we are deeply appreciative.

We received invaluable help from innumerable people, including (but most definitely not limited to) Jay Mathews of the *Washington Post*; Caroline Hoxby of Stanford University and other members of the Hoover Institution's Task Force on K–12 Education, as well as John Raisian and Richard Sousa from the Hoover high command; Chris Irvine and Mike Petrilli of the Fordham Institute; Stephanie Pace Marshall, President Emerita of the Illinois Mathematics and Science Academy; Rena Subotnik of the American Psychological Association; Jay Thomas of Aurora University; Patrick Keaton at the National Center for Education Statistics; Bernadette Hamilton with the Jefferson County (KY) Public Schools; Sarah Newell Usdin of New Schools for New Orleans; Jenny DeMonte of the University of Michigan; Cara Kranz of the Chicago Public Schools; Michael Schlesinger and Tonya Wolford of the School District of Philadelphia; Katie Brohawn of the New York City Department of Education; Linda Wallinger of the Virginia Department of Education; Philadelphia journalist Kristen Graham; Bill Jackson, Benjamin Jokerst, and Liz Richard of Great Schools.net; Robert Morse of *U.S. News*; Mary Ann Boylan of Dr. T. J. Owens Early College Academy; Holly McLean of Treasure Valley Mathematics and Science Center; and the hospitable, informative, well-organized, and helpful principals of the schools we visited: Kenneth Bonamo, Russell Davis, Evan Glazer, Steve Largo, Scott Lipton, Eric McLaren, Joseph Powers, Timothy Rusnak, Kathy Scott, Richard Trogisch, and Daniel Withers. Our sincere thanks to them all, to our tolerant and supportive families, and to Peter Dougherty and his terrific crew at Princeton University Press— including two anonymous reviewers whose editorial advice was both insightful and encouraging.

Part I

• • • •

The Big Picture

Chapter 1

History and Context

• • • • • • • • • •

The main trajectory of American schooling over the past century has been the gradual widening of access and raising of educational expectations for ever-larger portions of the nation's youthful population.

Though elementary schooling was nearly universal by 1910, just 13.5 percent of that year's adult population (twenty-five and older) had graduated from high school. Fifty years later, the corresponding figure was 41.1 percent. Today, about 87 percent tell the Census Bureau that they are high school graduates.[1]

This striking expansion of secondary schooling in the United States was driven by a quartet of forces, beginning with the human capital demands of a changing economy, which needed ever-more-educated workers for ever-more-sophisticated jobs. Pushing plows, joining nuts to bolts on assembly lines, and stitching garments in attic sweatshops would no longer suffice.

Second was the increasing prosperity that accompanied those more sophisticated jobs, which meant that more families could spare more children from work for more years even as states and towns could afford to pay for more schools and teachers.

Third were social justice and equity considerations, such that educational opportunities once open mostly to able-bodied, middle-class, white males were gradually extended to pretty much everybody.

And finally was the ceaseless quest by many Americans for upward mobility and a better life for their sons and daughters, accompanied by keen awareness that the more education their kids obtained, the better their prospects for advancement. (College-going burgeoned, too, especially after World War II.)

As time passed, we went from propping open the high school's back door to expecting just about everyone to spend three or four years inside and then emerge through the front door with a diploma in hand. In the three decades from 1930 to 1960, the ratio of graduates to 17-year-olds in the U.S. population soared from 29 to 70 percent. (It has since leveled at about 75 percent.) To keep pace with such swelling enrollments, the number of high schools rose, individual schools grew, and the overwhelming majority of them welcomed all comers.

One challenge posed by these expanding opportunities and rising expectations was—and remains—that not all young people want the same thing from high school, bring the same talents and interests with them to the schoolhouse door, or have the same post-graduation goals. Not all are equally prepared for advanced courses, and certainly not all enjoy the same resources and support structures in their lives. Nor can anyone say with certainty—though opinions on this vary widely—how many of the same things society can legitimately ask them all to learn, a dilemma that deepens as children progress farther in school. It's one thing to expect every eight-year-old to learn to read; it's quite another to declare that every sixteen-year-old must master biology, Shakespeare, or Mandarin.

Such complications have long confronted educators and policy makers with difficult quandaries about how to structure and organize high schools and their offerings. It wasn't so hard, back in the old days, to provide a smallish, elite population with the sort of classical education that was expected by a smallish number of elite colleges and universities, primarily on the East Coast. It was, however, a far more difficult challenge to decide what sorts of curricula, instructional programs, standards, and structures are best suited to mass secondary education.

Some educators held that high schools should fit young people for predetermined niches in life, while others insisted that everyone deserved a fair shot at multiple options. Some urged the schools to provide a single core curriculum for all; others declared that schools must specialize in "academic" or "vocational" (or other) programs; and still others favored multiple tracks within "comprehensive" high schools.

The "comprehensive-with-tracks" version gradually came to dominate the American secondary education scene, particularly after former Harvard president James B. Conant endorsed it in an influential 1959 book. Comprehensive did not mean uniform, however. Educators in the United States (and abroad) have long done battle over this, too. On one hand are those whose top priority is universality and commonality of curriculum, whether for civic ends (we must all learn the same things if we're to hang together as a nation and culture) or for egalitarian reasons (everyone should have access to the same opportunities and nobody deserves a "better" education than anyone else.) On the other hand are those who believe that individual (and sometimes group) differences ought to be recognized, celebrated, and accommodated by an education system committed to furnishing each person the course of study that is best suited to him or her.

By and large, public education has sought to have it both ways, trying to offer equal access to high-quality options but doing so through multiple routes and pathways. Hence our "comprehensive" high schools have nearly always offered multiple curricula tailored for students with differing interests and post-high-school plans. Everyone sat under the same roof but not always in the same classrooms. Most common were the "academic" or "college-prep" track for those aspiring to matriculate to universities; the "vocational" track for those who were headed to work after graduating and had a good idea of the trade they would pursue; and the "general" track for almost everyone else.

But comprehensive-with-tracking was never the sole model for secondary education. Many communities and some states also operated specialized high schools designed for particular missions, needs, or clienteles, particularly in the vocational realm—and often aligned with the human-capital requirements of local employers. Putnam, Connecticut, for example, established a "trade school" in 1915 to develop skilled workers for area textile mills.

Other high schools concentrated on educating exceptional students. These included disabled youngsters, beginning with those who were blind or deaf. (The Missouri School for the Deaf was founded in 1851.) In time, there also emerged magnet schools to foster integration by offering distinctive programs designed to draw youngsters of all races from multiple neighborhoods within the community. And, as we explain below, American education has long included a small number of supercharged high schools aimed at youngsters with uncommon academic talent and/or prior achievement.

How to Educate Smart Kids?

One source of the complexity of American secondary education is the reality that kids differ greatly in their strengths and abilities as well as in their levels of motivation and background experiences. Some come to high school quicker, keener, and more motivated than others—whether due to economic advantage, parental prodding, excellent teaching, genetic good fortune, or other factors.

We've devised a variety of approaches to educating such high-potential and high-performing students at the secondary level. Numerous options have been created within regular high schools via tracking, streaming, and special programs or course sequences. "Honors" tracks and Advanced Placement (AP) classes have provided additional opportunities for challenge and, in the case of AP, the chance to earn college credit. In some places, secondary pupils can also take courses at a local university, sometimes during the summer, sometimes online, sometimes as part of the regular school day. Early-entrance-to-college programs invite qualified teens to augment (or, in some cases, replace) their high school diploma with an associate's or bachelor's degree. Some high-potential middle schoolers gain opportunities for summer study on university campuses through programs such as Duke's Talent Identification Program and Johns Hopkins's Center for Talented Youth. And myriad extracurricular activities and competitions (e.g., Scholastic Bowl, Intel Science Talent Search) are intended to develop and reward academic promise beyond the classroom setting.

A less common approach to educating academically talented high schoolers has been to create entirely separate schools for them within the public-education system. These may be thought of as "whole-school" versions of the "honors track"—and are the focus of this book.

The Early Days

Some selective schools have been around for a long time (though not always with the admissions procedures that characterize them today). New York's original Townsend Harris High School (profiled in chapter 10) was founded in 1848. Louisville's Central High School (profiled in chapter 6) opened its doors—to "children of the African race"—in 1870. San Francisco's Lowell High School also began in the late nineteenth century. Worcester, Massachusetts, opened a citywide secondary program for children with advanced intellectual abilities in 1901. And the great-granddaddy of them all, the Boston Latin School, proudly traces its ancestry to 1635 and is recognized as our country's first public school. (Five of its former students signed the Declaration of Independence.)

Other schools were founded—or restarted or revamped—specifically to identify and serve youngsters of unusual ability, and in short order found it necessary to develop processes to screen and select among their would-be students. Cincinnati's Walnut Hills dates its selectivity and "classical" focus to 1919. The Bronx High School of Science was launched (for boys only) in 1938. New Orleans's Benjamin Franklin High School (profiled in chapter 9) started in the Sputnik year of 1957. The North Carolina School of Mathematics and Science opened in 1980 as a state-sponsored residential high school for exceptionally talented juniors and seniors—and inspired a dozen similar schools in other states. (In chapter 4, we profile one of these, the Illinois Mathematics and Science Academy.)

The number of such schools has never been large and, by our count, is only about 165 today, with the majority having begun in the relatively recent past. Of the 58 that supplied founding dates to us, only 13 existed before World War II and another 21 launched between Pearl Harbor and 1990. Surprisingly, half the schools for which we have this information are creations of the past two decades.

These schools arose in their different eras from a quintet of distinct yet overlapping challenges and policy objectives. Most straightforward was the desire to provide a self-contained, high-powered college-prep education for able youngsters, usually within a single community but sometimes on a county or regional basis, occasionally statewide. This impulse sometimes arose within the public-education system itself, such as a district superintendent or school board member particularly concerned with the acceleration or enrichment of gifted students. Elsewhere it emerged from government or civic and business leaders or from agitated parents concerned about educational opportunities for their own progeny.

Some universities chose to foster and occasionally to launch such schools, sometimes as "laboratories" for their own scholars and trainees, sometimes to accommodate faculty children, sometimes as a service to surrounding communities.

Philanthropic initiatives played a role, too, such as the Gates Foundation–funded effort to create specialized and distinctive "small high schools" and "early college" models to serve disadvantaged students, as well as the occasional benefactor (e.g., Nevada's Davidson Institute) with a keen interest in the education of exceptionally able youngsters.

A fourth driver of the establishment of such schools was the country's effort to desegregate—and integrate—its public-education system. Some of this was court ordered or sanctioned, while some was pushed by civil rights enforcers and activists or stimulated by federal "magnet school" dollars.

Finally, there were economic imperatives, particularly the need to strengthen the workforce, meet the human-capital requirements of a modernizing economy (e.g., STEM schools, which focus on science, technology, engineering, and mathematics), or develop individuals to work on the cutting edge of future innovation, invention, and scientific advancement. Though most such economy-boosting impulses were local, some came from the state level, often from governors keen to develop particular regions, strengthen the workforce, retain talent, or polish their states' reputations as places that took education and human capital seriously.

To the likely surprise of some readers, with rare exceptions (mainly in Louisiana), the schools we examine in these pages are *not* charter schools.[2] Although they're "schools of choice," they are operated in more top-down fashion by districts, states, or sometimes universities rather than as freestanding and self-propelled institutions under their states' charter laws. Perhaps they would be better off as charters, considering the ways that many are constrained by the larger systems of which they're part. But a central tenet of the charter movement holds that schools should *not* select among their applicants. If demand exceeds supply, charters in almost every state are obligated to use lotteries to determine which youngsters end up enrolling in them. This is not just a matter of doctrine among charter advocates but also a prerequisite for specialized federal start-up financing. As a result, some charter schools are academically high powered and some are high achieving. But almost none are academically selective.

The schools we're focused on *are* academically selective (though not all are high achieving). But they're all public schools, paid for and operated by governmental agencies and free to their attendees. Private schools—almost all of which are selective in various ways—don't qualify for our list. That does not, however, mean the public schools that do qualify are available to every youngster who might benefit from them.

In the early days, virtually all these schools had similar curricula— whatever courses and sequences the leading colleges of the time expected of their applicants, much as one would find at private prep schools like Andover or Deerfield. But they differed (from each other and over time) in how they defined eligibility and handled admissions. (We discuss today's admissions scene in chapter 3 as well as in parts II and III of this book.) Townsend Harris High School—originally a direct feeder into the City College of New York—began using entrance exams in the early 1930s and by 1940 was admitting fewer than one in six of its applicants. Stuyvesant, on the other hand, began in 1904 as a "manual training" school for boys but swiftly became known for its excellence in math and science and turned into a selective-admission academic high school by 1920. (It commenced entrance testing around the same time as Townsend Harris.)

Academic criteria aside, these early schools were typically limited to boys, and few welcomed black students (though a small number in the segregated south enrolled black youngsters exclusively).[3] They were rare in small-town and rural America, uncommon in suburbia, and almost unheard of in very poor communities. Some cities (and states) created options of this sort while others had none at all. (San Francisco did, Los Angeles didn't.)

As for wealth, one didn't have to pay money to enroll in such schools. Yet even where special-admission public high schools existed, they were not always within easy reach of poor families. That situation is better today: our data indicate that they enroll almost as large a proportion of low-income youngsters as are found in American public secondary education generally (table 3.4). But that does not necessarily mean that every individual school is easily accessible to low-income families.

For these schools to be realistic options for children, parents need sufficient means to transport their youngsters across town each day—and must *not* need them urgently to earn money, learn a useful trade, or help around the house. Moreover, to qualify for supercharged high schools, students must generally attend solid primary and junior high (or middle) schools. It also helps if their homes and neighborhoods are amply supplied with books, periodicals, and intellectually active people. That's true today—and has been since the beginning.

Can We Be Equal and Excellent, Too?

That was the question posed by Carnegie Corporation president (and future Health, Education, and Welfare secretary) John W. Gardner in his influential 1961 book *Excellence*, and it still speaks to competing policy priorities in American education and the extent to which we value (or deplore) the kinds of schools described in these pages.

But Gardner was not the first to probe this quandary. American democracy has always contained an inherent tension—some say a contradiction—between the pursuit of greater equality and uniformity for all and the quest to maximize individual achievement and prosperity via competition and diversity.

This tension has emerged repeatedly in U.S. education policy over the past half century, often framed as a competition between "quality" and "equality" (or "equity"). Educators and policy makers love to declare that we can do both without sacrificing either, and occasionally the dual objectives do get fused. Academically oriented "magnet" programs meant to foster integration by appealing to parents of every race who want an enriched or accelerated education program for their kids are one example. Today's move to widen access to AP courses and encourage more poor and minority youngsters to enroll in them is another.

Still, successful attempts to realize both ideals are rare. In the real world of limited resources and energies, most of our policy priorities and programs have tended to emphasize one mission or the other—and to shift between them as perceived needs and external catalysts changed.

Not surprisingly, academically oriented, selective-entry schools for high-achieving youngsters have generally enjoyed greater favor when "quality" has been in the ascendancy. But not always.

Sputnik-induced alarm about the country's intellectual prowess and technical competence gave a boost to such schools (as well as to honors and Advanced Placement programs within comprehensive high schools) in the late 1950s, but within a decade the education-policy pendulum was swinging toward egalitarianism. The Supreme Court first nudged it in that direction with 1954's *Brown v. Board of Education of Topeka* decision. Then Lyndon Johnson's "Great Society," with its civil rights, anti-poverty, and federal-aid-to-education programs, gave a strong shove to widen opportunities for low-income kids, take extra measures to prepare them for school, and compensate for the educational deficits of home and neighborhood.

Not long thereafter came the Bilingual Education Act (1968), Title IX of the Higher Education Act (1972), congressional passage of the Equal Rights Amendment (1972), the Women's Educational Equity Act (1974) and the Education for All Handicapped Children Act (1975), as well as ever-sterner efforts to integrate the schools (Judge Arthur Garrity's infamous Boston busing decree was handed down in 1974) and to back the growing pile of civil rights protections with federal enforcement muscle.

As more money and energy went into advancing equity in American K–12 (and higher) education, less was devoted to the pursuit of excellence, which is likely why few new selective-admission schools (other than magnets designed for racial integration) were launched between the mid-1960s and mid-1980s.[4] In fact, some of those that already existed came under attack for their "elitism." Boston Latin was swept into Garrity's ruling that the public schools of Boston were segregated, and, as part of the remedy, that city's school committee instituted a 35 percent "setaside" for minority students within the ancient school's exam-based admissions process.[5] So strong was the push to open up admissions to Bronx Science, Stuyvesant, and other selective high schools in New York City that a pair of alarmed lawmakers from the Bronx pushed through the state legislature in 1971 a measure shielding these schools from any tampering with their test-score-driven admissions process.[6]

In 1983, however, the United States was declared a "nation at risk" by a blue-ribbon commission, owing to the slipshod quality of its schools and the inadequate preparation of their graduates. The panel stressed the danger that this posed to "American prosperity, security, and civility." In its wake, attention began to shift back to educational "excellence"—mostly to higher standards and stronger achievement for all children in all schools, but also to the possibility of additional attention and opportunity being paid to exceptionally talented or high-achieving youngsters.

Although the National Association of Gifted Children (NAGC) dates to 1954—the same year as the *Brown* decision—and the U.S. Office of Education (now Department of Education) launched a small "gifted and talented" unit in 1974, the first major policy-level recognition that these kids, too, might deserve special attention was Congress's passage in 1988 (five years after *A Nation at Risk*) of the "Jacob Javits Gifted and Talented Students Education Act," named in memory of the late senator from New York.[7] That law defined (and today still defines) its target population as "Students, children, or youth who give evidence of high achievement capability in areas such as intellectual, creative, artistic, or leadership capacity, or in specific academic fields, and who need services and activities not ordinarily provided by the school in order to fully develop those capabilities." The foremost intent of this legislation was to help underserved populations deserving of such attention to gain access to advanced programs and schools that provided them.

While the federal program was never large (indeed, was "zero funded" by Congress in 2011), nor did it underwrite the actual operation of "G and T" classes or activities at the state or local level, it did lend a measure of legitimacy to such programs, which launched or expanded in many communities. Often politically vulnerable and fiscally fragile, yet fiercely sought out by determined parents seeking to enroll their children in them, gifted-and-talented programs in the early and middle grades were joined by widening honors and AP options in many high schools, as well as (after 1978) the International Baccalaureate (IB) program.[8]

In 1993, a panel headed by Pat O'Connell Ross concluded that the nation, having failed to develop its most talented students to their fullest potential, faced a "quiet crisis." That report, *National Excellence: A Case for Developing America's Talent*,[9] recommended tougher academic standards, beefed-up teacher training, and increased access to higher-level learning opportunities and early childhood education for all students, particularly minorities and the disadvantaged. It cannot be entirely coincidental that half the selective high schools for which we have founding dates were created in the wake of this report and the Javits Act, as well as *A Nation at Risk*.

Recent Reform Priorities

Over the past two decades, the excellence/equity balance has been tugged in both directions by a pair of newer reform strategies, which turned out to have quite different implications for academically selective high schools: the push for standards, testing, and accountability on the one hand, and accelerating efforts to widen school choice on the other.

"Standards-based" reform got underway in the 1980s as state leaders realized that the first step toward improving achievement was to specify the desired outcomes of their schools, that is, to spell out the skills and knowledge in various subjects that students should acquire at various points along the path to graduation. The next step was to develop assessments aligned with those academic expectations, in order to gauge how well schools and their pupils were doing at reaching the desired ends. In most jurisdictions, some sort of "accountability" system was then put in place to prod educators and students to strive toward those standards, reward them if they succeeded, and embarrass, intervene in, or "punish" them if they faltered.

By the mid-1990s, the federal government had become a major player on the standards-based reform stage, creating its own requirements and incentives for states to develop academic expectations, tests, and accountability regimens and its own cascade of interventions and corrective actions. This culminated in 2002's No Child Left Behind (NCLB) Act, which demanded that states (at least those seeking federal dollars, which turned out to be all of them) undertake to get every child to "proficiency" in math and reading within twelve years. No other level of achievement would count in determining whether a school was making "adequate yearly progress (AYP)," nor did any other subjects matter (except, in a minor way, science). This gave districts (in their budgeting) and teachers (in their allocation of classroom effort) powerful incentives to concentrate on lower-achieving pupils and schools.

Though one could fairly claim that NCLB sought to pursue both equity (by reducing achievement gaps) and quality (by boosting overall academic performance), the ways in which it pursued them turned out to pose unique problems for selective high schools. Because almost every state defined "proficiency" at a low level, which many kids in these schools were already well above, and because no academic achievement other than proficiency counted in determining a school's (or district's) fate in the NCLB-driven accountability system, high-performing schools and students were essentially sidelined.

NCLB also pushed against district-level selective schools by encouraging the distribution of high-achieving students among *all* schools in order to enhance their performance. Trying to fulfill the demands of this federal statute, a district would have little reason to create or sustain a selective high school that concentrated high achievers in one place if that heightened the risk of other schools not making AYP.

And although a lively argument rages as to whether NCLB's sharp focus on reading and math has narrowed the curriculum that's actually delivered by U.S. schools, there can be little doubt that contemporary accountability systems that reward performance only in two subjects provide little incentive for schools or teachers to pay equal attention to such other subjects as literature, writing, history, science, art, music, and technology. For selective high schools, this has raised the possibility that entering 9th graders might be underprepared for such courses owing to neglect of these subjects in the earlier grades. (As the school profiles in part II suggest, however, those we visited were striving not to retreat from providing a deep and comprehensive curriculum for their students, while keeping the academic-aspiration and curricular ceilings high enough to create growth opportunities for the very sharpest among them. In practice, Advanced Placement courses and exams were more apt to function as these schools' "NCLB.")

The second big reform strategy that consumed American K–12 education in the past twenty years was, on its face, better suited to selective high schools: the move to strengthen both quality and equity in K–12 education by creating new school options and widening the choices available to more youngsters, especially those from disadvantaged and minority backgrounds, and to recognize that individual differences, needs, and preferences deserve differing responses from an education system that had long focused on fitting everyone into a few standard offerings.

While the emergence of more and better choices was surely a boon to students and parents, however, it wasn't invariably a plus for pre-existing schools of choice. As kids got greater freedom to choose their schools, they could access more alternatives. Private schools came within range of more families that previously could not afford them, at least in the (slowly) growing number of states and cities with voucher or tax-credit programs. And a new supply of public schools emerged in the form of five thousand–plus charters, many of them specialized in various ways. Some (as in Milwaukee) may be termed "spontaneous," instigated by market forces. Others (as in New York City) were purposeful creations by school-system leaders bent on furnishing the children of their communities with more good options. At the same time, more neighborhood high schools concluded that they, too, needed to create special programs and "schools within schools" in order successfully to attract pupils and resources in this quickening marketplace.

Because every selective high school on our list is a "school of choice," one might fairly suppose that mounting support for choice—and for customizing education to the interests and circumstances of individual pupils—would also benefit these schools and their students. Certainly the widening acceptance of choice lends legitimacy to leaving one's neighborhood for a different school that might better meet one's needs, and the policies associated with a burgeoning choice movement make such moves easier.

But even as the schools on our list continue to have more applicants than they can accommodate—often many, many more—some of their leaders have begun to fret that their advantage within the education marketplace and their distinctiveness within the high school universe are diminishing as more quality alternatives emerge and become accessible to more youngsters. Others worry that letting students choose their schools will lead to "creaming" and resegregation along racial or other lines, and that selective schools are particularly apt to have that effect by taking the highest-performing students (and their test scores) and leaving the most challenging or least motivated (or worst parented) behind.

Despite their new competitors, their internal hand-wringing, and their external critics, however—and in the face of whichever direction the excellence and equity winds are blowing—selective public high schools continue to operate and in many cases to enjoy reputations as the best high schools in the land. Their numbers are small, but communities that have such schools often display them with pride to firms considering where to locate and to persnickety families judging where to educate their daughters and sons. The schools maintain support at the policy and political levels, not only because of the ardor of their alumni/ae and the determination of parents whose children benefit directly from them, but also because many are positioned as keys to America's prosperity and security. Their presence eases anxiety about international competitiveness, about developing intellectual leadership for the future, and about doing right by our "best and brightest" young people.

But how well grounded are such assumptions and opinions? Do these high schools deserve their lofty reputations? What really happens inside them? Who teaches in their classrooms? What are their students like, and how did they get chosen among myriad applicants? How different is their curriculum from what one finds in high-performing schools that admit everybody? How do they function within the larger public-education system? Selective high schools bear some resemblance to fine automobiles: prestigious in their way, admired by many, cherished by some, envied by others—but with few people understanding what goes on under their hoods. That's what we set out to learn. First, though, we had to find them.

Chapter 2

Searching for Needles in the High School Haystack

● ● ● ● ● ● ● ● ● ●

Defining a previously unexamined category of schools and identifying its members make for no small challenge. We began by thinking of them as elite institutions that require applicants to earn high scores on stiff entrance tests designed specifically for these schools. Some do, in fact, fit that description—and most incorporate exam results of various kinds in their admission process. But applying that filter alone would have excluded many other schools that seek to find, select, and serve high-performing, high-potential, and highly motivated students in self-contained (i.e., "whole-school") settings. And it would have included some schools that, on closer scrutiny, were not really what we were seeking.

The criteria we finally settled upon reflect an earnest attempt to be inclusive and consistent, without over- or underidentifying schools. For purposes of this investigation, an academically selective public high school is one to which these six statements apply:

First, it's a public school, predominantly (or fully) supported with tax dollars, does not charge tuition, is operated by or under the aegis of a public body, and is accountable to a duly constituted public authority.[1]

Second, it offers 12th grade and has a graduating class each year. That's what we call a "high school," even though it might also include elementary or middle grades. (This criterion barred a few new schools that were "growing" toward 12th grade but didn't have a graduating class as of 2009–10.)

Third, it's self-contained, not a program or school within another school. Hundreds of U.S. high schools contain academies, magnet or specialized programs, schools within the school, or distinctive course sequences that are selective or application based. Our list, however, is limited to schools where *all* enrolled students are selected through an admissions process.

Fourth, it offers an academic curriculum aimed at college readiness. The school may offer a variety of course sequences or specializations, but its overall curriculum is implicitly or expressly designed to give all of its students the skills and knowledge they will need for college-level work.

Fifth, it employs an admissions process that is academically *selective*. That process involves substantial attention to a student's academic potential and/or academic record, usually incorporating some attention to exam results. An array of other factors may also be weighed—such as attendance and behavior—but the process primarily emphasizes criteria such as grades, test scores, or writing samples.

Sixth and finally, its admissions process is academically *competitive*. We considered it to be so if more students apply than can be accommodated, or if a student's application could be rejected on the basis of his/her academic merit in relation to that of other applicants and/or the school's standards.

As straightforward as these criteria seem, in practice we found many schools that used admissions processes to select students for challenging academic settings but still did not make our list. They are, nonetheless, worth noting as public secondary-schooling options for academically advanced students. They include:

- *Partial-day schools, programs, and centers* that furnish students only with certain courses and enroll them for just a portion of the day, week, or year. While these institutions provide valuable opportunities to qualified students, high school diplomas continue to be conferred by their "home" schools. Most of the Governor's

Schools in Virginia fall into this category. Similarly, the Michigan Mathematics and Science Network supports thirty-three regional centers around the state, some of which offer advanced courses to students from area schools. Treasure Valley Mathematics and Science Center in Boise, Idaho, admits selected applicants from charter, private, district, and home school environments to take one or more courses. No doubt there are many more.

- *Competitive/selective programs within schools.* Because we were focused on whole schools, we excluded competitive or selective programs and schools *within* schools. We uncovered hundreds of these, including some magnet programs that operate inside larger high schools but have been assigned their own federal identification numbers. Schools such as Florida's Stanton College Preparatory and Paxon School for Advanced Studies, as well as numerous high-performing schools with exemplary International Baccalaureate (IB) programs, fell into this category.
- *Schools for the arts.* Because we sought academically oriented schools, we omitted selective schools that emphasize performing and visual arts curricula or programs. Such schools may also prepare students for a variety of post-secondary options (including college), frequently have rigorous academic programs, and often use academic criteria as well as auditions and suchlike as part of their admissions processes. A well-known example is New York City's LaGuardia High School of Music & Art and Performing Arts ("LaGuardia Arts").
- *Schools that admit via lottery.* Schools that use a lottery process to admit students are obviously not using an academically selective or competitive process and are therefore not included on our list. Hence most charter schools did not qualify—even high-performing ones such as The Preuss School (at the University of California at San Diego) and Pacific Collegiate School, also in California. But if a school uses an academically competitive process by which students become eligible to take part in a lottery, like Baton Rouge Magnet School in Louisiana, we included it. We also

included one charter school—International Academy in Bloom-field Hills, Michigan—that uses a lottery to delimit prospective students who then sit for a competitive entrance exam to qualify for entrance. The Charter School of Wilmington (Delaware), also included on our list, uses a combination of academic and extra-curricular criteria to gauge and assign point values to a student's interest in the school's teaching methods, philosophy, and educational focus. All students who meet the required threshold are enrolled. When demand exceeds the number of available seats—after residential, sibling, employee, and any other priorities have been applied—the school employs a lottery.[2]

- *Schools that skip the diploma en route to college.* We came upon a handful of schools and programs that don't actually confer high school diplomas on their students. Instead they slide them straight into college at an earlier-than-usual age. Examples include the Advanced Academy of Georgia and the Program for the Exceptionally Gifted (PEG) at Virginia's Mary Baldwin College.

The Messy Matter of "Screened" High Schools in New York City

New York's high school landscape presented a unique challenge for our list. The city uses a complex application-and-placement system for *all* of its 600+ high school programs, and hundreds of those programs (and entire schools) are "screened," meaning that those running them set various criteria or preconditions for admission to them. Sometimes those criteria involve prior academic accomplishment, but such prerequisites are set at various levels. About 75 such programs technically meet all six of our criteria, but in many cases their academic bar is set low. To make sure that our list was not overwhelmed by the largest city in the country—and to make sure that we identified within that city the schools that are its most academically selective—we included only those screened schools that require applicants to have minimum scores of 85 percent on the state assessments. This yielded fifteen "screened" high

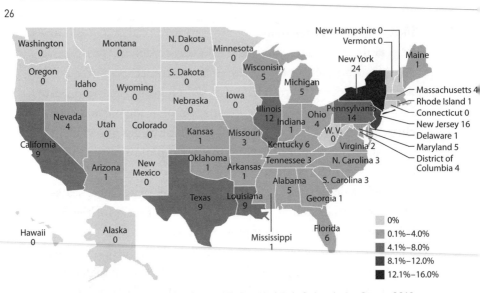

Distribution of Academically Selective Public High Schools by State, 2010. Numbers indicate how many of the schools listed in Appendix I can be found in each state. Percentages indicate what portion of the national total the numbers of schools in each state comprise.

schools, in addition to the city's eight specialized high schools that base their admission entirely on scores on their own separate test. (This complicated process is further described in chapter 10.)[3]

How We Searched and What We Found

We used several approaches to identify from the 22,568 public high schools[4] in the United States those that met our six criteria. We explain this process in appendix I, where readers will also find the list of 165 schools that finally qualified.

We found them in thirty states and the District of Columbia. Their enrollment ranges from 68 pupils (California's University Preparatory High) to 4,947 (New York's Brooklyn Tech), with a median size of just under one thousand students. The map shows how many of the schools can be found in each state. It makes plain that such schools are more prevalent in some jurisdictions than others, and in several cases (New

York, Illinois, Pennsylvania) they are further confined to individual cities within those states. A wide range of factors—historical, economic, and political—helps explain why, for example, there are more schools east of the Mississippi than west of it, or why Chicago, New York, and Philadelphia have many but Los Angeles, Denver, and Minneapolis have none. Suffice to say that most American teenagers do *not* live near an academically selective public high school.

Neither can families with access to a selective school always be confident that it's a reliable source of first-rate teaching and strong achievement. Because our intent was to identify schools by the nature of their *admissions* process—not to rank or judge them as educational institutions—readers will find on our list a small number of schools that would not be considered high *performing* by traditional indicators of student achievement. To make that distinction clear—and to provide context for issues discussed later in this book—we have included, next to each school's name in appendix I, its Great Schools rating whenever available.[5] We respect the care that this highly regarded national organization has taken to gauge and compare the performance of district, charter, and (when possible) private schools at the community, state, and (when possible) national levels, and believe that its individual school ratings are a credible, straightforward way to indicate a given school's academic performance (based on test scores) in relation to other schools in its state.[6]

Schools with lower Great Schools ratings may be academically selective—and may well be the best public high schools in their communities—but they are not particularly high achieving compared with other high schools as gauged by the state's own assessments. This may reflect the schools' actual performance and/or challenging circumstances that their students face and/or weak elementary/middle schools that "feed" youngsters into them.

As is already evident, even after we strove to apply consistent "decision rules" to the identification of schools that belong on our list, they turned out to differ from each other on many dimensions. Our next task was systematically to gather data that would illumine more of what these schools do and don't have in common.

Chapter 3

Exploring a New Constellation

● ● ● ● ● ● ● ● ● ● ● ● ●

Although some schools on our list are nationally renowned and many are locally famous, these schools as a group or type within U.S. education have rarely been examined or analyzed. Hence little is known about their demographics, their teachers, their education programs, their selection processes, et cetera. Here we explore this unfamiliar constellation within the vast universe of American secondary education.

School Demographics

To obtain basic information about student demographics, we drew data from the federal government's 2009–10 Common Core database for the schools on our list and compared them with all U.S. public high schools (table 3.1). The results both confirm and challenge some hunches and assumptions about selective high schools.

As expected, academically selective schools represent a tiny fraction of U.S. public high schools and serve slightly fewer than one percent of all students. Female pupils outnumber male 55 percent to 45 percent, whereas in the larger high school universe they're nearly the same. (More girls *apply* to these schools as well—see p. 41.)

Viewed in its entirety, the population of students served by these schools is more racially "balanced" than the population of students served by all public high schools. No ethnic group comprises more than 35 percent of total enrollment. Observe, though, that there are propor-

Table 3.1: Student Demographics, Academically Selective vs. All Public High Schools

	Academically selective public high schools[a]	All public high schools[b]
Number of schools	165	22,568
Total enrollment	135,700 ($n = 165$)	14,629,876
Male[c]	45% ($n = 161$)	51%
Female	55% ($n = 161$)	49%
White	35% ($n = 161$)	56%
Black	30% ($n = 161$)	17%
Hispanic (nonwhite)	13% ($n = 161$)	20%
Asian/Asian–Pacific Islander/Hawaiian	21% ($n = 161$)	5%
Native American	< 1% ($n = 161$)	1%
Two or more races	< 1% ($n = 161$)	< 1%

[a] Here and throughout this chapter, demographic data for the schools on our list are reported as obtained from the National Center for Education Statistics Common Core of Data, the U.S. Department of Education's Office for Civil Rights, district and school websites, and direct contact with administrators. Data were not always available for all 165 schools. In addition, demographic data for some schools did not reflect their total enrollments, resulting in percentage totals of less than 100% in some categories.

[b] See note 4 of chapter 2.

[c] For 16 schools on our list, there was a discrepancy between what the school reported as its total enrollment, and the sum of its male and female students. In these cases, we opted to use the latter sums as their total enrollment.

tionally fewer white and Hispanic students in these schools, and proportionally more black and (far) more Asian students.

As in American public education generally, however, while the combined population of the schools on our list is diverse in racial/ethnic terms, individual schools are often "imbalanced." In nearly 70 percent of them, half or more of the students are of one race (table 3.2).

For an African-American youngster, the integration picture in these schools resembles that of public schools generally. Fifty-one percent of black students in our schools have a majority of fellow students who

Table 3.2: Academically Selective Schools with Enrollment ≥ 50% of One Race
(*n* = 113)

	White	Black	Asian/Pacific Islander	Hispanic
Number of schools with 50%–59%	19	6	5	3
Number of schools with 60–69%	14	6	3	6
Number of schools with 70%–79%	12	8	2	0
Number of schools with 80%–89%	7	8	1	0
Number of schools with 90%–100%	3	12	0	0
Totals	55	38	11	9

are black. For public schools in general, that's the case with 52 percent of African-American pupils. On the other hand, white students in academically selective high schools are somewhat better integrated. Again, 51 percent are in schools where a majority of their classmates are also white—but in U.S. public education generally that's true for 77 percent of white pupils.[1]

Location is part of the explanation. As shown in table 3.3, 55 percent of "our" schools are located in large cities, which tend to be diverse places but also places where minority youngsters are generally concentrated. Those ninety-three largish schools enroll 70 percent of all the students in our school population, including 83 percent of the black students in that population, 75 percent of the Hispanic students, and 71 percent of the Asian pupils. A substantial fraction of these urban schools are designated "magnet" schools in the federal database or by their own principals, indicating that racial integration was likely part of the reason for their creation. Indeed, several were historically black schools that became magnets in the hope of attracting white (and other) students to their specialized offerings.[2]

Judging by eligibility for federal free and reduced-price lunches (table 3.4), the pupils in academically selective high schools are only

Table 3.3: Student Race/Ethnicity by School Location (2009–10)

	Large city	Midsize city	Small city	Large suburb	Rural/small town/exurban
Number of schools[a] (n = 156)	93	19	9	27	10
Total student enrollment	93,803	14,459	4,821	16,950	5,198
Male[b]	43%	45%	48%	48%	47%
Female	57%	55%	52%	52%	53%
White	29%	46%	46%	54%	63%
Black	35%	26%	11%	12%	11%
Asian/Pacific Islander	21%	17%	31%	21%	12%
Hispanic	14%	9%	10%	11%	11%

[a] This kind of locational information was not available for all schools.
[b] For 16 schools on our list, there was a discrepancy between what the school reported as its total enrollment, and the sum of its male and female students. In these cases, we opted to use the latter sums as their total enrollment.

slightly less poor than those in the larger universe of U.S. public education. Note, though, that some schools on our list are excluded here because they do not receive federal funding for these programs. (They are state-sponsored residential schools, university-affiliated schools, etc.)[3]

Based on the incomplete data we were able to gather, the schools on our list enroll fewer students with disabilities than do public high schools in general (table 3.4). Forty-five of the 120 schools reported having no IDEA-eligible students. About 75 schools have five or more students for whom special-education services may be provided.[4]

Although these comparisons at the national level are important and somewhat surprising, it's also important to look at the extent to which selective high schools reflect the demographics of their own communities. We therefore picked seven large cities that are reasonably well supplied with selective high schools and compared the racial/ethnic composition of students in all their public high schools with those enrolled in their academically selective schools (table 3.5). In New York, Chicago,

Table 3.4: Eligibility for Free/Reduced-Price Lunch and Students with Disabilities

	Academically selective public high schools	All public high schools
Students eligible for free/reduced-price lunch ($n = 148$)	37%	39%
Students with disabilities (IDEA-Eligible) ($n = 120$)	3%[a]	12%[b]

[a] Data from http://ocrdata.ed.gov/. Data were not available for all schools. Percentage includes some schools that enroll elementary and middle school students.

[b] Based on the number of students with disabilities for ages 14–17 in 2009–10 (www.ideadata.org) and on 14,865,347 students in grades 9–12 in 2009–10 (www.nces.gov/ccd).

Boston, and Philadelphia, black and Hispanic students are underrepresented in the selective high schools, while white and Asian students are significantly overrepresented. In those four cities, we also see that roughly one-quarter to one-half of *all* Asian and white students who attend public high school are enrolled in the selective schools. Given that these systems enroll far more Hispanic and black students, such numbers suggest that selective high schools may function as a kind of refuge from lower-performing or less desirable schools for significant numbers of white and Asian students. In those cities, the selective schools may also provide an incentive for the families of such students to remain within the public-education system.

The selective high schools of Milwaukee and the District of Columbia come closer to approximating district demographics. We note, though, that several of the selective schools in each of these cities are low performing (see Great Schools ratings in appendix I) and enroll mostly black students. (This is also the case for a number of schools in Philadelphia and Chicago.)

The demographics of selective high schools in Jefferson County, Kentucky, do, in fact, nearly mirror those of their district. But here, too, individual schools reveal a different picture: One of the five selective schools is 80 percent black, while the other four are predominantly white.

Judging by eligibility for the federal free/reduced-price lunch program, we find (in the six cities for which we could obtain such data) that

Table 3.5: Student Demographics in Selected Urban Districts

Chicago	*Native American*	*Asian*	*Black*	*Hispanic*	*White*	*Free/reduced-price lunch*
All students in [public] schools that include grade 12[a]	> 1%	4%	50%	38%	8%	72%
Students in 8 selective public high schools[b]	> 1%	14%	30%	28%	27%	52%
Proportion of subgroup enrolled in selective high schools	33%	36%	6%	7%	31%	8%
New York City	*Native American*	*Asian*	*Black*	*Hispanic*	*White*	*Free/reduced-price lunch[c]*
All students in public schools that include grade 12	> 1%	15%	30%	36%	19%	N/A
Students in 23 selective high schools	> 1%	37%	12%	12%	39%	N/A
Proportion of subgroup enrolled in selective high schools	6%	24%	4%	3%	19%	N/A
Boston	*Native American*	*Asian*	*Black*	*Hispanic*	*White*	*Free/reduced-price lunch*
All students in public schools that include grade 12	> 1%	10%	39%	36%	14%	66%
Students in 3 selective high schools	> 1%	25%	23%	15%	35%	41%
Proportion of subgroup enrolled in selective high schools	20%	53%	13%	9%	55%	18%

Table 3.5 *(continued)*

Philadelphia	*Native American*	*Asian*	*Black*	*Hispanic*	*White*	*Free/reduced-price lunch*
All students in public schools that include grade 12	> 1%	8%	64%	15%	13%	76%
Students in 13 selective high schools	> 1%	16%	54%	8%	22%	51%
Proportion of subgroup enrolled in selective high schools	28%	42%	17%	11%	34%	14%
District of Columbia	*Native American*	*Asian*	*Black*	*Hispanic*	*White*	*Free/reduced-price lunch*
All students in public schools that include grade 12	> 1%	2%	81%	13%	5%	66%
Students in 4 selective high schools	> 1%	3%	85%	5%	7%	46%
Proportion of subgroup enrolled in selective high schools	29%	21%	16%	7%	24%	9%
Milwaukee	*Native American*	*Asian*	*Black*	*Hispanic*	*White*	*Free/reduced-price lunch*
All students in public schools that include grade 12	> 1%	5%	63%	19%	12%	77%
Students in 5 selective high sch"ols	> 1%	7%	53%	17%	23%	62%
Proportion of subgroup enrolled in selective high schools	15%	31%	19%	20%	43%	17%

Table 3.5 *(continued)*

Jefferson County (KY)	*Native American*	*Asian*	*Black*	*Hispanic*	*White*	*Free/reduced-price lunch*
All students in public schools that include grade 12	> 1%	3%	37%	4%	61%	53%
Students in 5 selective high schools	> 1%	4%	34%	2%	60%	35%
Proportion of subgroup enrolled in selective high schools	35%	40%	23%	14%	27%	16%

ª We noticed that about 21 high schools in Chicago, most of them charters, did not report free/reduced-price lunch data for 2009–10. (This didn't appear to be the case with charters in the other cities.) To be consistent with the other cities, we included those schools in our total in this table. It's almost certain that all those schools have significant numbers of students who quality for free or reduced-price lunch. Nevertheless, we show the data as reported (or not). Removing those 21 schools' students from the CPS enrollment total yields a free/reduced-price lunch percentage of 83% among the remaining CPS high school students.

ᵇ Free/reduced-price lunch data were not available for one of these selective high schools.

ᶜ Free and reduced-price lunch data for New York City public schools are not reported in the NCES Common Core of Data for the 2009–10 school year, and data available through the city's Education Department website were not reported as student counts, which made it impossible for us to conduct an analysis.

the academically selective high schools also enroll proportionally fewer low-income students than do all high schools in their districts. That "poverty gap" is at least 15 percent. On the other hand, observe that 35 to 62 percent of the youngsters in every city's selective high schools *are* poor.

Surveying the Schools

To learn more about the characteristics of schools on our list—and to compare them in different ways—we asked their administrators to complete a lengthy online survey (reproduced in appendix II). We promised respondents that their responses would remain confidential, so in what follows we do not identify schools or administrators by name.

Table 3.6: Demographics of Survey Responders vs. All Academically Selective Schools

	Schools responding to survey	All academically selective public high schools
Total enrollment	36,115 ($n = 57$)	135,700 ($n = 165$)
Male	45% ($n = 55$)	45% ($n = 161$)
Female	55% ($n = 55$)	55% ($n = 161$)
White	38% ($n = 54$)	35% ($n = 161$)
Black	27% ($n = 54$)	30% ($n = 161$)
Hispanic/Latino	12% ($n = 54$)	13% ($n = 161$)
Asian/Pacific Islander	21% ($n = 54$)	21% ($n = 161$)
Native American	< 1% ($n = 54$)	< 1% ($n = 161$)
Two or more races	< 1% ($n = 54$)	< 1% ($n = 161$)
Eligible for free/ reduced-price lunch	35% ($n = 46$)	37% ($n = 148$)

We received fifty-seven substantially complete surveys, which represents 35 percent of all schools on the list.[5] The demographics of responding schools are shown in table 3.6, alongside the corresponding figures for all schools on our list (for which also see table 3.1). Observe that the survey respondents closely resemble the larger school population.

School Type

Because academically selective public high schools come in many ages, flavors, sizes, shapes, and with unique histories, a variety of terms (referring, inter alia, to a school's attendance area, funding source, educational emphasis, target population, and enrollment type) can be used to characterize them. We listed some of these terms in a survey question and also invited respondents to suggest one or more additional terms to describe their schools (table 3.7).

Most respondents reported that they serve students who live within the boundaries of a single city or school district (table 3.8), but a full 38 percent have countywide, regional, or statewide "attendance zones."

Table 3.7: School Descriptors Used by Administrators ($n = 57$)

Terms provided on survey	
Magnet	29
District-sponsored	17
STEM	15
State-sponsored	11
Residential	8
University lab	2
Charter	2
Governor's School	2
Regional center	1
Respondent-generated terms	
Early college/early entrance to college	6
Screened	2
Selective-enrollment	2
Vocational/technology	2
Career academy	1
Exam	1
Choice	1
School for gifted students	1

Admissions and Recruitment

The application requirements, processes, and selection criteria that these schools employ are of obvious interest—and some sensitivity. This was certainly the most challenging area to elicit clear information about. Some school officials are uneasy about the practice of selectivity, possible allegations of "elitism," and the student diversity that does or does not result from the admissions process. After all, these schools are public, yet many students living in the attendance area are not able to enroll in them. Some youngsters apply and are admitted; others are

Table 3.8: Where Do Students Live Who Are Eligible
to Apply to Your School? ($n = 56$)

Within a neighborhood or subdivision of a single city or school district	4 (7%)
Within the boundaries of a single city or school district	31 (55%)
Within multiple school districts in the same county or region	11 (20%)
Within the boundaries of the state	10 (18%)

not. Though the school's criteria are almost always public knowledge, the ins and outs of the selection process may not be obvious to would-be applicants and their parents, or to taxpayers and voters in the community. (How that process works was certainly unclear to *us* as we tried to parse the information about admissions requirements, procedures, and materials on various school and district websites—when we could even locate such information!)

How these schools handle admissions is also germane because many of them receive local, state, and national accolades based on various indicators of student performance (e.g., SAT/ACT scores, performance on state tests, number of AP exams taken and passed, graduation rates). One might predict that the selection methods and criteria that the schools use would yield students who are more likely to do well academically, which in turn raises questions about the *schools'* role in producing the results that come to define its reputation. (We examine these questions further in parts II and III of this book.)

The schools reported many different approaches, emphases, and criteria for admissions (table 3.9). A student's prior academic performance is the most widely used criterion, with nearly 80 percent of respondents saying that their process strongly emphasizes pupil academic records (e.g., grades). Applicants' scores on various tests also figure prominently. State- or district-administered tests appear to be the most widely considered, with nearly 60 percent of schools saying that they strongly or moderately emphasize scores on these assessments. About 40 percent of schools reported using tests developed specifically for their own use.

Table 3.9: Emphases in Admissions Criteria (*n* = 56)

	Strongly empha-sized in the admissions process	Moderately emphasized	Slightly emphasized	Not a criterion
Students' prior academic record (e.g., grades)	79%	16%	0%	5%
Scores from state/district tests administered in prior grades	43%	17%	6%	35%
Scores from an entrance exam customized for your school or district	40%	0%	9%	51%
Application essay responses	38%	17%	13%	32%
Other standardized achievement test scores (e.g., California Achievement Test, Iowa Test of Basic Skills)	32%	13%	11%	44%
Teacher recommendation(s)	30%	22%	15%	33%
SAT/ACT scores	24%	4%	8%	65%
Interview	17%	19%	10%	54%
Other recommendation(s)	13%	15%	13%	60%
IQ test scores	6%	4%	2%	88%
Portfolio or other work submission	4%	12%	6%	78%
Sibling(s) attend school	4%	16%	12%	67%

Eighteen schools reported taking SAT or ACT scores into consideration, a dozen of them in a major way. Open-ended responses indicate that some of those schools give students the option of submitting such scores but do not require them. Only six schools reported using IQ test scores in their selection process.[6]

The most widely used and emphasized *qualitative* criteria reported by schools are student essays (55 percent reporting strong or moderate emphasis) and teacher recommendations (52 percent reporting strong or moderate emphasis).

When asked (in open-ended questions) to identify additional criteria that are strongly emphasized in the admissions process, nine schools cited students' behavior and attendance records. Several respondents described these criteria as evidence of a student's maturity or ability to assume greater responsibility in a more challenging or flexible academic setting. Residential schools mentioned seeking evidence that the student has the emotional capacity to live away from home. One such process sounded highly individualized: "We ask students to shadow. They come in on a Sunday evening, stay with one of our Community Leaders and attend classes on Monday. The Community Leader then evaluates the prospective student."

Among other criteria that one or more schools strongly emphasize are a student's class rank, the *level* of previous courses taken, socioeconomic status, whether the student would be the first in his or her family to attend college, and the reputation of his/her previous school. Much as in admissions to selective colleges, some schools said they also ask candidates to submit evidence of involvement in extracurricular activities, leadership capabilities, and volunteer work. One administrator explained, "[We ask applicants to] submit a resume of honors won and community service done. Students [also] submit a project reflecting their creativity." Several schools also reported wanting to see a "passion for learning" or a strong interest in the school's focus area (e.g., STEM subjects).

Forty-one schools reported how many applications their schools received for the 2010–11 school year ($n = 52,482$ for the group). Many administrators who did not provide this information noted that appli-

Table 3.10: Ethnicity of Applicant Pool for 2010–11
(n = 28)

Total number of applicants	23,363
White applicants	33%
Black applicants	32%
Hispanic applicants	15%
Asian applicants	18%
Bi-/multiracial applicants	1%
Applicants of another race/ethnicity	< 1%
Applicants whose race/ethnicity is unknown	< 1%

cant data are not accessible to them because admissions are handled in the school district's "central office" or some other separate location. Not surprisingly, schools that reported the most applications—up to 7,000—are located in urban districts.

Thirty-four schools reported the gender of their applicants. For these schools as a group, 44 percent of applicants were male and 56 percent female—a distribution that parallels the actual enrollment of all identified schools (see table 3.1).

Table 3.10 indicates the racial composition of the applicant pool for 2010–11 for the twenty-eight schools that reported those figures. A comparison between the enrollment demographics of all academically selective public schools in 2009–10 (table 3.1) and applicant demographics in the same year for these twenty-eight schools challenges the easy assumption that, as a group, these schools do not attract the applications of a diverse population of students. As we saw above, however (tables 3.2 and 3.5), the ethnic profiles of individual districts and schools and their applicant pools may be notably less diverse.

The percentage of students to whom responding schools (n = 46) offered admission speaks directly to their selectivity (figure 3.1). Nearly two-thirds of the schools reported accepting fewer than half of their applicants. Notably, all of the schools that report an acceptance rate of 20 percent or less are in urban areas or draw applicants from across an

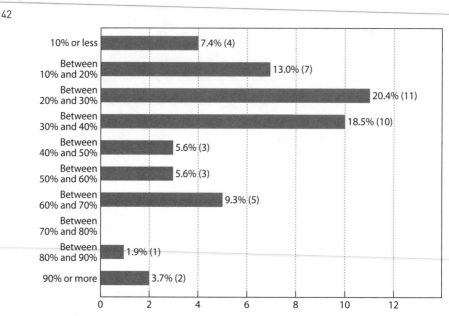

Figure 3.1: Acceptance Rates of Academically Selective Public High Schools (*n* = 46). (Survey question: To what percentage of applicants for the 2010–11 school year did your school offer admission?)

entire state. One of the two schools reporting a 90+ percent acceptance rate is among the "youngest" schools on the list. (The other offers admission to any student who wants to attend it who has passed a standardized test administered to all students in the district.)

Recruitment, Outreach, and Diversity

We asked respondents to note changes in their applicant pools over the past five years. Forty-one schools answered that question. Eleven reported receiving more applications over that period, with some linking that increase to factors such as media attention, awards, school performance, population growth, and the closing of underperforming schools in the area. One urban principal noted that 2010 was the first year that a majority of accepted students came from charter, private, and parochial schools—a pattern that perhaps speaks both to dissatisfaction with other available options and to the weaker economy.

Responding schools also noted a number of changes in the demographics of their applicant pools. Most frequently cited were increases in the number of applicants who are female, Asian or Hispanic. Several schools reported a decrease in the number of white applicants in recent years. Three schools mentioned that they had begun accepting applications from foreign and/or out-of-state students who promised to move into the attendance zone should they be accepted.

One administrator reported that "the school's applicant pool over the past two years more closely approximates local demographics," alluding to the "representation" and "diversity" challenges that academically selective schools often face. Mindful of that challenge, we asked respondents to briefly describe any strategies that their schools or districts use to foster racial, ethnic, socioeconomic, gender, or geographic diversity. Several interesting themes emerged from the fifty-two responses.

Some were ambiguous or vague, whether intentionally so we cannot judge. For example, one respondent said, "Currently variables of diversity do not play an overt role in admissions decisions," and another that "[Applicants] are looked at through a diversity lens." Other responses suggested that there is attention paid to maintaining diversity in the admissions process but do not divulge specific strategies (e.g., "We try to match the ratio of the state's diversity to our school's diversity," and "We are all racially inclusive to foster diversity and grant admission in an effort to have a diverse school").

Sixteen schools reported that they use no strategies to foster diversity, with several citing exclusive reliance on quantitative evidence in making admissions decisions. "The numbers are the only thing used in admissions," said one administrator. Other respondents noted that their applicant pool is sufficiently diverse without extra effort. For example, "Diversity is not mandated for our school, but is always maintained without quotas or other mechanisms," and "Our admissions policy is background blind. We have always been successful in attracting a diverse student population across all descriptors."

Thirteen schools elaborated on their strategies for ensuring *geographic* diversity across the district or state (which probably also boosts their ethnic and socioeconomic diversity). Approaches include drawing from a range of schools across the attendance area; limiting the number of students from any given neighborhood, town, zip code, high school zone, or congressional district; and limiting the number of students from any one feeder school. For example, one respondent explained: "Students are grouped by high school zone (= neighborhood) and ranked by the formula within their zones. Ranking is done in rounds, taking approximately the same number of students from each zone in each round, until all qualified students are ranked." Another reported: "We select by score earned on the portfolio submitted and by geographic area with a certain percentage coming from all four quadrants of the city."

Some respondents also mentioned recruiting students from public, private, parochial, charter, and independent schools. Since nearly all the schools on our list are already oversubscribed, such outreach suggests a purposeful effort to diversify and/or strengthen their applicant pools.

A smaller number of schools described fostering diversity by accounting for differences in applicants' academic preparation. One respondent explained: "Once the applicant pool is built, we examine [the applicant's grades, test scores, etc.] to identify students within their specific context. We understand that not all schools and districts in the state provide the same kind of learning environment and experiences. We also understand that access to additional programming is dissimilar across the State." Some schools described "summer bridge" programs or other support services that prepare prospective applicants or provisionally admitted students who may not have had access to challenging or high-quality educational opportunities.

Many schools pointed to recruitment efforts as ways to boost diversity in their applicant pools. Among the approaches noted were sending school representatives (e.g., counselors, students, parents) to feeder schools with underrepresented populations, high-poverty schools, or underperforming schools; hosting open houses and social events on campus and in homes of current students at times convenient for parents; offering weekly tours; and staging neighborhood recruitment events. Involving leaders, teachers, students, and parents from a range of racial and cultural backgrounds in these recruitment efforts was also viewed as a

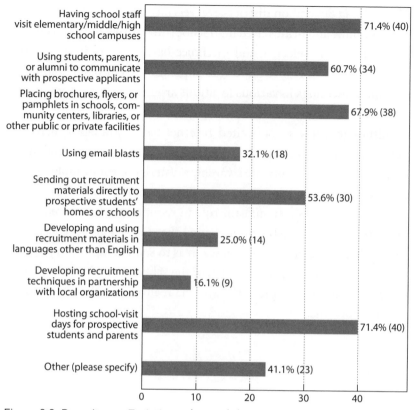

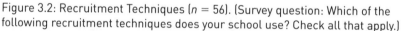

Figure 3.2: Recruitment Techniques ($n = 56$). (Survey question: Which of the following recruitment techniques does your school use? Check all that apply.)

way to invite a more diverse applicant pool. Several respondents reported relying heavily on "word of mouth" in and around the school community ("That's one of our strongest suits," commented one principal).

Figure 3.2 depicts responses to a separate question about recruitment techniques. School-to-school visits and open-house-style events were the most frequently cited strategies. A "word of mouth" approach is implied in the second option. Printed recruitment materials, distributed through multiple means, are widely used among responding schools, although few print these materials in languages other than English.[7]

Because larger cities tend to centralize the admissions and placement process, some schools in places like Chicago, New York, and

Philadelphia depend on district-level recruitment strategies and tools, such as online and print-based high school directories and citywide fairs that showcase all selective and/or choice-based schools in the district. Schools that draw from a statewide population mentioned holding recruitment meetings in various locations around the state. Two schools said they place notices in local newspapers.

Although a few schools cited Internet-based strategies such as e-newsletters and websites, no school suggested that it uses social media or networking tools to create awareness of and interest in applying to it. Some reported using e-mail as a recruitment tool ($n = 18$). Direct mailing, however, plays a significant role in recruitment for more schools ($n = 30$). One administrator explained that the school purchases lists from college-recruitment databases so as to send materials to prospective students. Another described how the school provides information to new families moving into the area via realtors and the city's visitor-information office.

Teachers

One assumption about academically selective public schools is that surely they are better resourced—which includes having more and "better" teachers.[8] As for *more* teachers, we found that the pupil-teacher ratio in the high schools on our list is actually a bit higher (17.3:1) than in all public high schools (15.1:1).[9]

But are their teachers different? As shown in table 3.11, the percentage with doctoral degrees is notably higher in these schools than in high schools generally (11 percent vs. 1.5 percent), as is the percentage with masters degrees (66 percent vs. 46 percent). We suspect that these percentages might be higher still if we had data from more schools.[10] Note, too, that students at a number of our schools take some courses from college professors, whose credentials probably don't turn up within our survey data.

As shown in table 3.12, nontrivial numbers of teachers in our schools also have experience in industry, extensive backgrounds in science or technology, and/or have taught at colleges or universities, though we

Table 3.11: Teachers with Advanced Degrees or Alternative Certification ($n = 51$)

	Teachers in academically selective schools	All public high school teachers[a]
Teachers with an earned doctorate degree	11%	2%
Teachers with an earned masters degree (but not a doctorate)	66%	46%
Teachers who did not attend a traditional teacher-preparation program	16%	18%[b]

[a] U.S. Department of Education, National Center for Education Statistics, Schools and Staffing Survey (SASS), "Public School Teacher Questionnaire," 2007–8.

[b] Percentage of grades 9–12 public-school teachers who entered teaching through alternative certification.

have no data by which to gauge how this may compare with the overall U.S. high school teaching force. (Note, too, that several of our questions emphasized "*extensive* background.")

Despite these varied backgrounds, however, the percentage of teachers in our schools who did not attend a traditional teacher-preparation program is slightly lower than the percentage of all public high school teachers who entered via alternative certification (table 3.11).

Teacher Demographics and Selection

Much as in U.S. high schools generally, a thin majority of teachers in schools responding to our survey are female (56 percent). Over three-fourths (78 percent) are white, slightly lower than the 83.5 percent found in public high schools generally. The comparisons in table 3.13 suggests that academically selective public schools also have a slightly higher proportion of black (and slightly lower of Hispanic) teachers than are found

Table 3.12: Teacher Backgrounds in Academically Selective Public High Schools (*n* = 51)

Teachers that have a teaching certificate that is valid in your state	91%
Teachers who currently teach or have taught in college/university settings	11%
Teachers who currently teach or have taught in private schools	5%
Teachers with extensive backgrounds in business or industry	9%
Teachers with extensive backgrounds in science or technology fields	10%
Teachers with extensive backgrounds in nonprofit organizations	2%
Teachers with extensive backgrounds in the military	3%
Teachers with extensive backgrounds in other public-sector careers	2%
Teach for America corps member/alumnus/a	1%

in all public schools, not unlike their pupil demographics (see table 3.1). Similarly, teachers of Asian heritage constitute a larger percentage than they do in high schools generally.

One might reasonably expect schools that select their students on academic grounds also to apply different or more rigorous criteria when

Table 3.13: Teacher Demographics in Academically Selective vs. All High Schools

	Academically selective schools (*n* = 54)	All public high schools[a]
Male teachers	44%	42%
Female teachers	56%	58%
White teachers	78%	84%
Black teachers	10%	7%
Hispanic teachers	5%	7%
Asian/Pacific Islander teachers	6%	2%
Bi-/multiracial	< 1%	< 1%
Other	< 1%	< 1%
Unknown	< 1%	N/A

[a] Percentage of public-school teachers of grades 9 through 12, by field of main teaching assignment and selected demographic and educational characteristics: 2007–8. (Source: NCES *Digest of Education Statistics 2010*.)

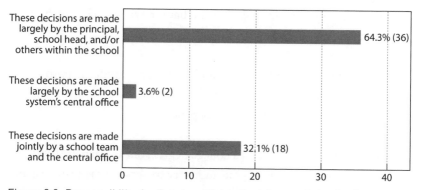

Figure 3.3: Responsibility for Teacher-Hiring Decisions at Selective Public High Schools (*n* = 56). (Survey question: Which of the following statements comes closest to describing how hiring decisions about teachers at your school are made?)

selecting their teachers. We explored this hypothesis by asking survey respondents about their hiring processes.

Nearly two-thirds of the fifty-six responding schools indicated that teacher-hiring decisions are made at the school level (figure 3.3). This seems to defy the widespread perception that public-school principals have little say about who teaches in their schools, and it may well be that the schools on our list are exceptional in that regard. Note, though, that some of them operate as independent state agencies, university-affiliated institutions, philanthropic or charter endeavors, or within systems that are not tightly controlled by the central office. Still, taken with the additional number of respondents indicating that they *share* decision-making responsibilities with the central administration, the schools responding to the survey do appear to exercise considerable autonomy in the teacher-hiring process.

A few respondents noted that their hiring process is guided by other external factors. One explained the influence of the teacher-union contract:

> We are held to the [district] policies regarding hiring. In years of lean budgets, when permanent teachers are losing positions in other schools, if we have an opening, we are limited to choosing from teachers who have been "excessed" from other schools. These teachers, according to

the collectively-bargained agreement, have the right to choose the positions based on seniority.

Another respondent from a school that grants students both an associate's degree and a high school diploma described a somewhat different version of autonomy in the hiring process:

> Because [our school] grants a college degree, our [agreement] with the [district] gives [our school] the authority to appoint the principal and hire the faculty qualified to teach the college classes as well as the high school classes. If [teacher union] members are qualified, we consider them for positions. All faculty hired and paid through DOE funding become members of the [teacher union].

The criteria that schools stress in selecting teachers obviously signal what they value in their instructional staffs. Table 3.14 outlines the extent to which responding schools say they emphasize various criteria. Subject-matter knowledge, pedagogical knowledge/expertise, and the ability to relate to, understand, and/or engage adolescent learners are most strongly emphasized. Education level, type of teaching experience, and recommendations from previous employers are also taken seriously. In general, these results reflect what one might expect conscientious high school leaders—selective and otherwise—to seek when choosing their teachers, provided that they have the authority to make such decisions.

Respondents also cited other factors that matter to them. Some of these would likely count as evidence of a candidate's potential at any school (e.g., classroom management strategies, teaching philosophy and instructional skills, reflective nature, technology prowess, collegiality). Others may be peculiar to schools that take unusual pains in the selection process (e.g., demonstration lessons, teacher/student committee interviews).

Factors that are perhaps more specific to (or could be expected from) academically selective schools include experience or credentials as a practitioner in a relevant field (e.g., business, medicine, Ph.D. in

Table 3.14: Teacher-Selection Criteria ($n = 55$)

	Strongly emphasized	Moderately emphasized	Slightly emphasized	Not a criterion
Subject-matter knowledge	93%	6%	0%	2%
Ability to relate to, understand, and/or engage adolescent learners	84%	11%	2%	4%
Pedagogical knowledge/expertise	68%	26%	4%	4%
Type of teaching experience	46%	40%	9%	6%
Education level	44%	47%	6%	4%
Recommendations from previous administrators or supervisors	33%	51%	15%	2%
Reputation of previous places of employment	31%	35%	27%	7%
Portfolio (e.g., sample unit/lesson plans)	15%	49%	20%	16%
Years of teaching experience	15%	44%	33%	9%
Recommendations from previous teaching colleagues	7%	47%	38%	7%

biology) and training in Advanced Placement instruction. A number of respondents volunteered that a candidate's ability to work with and relate to gifted students is important. According to one, "A program with high-achieving students needs faculty that can and will challenge students. However, teenagers are a unique entity and education needs to be age-appropriate and engaging." Several schools noted that their hiring processes strongly emphasize formal training in teaching such pupils, as well as considerable expertise in the subject matter (as one respondent put it, a teacher's "passion as a scholar"). On the other hand, no one indicated that they seek teachers with a prior track record of boosting student achievement.

Building on the theme of willingness to teach in different ways or otherwise adjust to setting- and student-specific needs, two respondents described less conventional approaches to teacher selection:

> We oftentimes are more comfortable hiring someone who has not taught in a regular classroom, as our methods of instruction are atypical of the average high school.

> Aside from the criteria listed, we have an extensive curriculum and methods analysis questionnaire that we designed specifically for our setting and which is based on the particular concerns we have had with the recruitment process since our first year of operation. Responses to this questionnaire along with performance in multiple teaching auditions are strongly emphasized. The additional criteria we seek are flexibility, creativity, intuition, strong commitment to team teaching, and novel approaches to problem solving.

Although one item on our survey spoke to a candidate's ability to relate to adolescents, six respondents provided additional comments about this factor. Among these were "a passion for working with young people" and "teachers who care about students and want to develop positive relationships [with them]."

Exemptions and Waivers

Because many of the schools on our list occupy distinctive niches within their local communities, districts, or states, we were curious whether their teachers are fully subject to the provisions of teacher-union contracts. Most certainly are. We aren't sure how much to make of the exceptions indicated in figure 3.4. Colleagues at the National Council on Teacher Quality state that it *is* extraordinary to find, for example, that six of thirty-three responding schools are not (or not fully) subject to seniority-based staffing decisions. But these numbers are all small,

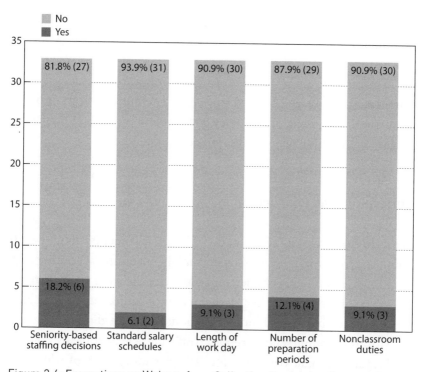

Figure 3.4: Exemptions or Waivers from Collective-Bargaining Contract Provisions (*n* = 33). (Survey item: Indicate whether your school has exemptions or waivers [full or partial] from the provisions of the collective bargaining contract in any of the following areas.)

and it's hard to know what to compare them with in the larger high school universe.

In open-ended responses, several administrators noted other exemptions that apply to their schools. Five described provisions related to time, including more (or less!) preparation time, fewer nonclassroom duties, extended teaching days, and flexibility in reconfiguring the school day to accommodate special activities and scheduling needs.

A handful of responding schools said either that they are not required to hire teachers with state certification or that other credentials (e.g., Ph.D. in relevant field) pre-empt certification, at least for several years.

> We follow the [collectively bargained] contract. As a new school, however, we negotiate with teachers at the school level apart from the contract. We have no formal exemptions, but we do not follow the contract

to the letter in many areas through negotiation with teachers at the school level.

In general, however, we were struck by how *few* of these schools reported that they have obtained waivers or exemptions from ordinary regulations and procedures. Survey questions 24 through 27 (appendix II) gave them ample opportunities to do so.

Curriculum and Instruction

What do these schools actually "do" with their students, and how different is it from what these youngsters might encounter at another high school? We examine these questions more closely in the school profiles in Part II (and reflect further on the matter of "differentness" in chapters 15 and 16), but several survey questions provide a glimpse.

Most responding schools reported offering at least some AP courses or the International Baccalaureate (IB) program—both of which are increasingly viewed as indicators of a school's academic rigor and quality. Several commented that they "only offer honors and AP courses." In effect, those schools consist entirely of what would be considered an "advanced track" within a comprehensive high school.

On the other hand, five schools noted that their students do *not* take Advanced Placement courses per se, either because they take actual college courses (at host colleges or through dual enrollment arrangements) or because they earn college credit for advanced courses taught in the school building by qualified instructors.

Numerous respondents highlighted *other* kinds of highly specialized and advanced courses, either in addition to or in lieu of AP courses or the IB program. Schools with a STEM focus and/or those with university affiliations, in particular, reported a wide array of upper-level science and math courses that few ordinary high schools—even very large ones—could offer. For example: Human Infectious Diseases, Chemical Pharmacology, Logic and Game Theory, and Vector Calculus.

Another recurring theme is an emphasis on independent research projects by students, ranging from classroom-supported guided-inquiry

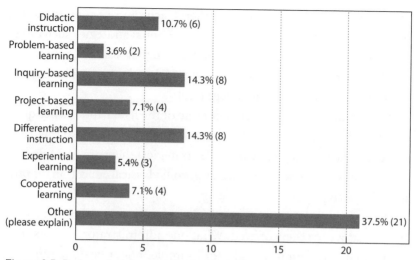

Figure 3.5: Pedagogical Approaches in Academically Selective Public High Schools (*n* = 56). (Survey question: Which term best describes the pedagogical approaches or strategies that guide most of the instruction at your school? If none of the terms are good descriptions—or a combination of terms applies—please select Other and briefly explain.)

models to extended team-based problem-solving challenges to collaborative research with university student and professors. Many of the mentorship and internship opportunities that these schools afford their students rival those typically offered through universities, fellowships, or in the job market.

Notably, many of the innovative and advanced-level opportunities that these schools provide to their students take place *outside* the classroom—in some cases (especially in junior and senior years) outside the school building itself, as students go off for internships, mentorships, and independent projects of many kinds. Two factors may facilitate this relative freedom to offer in-depth courses and individual exploration. First, a number of schools report using daily or weekly schedules that mimic the structure of a college schedule. Second, about 20 percent of respondents indicated that their school is not subject to state curricular guidelines or graduation requirements.[11]

We were interested in pedagogy, too, so we asked administrators to identify a term that best describes the approach or strategy that guides most of the classroom instruction at their school (figure 3.5). Predictably, many chose "other" to explain that their teachers use a combination of the approaches we listed, as well as instructional strategies such as Socratic seminars. Several administrators noted that teachers' approaches vary by department (e.g., math, history) and by whether an instructor is teaching or has taught at the college level.

One respondent suggested that none of the listed approaches quite captures the essence of his/her school's instruction, explaining that, while its teachers use many of these strategies, their use is "tempered by our commitment to delivering a rigorous classical education for profoundly gifted pupils."

To be sure, we cannot know exactly *how* respondents construed the terms that we (or they) offered. What one administrator believes "differentiated instruction" entails, for example, might be quite different from how another understands it. Moreover, in many cases, the person completing the survey was not in a position that entailed much direct observation of classroom teaching (e.g., school counselor, admissions director).

Part II

• • • • •

Inside the Schools

Introduction

While identifying and surveying academically selective public high schools gave us a bird's-eye view of this distinctive corner of the secondary-education world, we were left with questions that could only be addressed by going inside the schools themselves. So we resolved to visit up to a dozen of them. Our plan was to spend time in schools of varying kinds in different parts of the country.

To select them, we reviewed the list of those that had responded to our survey, assuming that administrators who had taken thirty to sixty minutes to share information about their school might be more willing to host a visit than those who had not replied.

Of the eighteen schools we contacted, we were able to schedule and complete visits to eleven (five for Hockett and six for Finn). Most of the schools that declined did so because of our timing (April–May, when many schools are besieged by state tests, AP/IB exams, and other end-of-year activities). Some schools that we visited required that we secure permission from the central office. In those cases, we complied with all district guidelines for proposing and gaining approval to conduct research.

Each visit lasted from most of a day to two full days. To eke the greatest benefit from that time, we sent the principal (or other contact) a detailed description of our project, including what we hoped to accomplish during these site visits, and a list of proposed activities that included interviews with leaders, teachers, parents, students, guidance counselors, board members, community members, and alumni/ae, as well as classroom observations. Nearly all schools were able to accommodate most of these requests, although the numbers and kinds of individuals we interviewed and the classrooms we visited differed by school.

In many cases, we followed these visits with calls and e-mail exchanges with school heads and other knowledgeable individuals.

We do not claim that the eleven profiles that follow are representative of this school universe, but they illustrate many features of what turned out to be an exceptionally varied set of educational institutions. They are located in nine states and the District of Columbia, in every region of the country except the Northwest (which has few such schools—see map on p. 26).

One is a statewide residential school. One is a grades 2–12 school for gifted students. One is a historically black school, now a selective-admissions magnet. One is a charter school, converted from district magnet. One started as a vocational school and evolved. One began as a magnet program within an ordinary high school and turned into a full-fledged high school. Four have close university ties. The years of their founding span a century and a half, and their sizes range from 600 to almost 2,200 pupils. Six are urban schools, three are suburban, and two are located in small cities or towns. Their Great Schools ratings range from a mediocre 4 to a top-of-the-line 10. (One is unrated.)

No two visits went quite the same way, as we were granted access to different sources at each school, had different amounts of time, and some visits were more structured in advance by our hosts than others. The co-authors' approaches to such visits differed, too. Hockett was more systematic, Finn more impressionistic. Note, too, that while these profiles emphasize particular features of individual schools, many of the same features were also found in other schools—leading to a discussion of common themes and takeaways in chapter 15.

Chapter 4

Illinois Mathematics and Science Academy

● ● ● ● ● ● ● ● ● ● ● ● ● ● ● ● ● ● ● ●

Aurora, IL

A Statewide Investment

Carl Sagan called the Illinois Mathematics and Science Academy (IMSA) "a gift from the people of Illinois to the human future." Reflecting this challenge, IMSA is more than a public boarding high school for 650 talented 10th–12th graders from across the Prairie State: it's a research institution, professional-development provider, outreach facilitator, and, according to its self-confident mission statement, "the world's leading teaching and learning laboratory for imagination and inquiry."

Situated in the Fox River Valley, thirty-five miles west of Chicago and not far from several national science laboratories, IMSA is technically a state agency that operates independently from the public K–12 system. It's governed by a board of trustees, not the Illinois State Board of Education, and is exempt from all ISBE regulations. Its budget is appropriated annually within the Illinois Board of Higher Education System. As a state-funded public institution, IMSA does not require students to pay tuition or for housing, but they do pay fees, adjusted for family income and size.[1]

In its twenty-five-year history, IMSA has graduated four thousand students—far fewer than many comprehensive high schools in the state. Since its inception, however, IMSA has been charged not only with offering "a uniquely challenging education for students talented in the areas of mathematics and science" but also with "a responsibility to stimulate further excellence for all Illinois schools in mathematics and science." Nearly fifty thousand elementary, middle, and high schoolers have participated in IMSA's varied outreach programs, and hundreds of Illinois educators have been through its professional-development workshops (on problem-based learning) and programs for preservice teachers. Three field offices—in Chicago, Rock Island (northwest Illinois), and Edwardsville (southwest Illinois)—bring IMSA-run enrichment and professional development programs to students and teachers who might not otherwise have access to advanced learning opportunities in science and math.

IMSA was conceived by Leon Lederman, a Nobel laureate in physics and former director of the Fermi National Laboratory. In 1982, he gave a speech to an audience of business and educational leaders, envisioning a high school that would funnel more talent into STEM-related fields (i.e., science, technology, engineering, and mathematics). Stephanie Marshall—then a local school-district administrator and later IMSA's first president—was among those inspired by what she heard. She and other supporters forged ahead with the idea for an Illinois counterpart to the first two state-sponsored residential high schools: the North Carolina School for Science and Mathematics (founded in 1980) and the Louisiana School for Math, Science, and the Arts (1983).

Two local groups, Friends of Fermilab and the Corridor Partnership for Excellence in Education, drew up a concept paper for the school and presented it to then–Illinois governor Jim Thompson. Support extended to leaders in the state legislature—among them future Speaker of the U.S. House of Representatives Dennis Hastert, in whose district IMSA would be located—as well as industry leaders and higher educators. The release of *A Nation at Risk* in 1983 provided further impetus for such a school aimed at developing talent in math and science.

The following year, the state superintendent conducted a feasibility study that led to a bill to create IMSA. Concern over the school's proposed exemption from the Illinois school code—as well as brain-drain anxieties—ultimately defeated that measure. A second attempt, which included the project within an omnibus measure, succeeded in 1985. It established IMSA as "a symbol of [the] cooperative endeavor" among the state's educational, industrial, and scientific communities to provide excellence in science and mathematics education, and earmarked $500,000 for a pilot program. IMSA moved into a vacant school in a local district and opened with its inaugural class of 210 students in 1986. Dormitories were eventually built, but the first students lived in the school building itself.

Halfway into that first year, state-funding cuts threatened to close IMSA. Marshall took the entire student body with her to Springfield and successfully pleaded the school's case before the General Assembly, securing the money for another year. Twenty-three years later, in 2009, IMSA won the prestigious Intel Star Innovator Award (and $270,000 in cash and prizes), besting seven hundred other high-performing schools to be named the one with the most "comprehensive program incorporating innovative and effective use of technology, engaging parents and community in students' education, fostering professional development and teamwork, and delivering consistent achievement of high academic standards."

Although IMSA's financial position is considerably more stable today than in its early years, its leaders know that the school is never far from the cutting-room floor. Today, the school's annual operating budget is nearly $22 million. About $18 million comes from the state, the rest from philanthropic sources, grants, and student fees.

On a Mission

IMSA's mission statement (currently in its third iteration since the school's founding) contains none of the typical phrases like *academic excellence*, *college preparation*, *critical thinking*, or *lifelong learners*. Instead IMSA boldly aspires to "ignite and nurture creative, ethical scientific minds that advance the human condition, through a system distinguished by profound questions, collaborative relationships, personalized experiential learning, global networking, generative use of technology and pioneering outreach." This ambitious creed isn't relegated to the school website but, as conversations revealed, is woven into the language of staff and students. One student joked, "They brainwash us with our mission statement here," adding, "but it's made me think about what success means. I want to make a difference in what I'm doing—not just make money."

Lofty goals are also apparent in IMSA's five-year strategic plan. Objectives like "Each IMSA graduate lives a life of exemplary service to humanity" and "All learners achieve their personal aspirations and explore their potential to contribute to the common good" suggest aspirations and expectations that go far beyond those measurable by test scores.

In addition, the academic program at IMSA is framed not by the state's K–12 academic standards (though it is aligned with those standards) but by the school's own Standards of Significant Learning (SSLs)—an extensive set of expectations for IMSA graduates that "articulate valued habits of mind which contribute to integrative ways of knowing." Each department has its own curricular standards that translate the SSLs into content-specific goals. Developing ways to assess whether students have attained the SSLs is part of the school's strategic plan.

Learning Opportunities

Stephanie Marshall, who stepped down from the president's office in 2007, talks about the need for IMSA and schools like it to develop "decidedly different minds" for the twenty-first century that are knowledgeable, creative, innovative, ethical, and wise. The school feels decidedly different, too. A competitive aura is perceptibly absent from classrooms—the focus here is not on collecting As or earning 5s on AP exams. As one student put it, "I feel like there's more of an emphasis on discovering your life calling here—not on college admissions. In three years, I've never felt like anyone has made it seem like what college you get into is important."

In line with the school's vision of "advancing the human condition," all students are required to perform one hundred hours of community service. (Some members of the graduating class of 2010 gave over three hundred hours during their three years.) In the name of "promoting collaboration, exploration, and discovery," IMSA does not calculate grade point averages (GPAs) or class rankings.[2] There is no valedictorian, either; students vote on a graduation speaker from among their peers.

Time is a flexible commodity at IMSA, allocated to accommodate a range of "learning opportunities" (the school's term for "courses"), out-of-class experiences, meetings with mentors, teachers, and advisers, and peer collaboration. The official day is long, running from 7:30 a.m. to 4:15 p.m., but most students aren't in class that whole time. An innovative schedule divides the day into 20 modules ("mods") of 20 minutes each with five-minute breaks in between. Classes run in 2-mod (45 minutes), 3-mod (70 minutes), or 4-mod (95 minutes) increments. Much as in college, students have a different schedule each day (designated A, B, C, D, and I). No classes are held on Wednesdays, also known as Inquiry (I) days, when students engage in yearlong independent and collaborative research projects on and off campus.

Between the first and second trimesters, students participate in a one-week break from regular classes that is designed as an opportunity to explore an interest, idea, or question related to specialized topics, including some that border on the grandiose or trendy. Taught by faculty, staff, and even alumni/ae, Intercession offerings in 2011 included such academic and nonacademic options as Nuclear Weapons and WMDs; Asian Antagonisms: Current Diplomatic Confrontations in Asia; Molecular Gastronomy; Dystopian Film Festival; So You Wanna Be a DJ?; and How to Change the World. Students can also use the time to work on their Student Inquiry and Research projects (see below) or take an AP exam prep course.

IMSA students are taught by a well-credentialed and widely experienced team of sixty-one full- and part-time teachers: thirty have doctorates, and the rest have at least one master's degree, usually in the discipline they teach. Twenty-eight teachers have experience teaching at the college level, and many have published in scholarly and professional journals.

Unlike many high-performing high schools, IMSA does *not* treat Advanced Placement courses as the cornerstone of its academic program. No classes are designed around AP syllabi; however, a number of courses designed at and beyond the college level equip students with the knowledge and skills necessary to take a related AP exam. In 2009–10, students took 670 AP exams, with 536 of those earning a score of 3 or higher.

Perhaps the most "advanced" study a student can undertake at IMSA is Student Inquiry and Research (SIR)—a program that facilitates independent, interest-based inquiries. Juniors and seniors can opt to undertake these yearlong investigations alone or with peers under the guidance of advisers whose ranks have included university faculty, scientists, and other professionals from medical, legal, and technology fields as well as IMSA instructors. Students share their results at a spring showcase called IMSALoquium and, in many cases, with relevant professional, scholarly, and real-world audiences. One student we spoke with credited her junior-year SIR with helping her realize "how much more I had to learn" and "envisioning my future."

Aggregating Talent

One IMSA leader characterized the school's selection of some of the brightest, keenest young scientific and mathematical minds in the state as "aggregating talent." In a given year, the school receives roughly 800 applications for 220–250 slots.[3] (All students enter as sophomores.)

Applicants submit a comprehensive body of evidence—rivaling a college admissions portfolio—in support of their performance, potential, and interest in math, science, and technology. This includes SAT scores; school transcripts; awards, accomplishments, and other evidence of achievement or interest in STEM-related endeavors; essay responses to questions posed by IMSA; and evaluations by applicants' current or past teachers and counselors.

IMSA's selection process is systematic and rigorous. All the qualitative evidence (i.e., everything except SAT scores and grades) goes through a Review Committee Evaluation process. Committees are composed of three or four individuals, including at least one IMSA staff member, one representative with a multicultural background, and one person from outside the Chicago metro area. Over one hundred "outsiders" are involved—among them scientists, university professors and counselors, superintendents, alumni/ae, and parents of alumni/ae. They are trained to use rubrics for rating candidates on five dimensions: potential for mathematical reasoning, potential for scientific reasoning, communication skills, interpersonal relations, and skill application. The committees assess applicants "contextually," mindful that their prior access to educational opportunities varies, depending on where they have lived and attended school.

Then the contents of each applicant's file go to one of five admissions counselors, each of whom reviews two hundred or so applications and determines which to recommend for admission when the Selection Committee convenes. This committee is composed of the counselors and additional IMSA staff. They spend days making final decisions about each candidate in light of the reviewing counselor's recommendation and data on all candidates rank-ordered by test scores and grade point averages. The committee also considers additional factors, ranging from more objective variables such as class and applicant pool demographics and a candidate's first language to subjective considerations such as maturity or a "demonstrated pattern of ethical decision-making." Ninth-grade applicants are usually chosen over 8th-grade applicants (who have another year to apply); occasionally, a qualified 8th grader may be offered the chance to enroll the following year.[4] In all, no fewer than sixteen people "touch" a student's application before a decision is made.

IMSA's written admissions policy[5] provides not only a transparent and thorough description of the school's criteria and procedures but also an extensive rationale for each criterion, provisions for students who have been homeschooled or radically accelerated, and detailed descriptors of qualified candidates. This comprehensiveness can be attributed at least in part to a 1999 state audit of IMSA's admissions policy that was sparked by controversy over a rejected applicant.[6] In response to the audit, IMSA officials resolved to review and modify the admissions policy as necessary at least every other year. Since then, the policy has been revised seven times. Administrators say these changes have yielded a process better aligned with the school's mission and its beliefs about talent. Whereas the school used to identify kids who were more "globally talented," the current process is more specific to youngsters'

Table 4.1: Student Demographics, IMSA vs. Illinois (grades 9–12)

	White	Black	Hispanic	Asian/Pacific Islander	American Indian/ Alaska Native
IMSA[a]	42%	8%	5%	42%	< 1%
Illinois[b]	57%	20%	18.5%	4%	< 1%

[a] Source: National Center for Education Statistics, Common Core of Data, 2009–10.
[b] Ibid.

aptitude, achievements, and interest in math and science—what IMSA seeks to develop.

One issue that surfaced in the audit—and that IMSA continues to grapple with—is the extent to which the school's enrollment does (or should) reflect the demographics of Illinois. State law requires it to employ admissions criteria that "ensure adequate geographic, sexual, and ethnic representation."[7] IMSA's present enrollment does not, however, reflect the state's demographics (see table 4.1), despite the school's exhaustive efforts to recruit a more diverse pool of high-quality applicants. Admissions personnel indicated that the student body more closely resembles the ethnic breakdown of the applicant pool and—as in many of the schools we visited—that the number of Asian applicants has increased in recent years. There are slightly more males (51.5 percent) than females at IMSA. Almost 75 percent of the student body hails from the Chicago metro area, the rest from other parts of the state.

Living at School

Perhaps IMSA's most unique attribute from the perspective of would-be applicants and kids who attend other schools is that students who go there also live there. Seven dormitories house about one hundred students apiece. There are three female halls, three male, and one co-ed, each divided into four wings. Adult supervision includes, for each of the seven dorms, a hall coordinator, a residence counselor for each wing, and a day hall supervisor. There are two student leadership positions for juniors and seniors as well. Students live two per room, and share a bathroom. Incoming sophomores are paired with roommates based on an interest survey; juniors and seniors can choose their roommates.

Like the classes at IMSA, residence life is guided by the Standards of Significant Learning and has its own curriculum. A number of practical policies shape it, too, including rules for leaving campus, curfew checks, hosting members of the opposite sex in the room, having off-campus guests and overnight visitors, and cleaning one's room. Students are also encouraged to practice "sustainable living" by limiting their consumption of water and energy, and by recycling. To help sophomores adjust, mandatory study hours are enforced between 7:00 and 9:00 p.m. This restriction (and some others) eases, and privileges increase, with time and as students demonstrate responsible behavior.

Technology and social media have significantly changed how students live at IMSA. Principal Eric McLaren recalled that, in IMSA's early years, "There were no cell phones, no Internet. Our kids now are so connected . . . it's changed the nature of the student experience." Students can readily (and cheaply) contact friends and family, which can help them adjust to living away from home and provide support during stressful times. On the other hand, while laptops and such devices certainly facilitate learning and research in the dorm, they can also deplete and distract from study time. In fact, according to student life director Bob Hernandez, most minor disciplinary infractions involve coming late to or missing class because of oversleeping. Students will say they were "up late studying" when in fact they were using the Internet to surf the Web or chat with friends. One IMSA student wrote in a blog entry (ironically) that she'd recently installed a program on her computer that would limit the amount of time she spent on time-wasting websites. And a graduating senior told us she wished the school had actually been *stricter*—especially during sophomore year—to "condition" her to better time management. For the 2010–11 year, a new practice was introduced: school-supplied Internet access shuts off at 11:00 p.m. Monday–Thursday.

The school's residential character naturally influences who applies, enrolls, and chooses to continue at IMSA. For some parents, having a son or daughter leave home as a young teen to live at school conflicts with cultural and personal beliefs and expectations. (One administrator said that anxiety about the residential component is the foremost deterrent to Hispanic applicants.) Arguably, families that live within reasonable driving distance from the school make a different kind of decision in sending their child to IMSA than those who live way downstate.[8] Approximately 15 percent of incoming students withdraw from IMSA before graduating.[9] One big reason? Homesickness.

Return on the State's Investment?

With a per-pupil spending level of over $30,000 per year, IMSA is frequently—and understandably—asked to justify its worth.[10] On the one hand, achievement test and AP scores, and the numerous awards the school and its students have received (not to mention alumni/ae who were responsible for the likes of YouTube and Yelp), might convince any reasonable citizen that IMSA does well by its graduates. On the other hand, there is no "hard" evidence that it does better at educating them than their "home schools" might have done. One school leader observed, however, that the indicators of success that IMSA favors (e.g., SIR projects, students' contributions to alternative energy) aren't necessarily those that legislators (and critics) look for.[11]

The school is participating in a rigorous study by researchers from the American Psychological Association and the University of Virginia that its administrators and supporters hope will provide valuable data on whether IMSA graduates are more likely than graduates of other (STEM and non-STEM) high schools to pursue STEM-related studies and careers, among other things. School leaders anticipate that the results will help them convince both legislators and those who control other, less precarious sources of funding that past and future investments in IMSA do indeed yield, and will continue to yield, a high return. As current president Glen "Max" McGee put it, IMSA's "value-added" is "harder to quantify but almost impossible to refute."

Chapter 5

School Without Walls

● ● ● ● ● ● ● ● ● ●

Washington, D.C.

Little-Noticed Gem in a Troubled System

Founded in 1971, School Without Walls Senior High School (SWW) gradually evolved from a small (fifty-pupil) "alternative" school designed for District of Columbia pupils who didn't fare well in conventional schools into a larger, highly selective, and academically rigorous college-prep high school for bright, motivated youngsters. In its fortieth year when we visited, it is now one of three academically selective public high schools in D.C.[1]

Adjoining the campus of George Washington University (GW) in the Foggy Bottom neighborhood, SWW spent decades in a decrepit and leaky, albeit historic, school building. (Student tour guides love to point out a quote on the wall from Eleanor Roosevelt decrying the state of the school facility back in the 1940s.) Thanks to a major gift by GW, however (in return for SWW surrendering a small parking lot for university use), plus plenty of additional District money, a massive two-year renovation was undertaken. This finally led, in 2009, to SWW reoccupying a smashing, modern facility that combines the old school (boldly made over within the strictures of historic preservation) with a spacious, bright, attractive, and functional new building. Though the process was arduous and slow—besides the money, plenty of politics were involved within the university, the District of Columbia Public Schools (DCPS), and the D.C. government—the outcome is indeed impressive.

Admissions and Demographics

SWW enrolled 470 students in 2010–11 and is growing to 500+, partly in response to increased demand for admission but also to bring in enough revenue to sustain its academic program as the District cuts its per-pupil funding. Even with that growth, however, the principal expected (as of April 2011) to be obliged to lay off several teachers in order to balance the school's budget.

There's plenty of demand for SWW, with 700 applicants for about 120 openings. (Nearly all students start in 9th grade, with older pupils admitted only to fill empty slots, accommodate special circumstances—such as families that move back to D.C., including State Department and military families—and handle a few foreign exchange pupils who come for a single year.) It draws students from private and charter schools in the District as well as from DCPS. Indeed, the 2010 entering class was the first in which a slight majority of youngsters came from private and charter schools. (Among 2011 entrants, however, 60 percent hailed from DCPS.) Several people commented that the school's grand new facility has attracted a number of "private school families" that find SWW a more appealing option now. From those parents' standpoint, it's obviously a bargain, too, compared with area private schools, and this may have mattered more than usual during the economic downturn. Some speculated, however, that "Walls"—as everyone calls it—could lose some of its allure when the District's well-regarded Woodrow Wilson High School moves into its own new state-of-the-art facility, complete with swimming pool, athletic fields, and an academic program that includes numerous honors and Advanced Placement classes.

SWW uses a multistep admissions process. Even to cross the eligibility threshold, a youngster must have at least a 3.0 average in 7th grade and the first quarter of 8th grade, and be "proficient" in both math and reading (and a written essay) on the District's standardized achievement test.[2] About 460 of the initial 700 applicants typically meet those criteria and are eligible to take SWW's own admission test, which it has adapted from well-regarded high school achievement (and exit) tests used in other states.[3]

Using a cutoff of 41 or more questions answered correctly on the 50-item test generally produces a pool of 200 finalists, all of whom are then interviewed by a school panel consisting of teachers and current students. The interview determines which of the finalists are actually admitted. Of those, 70–80 percent actually enroll.

Demographically, SWW is not fully reflective of the D.C. population. Though students come from every ward in the city, not quite one in five is eligible for the federal free/reduced price lunch program. (Administrators note, however, that many high school students don't even apply for it, especially at this "open campus," where they can leave for lunch outside. Hence these ratios may be misleading.) Only a few pupils (six, when we visited) have special-education plans, and the school does not claim to provide a full battery of special-ed services, though it has a part-time coordinator on staff as well as a visiting psychologist and other such personnel.

When we visited (toward the end of the 2010–11 school year), 58 percent of SWW students were African-American (down from 66 percent a few years back), 28 percent were white, 12 percent Latino, and a few came from Asian or mixed-race backgrounds. Perhaps the most notable demographic feature of the school is that two-thirds of its pupils are girls.[4]

Though we saw no evidence of preferential admissions in the name of diversity, SWW works hard to recruit students from all over town, sending counselors to visit middle schools around the District, especially those located in neighborhoods whose youngsters might not know about it or not think it's a good fit for them.

Academics

To remain at School Without Walls, students must maintain a solid academic record, and SWW makes available all manner of tutoring and other forms of special assistance for struggling pupils. The administrative team is proud of its retention rate; it reports that 90–95 percent of those who enter in 9th grade stay to graduate. (The kids don't entirely agree. Twelfth graders guestimated during our visit that roughly one-quarter of those who had entered Walls with them were no longer there.)[5]

Though SWW follows the essentials of the D.C. high school curriculum, including the requisite number of Carnegie units to graduate, its own curriculum ranges far beyond. It includes mandatory community service, an ambitious senior research project, and most recently a required 10th-grade AP course in world history. (The school's Advanced Placement offerings are many—students take some five hundred AP exams every year, with fees covered by DCPS.) Field trips are frequent and overseas journeys increasingly common. (Parents pay part; grants are sought; and fund-raising is extensive.) The school that initially viewed the urban community as its expanded classroom "without walls" now thinks of the world that way.

SWW offers a full complement of science and math classes but is forthright that its curricular focus is "the humanities."[6] And it enjoys a close and multifaceted relationship with George Washington University, ranging from undergraduates who tutor its students to tuition-free opportunities to take GW courses, even (for a handful of qualified students) to spend their 11th- and 12th-grade years in an "early college" program that yields a GW-conferred associate's degree as well as a high school diploma.[7] GW's school of education is located right next to School Without Walls, though knowledgeable observers say that this proximity has not yet led to the kind of close ties between the two institutions that former GW president Stephen Trachtenberg hoped for.

SWW's classes are relatively small—with 38 teachers for 470 students, the simple teacher/pupil ratio hovers just above 1:12. "Core courses" don't exceed 25 students, and AP classes are kept to 20. SWW's principal is an unabashed advocate of small classes, and would rather offer some courses only in alternate years (in response to budget cuts) than make them bigger. Also noteworthy for a school this size is the presence of four full-time counselors. Each entering class is matched with a counselor who sticks with it for the full four years. By grades 11 and 12, that individual is consumed largely by the college admissions process, an endeavor that the school team takes seriously—both the entrance part and the financial-aid part. On the other hand, parents with whom we spoke indicated that they felt primarily responsible for shepherding their daughters and sons through the college quest and mildly complained that they didn't get much real guidance from the counselors.

There's little staff turnover here. A seven-year teaching veteran said she could recall only once that an instructor had left involuntarily. Initial faculty selection is taken seriously—it's a major focus of the teacher-dominated "personnel committee," as well as the principal—and those who depart have typically retired, gone back to graduate school, or left for other personal reasons. Teachers really like being part of the SWW "family," though they acknowledge that the first year can be rocky as they adjust to classes full of motivated, bright, hard-working students whom they must keep up with—or move ahead of. That's why the recent round of budget reductions—and attendant need to let some teachers go—proved especially painful for all parties. This sort of thing had really never happened in recent memory. And whereas any past layoffs would have been dictated by seniority, in the era of D.C.'s new and much-discussed teachers' contract an elaborate committee process must yield actual judgments—and recommendations to the principal, which he is all but obligated to accept—regarding which of their peers will be laid off.[8] This the faculty found stressful and unpleasant.

On the extracurricular side, SWW offers a goodly array of activities but only limited sports. (It has no immediately accessible outdoor athletic space. This, plus the humanities focus, may account for its disproportion of female students.) When we asked about football, for example, the response was "Well, we recently added a lacrosse team!" SWW students may, however, join teams at other DCPS schools, including, for instance, the crew and swim teams at Wilson High School.

The school's atmosphere is relaxed and friendly. Students move about freely and seem to know all the teachers and administrators. (When we interviewed the principal, he invited our youthful tour guides to linger in his office and take part in the conversation.) Students enjoy quite a lot of freedom—and, in return, must shoulder a high level of personal responsibility. Though the school wants to know where they are, the campus is open, and many pupils spend sizable portions of their time elsewhere. Yet we were told that most "come even when they're ill" because, with many classes meeting just twice a week (for extended blocks of time), missing a single day can mean falling way behind. This is, self-evidently, a school for highly motivated young people who can deal responsibly with freedom. Indeed, staff remarked that some entrants from the District's best-regarded middle schools, including the KIPP charters, are accustomed to such a tightly structured and disciplined environment that they have difficulty adjusting to SWW.

Budget, Politics, and Policy

Parents (and mentors and other adults involved with students' lives) play a large role in School Without Walls and are kept in close contact by teachers and school staff. An active parents' association also helps with fund-raising ($30,000–40,000 per year, sometimes more) to assist with everything from textbook purchase to paying for additional teachers, tutors, or aides.

These parents can also be fussy, critical education consumers. Despite the humanities focus, for example, when we asked a group of them whether any elements of the school had proven disappointing, they quickly mentioned foreign-language instruction as a notable weakness within the curriculum. (As noted above, they also cited shortcomings in the college-admissions counseling realm.)

The school team is outspokenly proud of its track record but can be self-critical, too. SWW enjoys high *Newsweek* rankings, a recent designation by the U.S. Department of Education as a Blue Ribbon school, and virtually 100 percent acceptance of its graduates into four-year colleges, many of them with scholarship assistance. School leaders are also pleased with its recent reaccreditation by Middle States. Though this is not obligatory for D.C. schools, and is indeed burdensome and expensive to obtain, the SWW team believes that "coming from an accredited high school" gives its students an edge in college admissions. The self-study that is required as part of the accreditation process also gave the school team ample opportunity to reflect on its own strengths and shortcomings—and prompted it to make some adjustments to address the latter.

Despite its many strong points, its able faculty, and its impressive performance, the SWW team feels like something of a stepchild of DCPS. Even receiving a Blue Ribbon designation from the federal Education Department, ordinarily regarded across American K–12 education as a big deal, elicited barely a murmur of satisfaction from the District. And while U.S. education secretary Arne Duncan, U.N. ambassador Susan Rice, and other notables have come to visit, apparently former DCPS chancellor Michelle Rhee never turned up and paid little mind to the school, its achievements, or its needs. The SWW principal, nearing the end of his fifth year in that role, acknowledged that he was not a "Rhee[-appointed] person" and indicated that she barely gave him the time of day. (Asked about her successor—the current chancellor—he diplomatically replied "It's too soon to know.")

We asked about waivers and exemptions from conventional regulations and union-contract provisions and were told that SWW has none. On the other hand, it seems simply to disregard those rules that it finds dysfunctional. The principal firmly adheres to the view that, in a bureaucracy like DCPS, it's far "better to seek forgiveness than to ask permission." And so, for example, GW faculty members sometimes teach SWW classes even though they're not "certified" to do so.

Though there's ample evidence of unmet demand from qualified students residing in the District, DCPS has—to the mystification of SWW administrators—made no effort to expand or replicate the school and its program. That the school is gradually growing on its own is, as noted above, partly a response to demand and partly a way to offset budget cuts, even though the additional pupils will likely be housed in other locations.[9]

As those budget cuts got made "downtown," SWW felt singularly put-upon. "It's all political," we were told several times, and the initial round of reductions would have inflicted on this school the largest per-student cuts in DCPS—a reduction from $10,600 to $8,455, which would have meant shrinking the 57-person staff by 11 or 12 positions. Appeals have mitigated this—when we visited, administrators expected the total forthcoming cut to be about $500,000, which translates to a loss of 4 or 5 teachers.

Politics may not tell the full story, however. DCPS is in the middle of a multifaceted struggle to reform its public schools, and the priorities it set for the last budget round emphasized targeting resources on "students at risk" and on enhanced equity. Though this is faithful to the precepts of "weighted student funding"—another reformers' dream—it obviously causes trouble for schools that don't enroll a lot of at-risk youngsters and many of whose pupils are relatively privileged.

D.C.'s School Without Walls is not perfect, and it's clearly not a school for everyone, but, particularly in a city with a famously troubled school system in continuing need of a makeover, it's remarkable what a fine educational institution it is—and yet how little notice or priority it has received in its own community.

Chapter 6

Central High School Magnet Career Academy

• •

Louisville, KY

Career or College Readiness?

When Central High School Magnet Career Academy's current build-ing was completed in 1952, at the corner of Chestnut and 12th streets in the West End of downtown Louisville, its facilities were "unsurpassed in the city's schools."[1] As the neighborhood around the school became increasingly crime-ridden and marked by a combination of housing projects and vacant buildings, one might predict that the school would fall prey to its surroundings. But the yellow-tinged brick building with midcentury-modern touches is more or less "preserved" in something very close to its original state.

A historically black school founded more than 130 years ago, Cen-tral is now one of five magnet high schools with academically selective admissions in the Jefferson County Public Schools (JCPS). In its lobby area, a mural of Muhammad Ali introduces visitors to the school's most famous graduate. Principal of nine years Daniel Withers gradu-ated from Central before becoming a teacher there, and then assistant principal. Although Central is academically selective, unlike some of its district counterparts it's not a high-performing school by traditional measures and doesn't appear at the top of national "best high school" lists. Its Great Schools rating is 4 (out of a possible 10). The average

ACT composite score for its graduating seniors in 2010 was 16.5, two points below the district average and almost 10 points lower than the district's most selective magnet high school, DuPont Manual (25.4).[2] When we visited, the school was in its third year of restructuring under the No Child Left Behind law for failing to make adequate yearly progress. Athletically, Central is a standout, with multiple state championships over the years in football, basketball, and track and field.

In 2010–11, Central received some nine hundred applications for three hundred spots. The main draw, according to school and district staff, is the career magnet academy, consisting of nine career-focused programs from which students choose a "major": Banking/Finance, Business Management, Computer Technology, Law & Government, Pharmacy, Nursing, Dental Science, Pre-Medical Science, and Veterinary Science. In 9th grade, students sample all magnets for three weeks each. Toward the end of the year, they apply for and rank their top three choices. The teacher in charge of each magnet determines its entrance criteria. Students take the magnet courses in addition to schoolwide core subjects, and all magnet courses have college-prep components. Many magnets also involve partnerships with business and professional organizations, among them Papa John's Pizza, Speedway, and Fifth-Third Bank. Students complete most of the programs with certifications that permit them to land entry-level jobs after graduating as, for example, a certified nursing assistant or a pharmacy technician.

The only magnet that is not, strictly speaking, a career-prep pathway is Law & Government.[3] It's one of the most popular, however, with roughly thirty spots available for sixty students who apply. "I'd like to take every kid," said the program instructor, a former prosecutor of twenty years. "You never know whose fire could really be lit." He considers applicants' grades and behavior, as well as their attitude and maturity level, and has students already in the program interview applicants to it. As part of an enhanced partnership with the University of Louisville, students are able to take a college course that he teaches, alongside university students, for dual credit. Internships involving clerical work with private law firms are another opportunity that students in this magnet benefit from. "Law is a lily-white profession," the teacher noted. "If we're ever going to change that, we need to create pipelines to law school."

Although the magnets occasionally take time away from core subjects (e.g., with field trips and special events), in general they are seen as valuable ways to help students make better-informed choices about their futures. As one administrator put it, "The magnet gives kids an alternative if college doesn't work out, for whatever reason." Of about twenty-five graduating seniors in a nursing class, half said they were planning to go into a health-related field, through either college study or the workplace.

History

Central's heritage as Louisville's sole high school for black students is a source of pride among many alumni/ae; consequently, a good number of students apply to Central at the urging of parents or relatives who went there.

According to its website, Central High School began "in a time dramatically different from now: a time of separation, injustice, and inequality for many people." The "time" was just after the Civil War, in 1870, when a group of prominent black citizens petitioned the Louisville Board of Education to establish free schools for their children. A school for "educating children of the African race" was opened, financed by taxes collected from all black-owned property. What became Central Colored High School grew from the original grades 1–8 building and occupied several different locations in its first seventy years before moving to its current address.

In the first decade of the twentieth century, following the urgings of Booker T. Washington and other national black leaders, the school's academic focus was augmented with training in "useful" skills such as dressmaking, automobile mechanics, and plumbing. Parent and student protests in 1945 led to the word "colored" being dropped from the school's name. By 1950, the school had grown to almost 1,300 students. Both the academic and vocational programs remained intact.

Brown v. Board of Education of Topeka eventually led to controversial changes both at Central and in the Louisville schools generally, all centering on desegregation efforts. Central was still the only black high school in September 1975, when court-mandated busing began. Many Central alumni/ae, teachers, and then-current students strongly opposed the desegregation effort, fearing that it would erode the excellence, spirit, and tradition of the school. Indeed, a kind of "enrollment chaos" ensued over the next twenty-five years.

As a result of busing and racial quotas, Central was 70 percent white by 1982. According to one faculty member, between 1975 and 1991 it was "pretty much an empty school," with some black families moving to the suburbs. To draw black students back into the school, in 1986 Central started offering magnet courses.

Jefferson County's school-integration plans were revised multiple times over the years in response to various court rulings, and in 1991 all schools were required to be 15–50 percent black. Career programs and magnets were used throughout the district to encourage further integration. Central adopted its magnet programs in 1992 under the guidance of then-principal Harold Fenderson.

By 1997, the school was nearly 50 percent black and yet also about 50 percent below capacity: it had almost six hundred openings owing to low enrollment of white students. Because of the racial quotas, Central could not fill these openings with black students and had to turn many black applicants away. According to one administrator, at that time, "If you were white and breathing, you were in." The school board denied community members' requests to exempt Central from the quota. Dr. Withers, assistant principal at the time, was opposed to the idea of quotas preventing students from coming to Central. "I want diversity," he said, "but I want kids who want to be here." In 1998, parents of six black students who had been denied admission to Central brought a lawsuit against JCPS. Two years later, the federal district court ruled in their favor and struck down the use of racial quotas for the district's magnet schools. *Meredith v. Jefferson County Board of Education*, the case that even-

Table 6.1: Enrollment in Jefferson County's Academically Selective Magnet High Schools (2009–10)

	Central	DuPont Manual	Louisville Male	Butler	Brown (K–12)
Total enrollment	1,036	1,856	1,782	1,655	635
White	8%	70%	66%	70%	58%
Black	78%	17%	30%	26%	33%
Hispanic	8%	2%	1%	1%	1%
Asian/Pacific Islander	3%	10%	2%	2%	2%
Eligible for free/ reduced-price lunch	84%	15%	23%	39%	21%

Source: NCES Common Core of Data, 2009–10.

tually went to the U.S. Supreme Court, challenged the county's use of quotas in its regular schools. The plaintiff was a white kindergartener who had been denied admission to a school close to his house, even though space was available there.

Today, no racial quotas are in place for the JCPS magnet high schools, including those that are academically selective. And all now enroll 50 percent or more of one race (see table 6.1). In four out of five cases, that means mostly white.

Most people we spoke with believe that Central's demographics influence how people view it. "[Central] has a positive image," said one administrator, "but we're still seen as 'the black school.'" Though some staff members feel the school's reputation in the district has improved ("We used to be the doormat," said one longtime faculty member), others think the school is still not given due respect. Bernadette Hamilton, director of the JCPS Optional, Magnet, and Advance Programs (and a Central graduate), agreed: "Central is still living under the stigma of 'that's where the black kids go.'" Students and teachers also complained that television news reporting detracts from the school's image by associating it with crimes in the neighborhood. "They always show Central on camera, to give people an idea of where the stuff happened," one student said. "But then people think that Central students were involved, or that things are happening at the school. I wish they wouldn't." When asked how often Central is compared with the other magnets, one teacher said, "Not as often as we should be!" and suggested that the "schools with different populations" tend to get more positive press.

Admissions

Attending any high school in JCPS today means filling out an application. Beginning in 2010–11, all nonmagnet high schools were divided into three "networks." Each school has its own Professional Career Theme and programs designed to attract applicants. Students can apply either to any school in their network or to any districtwide magnet high school. In the fall, JCPS holds a "Showcase of Schools" at the Louisville Convention Center, essentially a recruitment fair for elementary, middle, and high school magnet schools and programs.

The process for applying to a magnet high school, including Central, involves two steps. First, students submit a general application to the district office, indicating two school choices. There are questions related to race,[4] but also—in deference to the Supreme Court's *Meredith v. Jefferson County* decision—the statement that "*Information on race will not be used in the assignment of an individual student*" (emphasis in the application form).

The rest of the process is handled at the school level (and without further questions about ethnicity or race). Students receive a letter from the schools to which they are applying with additional direction about what other materials to submit. Each school designs its own application, and all schools must keep the Office of Optional, Magnet, and Advance Programs abreast of the criteria they are using and any changes they make to those criteria or their admissions procedures. Central requires a writing sample, recommendations from math and science teachers, a recommendation from a guidance counselor or principal, a middle school transcript, attendance records, test scores, and a behavior report.

Ms. Hamilton, who oversees the application process at the district level, reflected on the selectivity of some of the magnet high schools:

"Anytime you say, 'Yes, we want you. No, we don't want you,' there are challenges." She felt that, ultimately, decentralized admissions allow schools to "see" the kids who are applying to them and that it would be difficult for personnel who are not actually in a school to select students for someone else's programs.

At Central, a teacher committee reviews applications and votes on whether to accept or reject each applicant. For the 2010–11 academic year, the school received about 900 applications and accepted 310. The coordinator in charge said: "Our goal is to get the best possible kids in here. . . . And because we can choose our kids, why not choose better kids?" For the previous year, the school took about 50 more applicants than its 300 guideline, choosing to increase its entering class by over 15 percent. In retrospect, the admissions coordinator surmised maybe "there's a law of diminishing returns," as that class of students, he said, wasn't faring as well academically. Since then, the school has admitted closer to 300 students per year.

College vs. Career?

The emphasis on career-oriented magnet programs at Central raises the question of whether this approach detracts from preparing students for college. Staff are undeniably proud of their magnet programs but, as one teacher said, "Central has always 'straddled the fence' [between college prep and career prep], to our detriment. In the face of high-stakes testing, we've increased our college focus, like on how kids are doing on the ACT." (For his own part, he said, he tries to emphasize transferable skills, like organization, that kids will need regardless of where they end up.) A central office administrator reported that some parents mistakenly perceive that Central doesn't emphasize college readiness. For core subjects, students can take one of three levels of classes —regular, honors, or "Advance"—in addition to five Advanced Placement courses (far fewer than at most schools on our list).

According to data on Central's School Report Card for 2009–10, although the school has a 92 percent graduation rate, the later paths of

Table 6.2: "Transition to Adult Life" Data for Central High School, Jefferson County Public Schools, and the Commonwealth of Kentucky

	College	Military	Work	Voc/tech training	Work & part-time school	Not successful[a]
Central HS	60.0%	1.7%	9.6%	1.7%	7.0%	20.0%
District	66.6%	1.8%	16.4%	5.7%	4.7%	4.7%
State	56.4%	2.4%	22.8%	6.3%	6.5%	5.6%

[a]The Kentucky Department of Education defines a successful transition in these terms: enrolled as a full-time student at a postsecondary school (a minimum of 12 units per semester); employed at least 30 hours per week in a permanent position; employment includes paid work (self- employed or for a business), caring for children/family in the home, community service, or religious duties; an active member of the United States military; or involved in any work/school combination adding up to at least 30 hours per week. Graduates who are un- or underemployed, and graduates who could not be found or verified, are classified as "not successful."

its alumni/ae are less certain, with only 60 percent going to college full-time and 20 percent classified "not successful" (table 6.2). During our visit, school personnel said that only 30 percent of those who do attend college complete their sophomore year.

Faced with such data, Central's teachers and guidance counselors must decide how to help students plan for their futures, especially when, as one teacher put it, "some kids have immediate needs that are so great they have no time to devote to education" and may not anytime soon.

On the one hand, some faculty felt that not all Central students can go to college, or are college-bound. "Kids need to know, 'Hey, it's okay if I become a truck driver,'" one said. Another perspective is, "Aspiration [to go to college] is one thing, but let's see what your skill set is. . . . What are they really ready for?" However jarring, these sentiments seemed to be rooted in genuine concern for students. "I want a kid to leave high school wanting to be good at something," a teacher said, feeling strongly that the "something" need not necessarily involve college.

One guidance counselor offered a different view. New to Central from another high school in JCPS, she felt that directing students into careers is perhaps easier than helping them with the process of applying to college but that, with support, most students at the school can get into, pay for, and succeed in a college of their choice. Rather than blame lack of parent support or kids' circumstances, she felt a more productive path would be to prepare students for a range of possibilities. "Regardless of your background," she said, "all seniors should have choices—they should all have to make decisions. . . . Life happens. Now is the time to take advantage of the support, while it's still available." Kentucky offers numerous scholarships to state schools for minority students who meet minimum GPA requirements. The counselor proudly opened a binder of acceptance and scholarship letters for this year's seniors—many with financial aid packages in the tens of thousands of dollars. "I tell kids, go where you have the least to pay."

Despite different views among staff members as to whether Central should expect all its students to prepare for college, everyone seems to feel a strong obligation to prepare students for "the real world." During our visit, a number of students were participating in a yearly simulation designed for this purpose called "The Reality Store." Each student received a role (e.g., "married with two children") and a job before visiting "stations" that simulated different financial obligations in the real world (e.g., buying insurance, paying for rent/utilities). Like most high schoolers of any background, students emerged from this experience surprised by how quickly a paycheck gets spent. But it appeared that this "dose of reality" was more targeted at keeping students from dropping out of high school rather than at teaching them practical economic principles or the value of going to college.

Perhaps most telling about Central High School is that leaders, teachers, and students consistently characterize it as a "family." And like a family, they protectively defend one another and the school. "We aren't ashamed of this school," said Dr. Withers. "We're proud of it, and the community is proud of it."

Chapter 7

Liberal Arts and Science Academy

● ● ● ● ● ● ● ● ● ● ● ● ● ● ●

Austin, TX

Upstairs, Downstairs: From Program to School

Although its origins date to 1985, Austin's Liberal Arts and Science Academy, known to all as LASA, has been a full-fledged high school only since 2007.

It began as a magnet program with a math, science, and technology focus back when the Austin Independent School District (AISD) was getting serious about desegregation. Those in charge at the time judged that situating a rigorous, academically selective magnet within the Lyndon B. Johnson High School—in a then-mostly Black neighborhood on the lower-income "east of I-35" side of town—would draw white students to the school and boost its overall performance while advancing integration. In fact, they created two such programs for this purpose, the second a "liberal arts" magnet (i.e., English and history) within another comprehensive high school, also located in a poor minority neighborhood.[1]

In 2002, led by then-superintendent Pascal Forgione, the two programs were merged into a single magnet, thereafter known as LASA and housed at LBJ.[2] Five years later, also under Forgione's leadership, the district turned LASA into a full-fledged high school in its own right, with a complete curriculum and its own identifying number within the Texas school tracking system.[3]

The school is still housed on the LBJ campus, however, where its 880 students occupy the second floor, leading to something of an "upstairs-downstairs" divide and occasional tension between the two institutional housemates, not least because several key parts of the facility and program are still shared. (These include the auditorium, gym, and cafeteria as well as athletic teams, yearbook, and a number of other extracurriculars.)

Downstairs, LBJ high school is almost entirely low-income and minority—today about half black and half Latino, though the Hispanic portion is rising in concert with Austin's changing demography. LBJ also teeters on the brink of unsatisfactory academic performance under the Texas school-accountability system.[4]

Why LASA was turned from magnet program within LBJ into full-fledged high school is a multichapter tale, but was in part a response to state and federal policy, as well as the seductions of private philanthropy. When the magnet students were included within LBJ's outcomes data, their high scores tended to mask the weaker performance of the kids downstairs—not a good thing if one wants to strengthen that performance. At the same time, because Texas guarantees state-university admission to students in the top 10 percent of their high school graduating class—a way to foster diversity in higher education without using racial criteria—the LASA students tended to soak up all those slots, leaving few or none for the less advantaged (and mostly minority) youngsters downstairs. This fostered considerable resentment, particularly in the immediate vicinity of LBJ where those kids lived.[5] Turning LASA into a separate school meant that LBJ would have its own "top 10 percent."

Admissions, Demographics, and the Middle Class

Admission to LASA resembles that of a selective college. The five-part entrance "rubric" includes applicants' middle school grades, teacher recommendations, and test scores, plus the school's own aptitude exam, state achievement test results ("TAKS" scores), and several essays.[6] This process winnows about 300 acceptances from the 500- to 600-child applicant pool that the school usually gets, and some 90 percent of those offered admission actually enroll. Included in the new admits are about twenty 10th graders—mainly to fill vacancies created by the 10 percent or so of 9th graders who opt not to return to LASA. Also included are a handful of "probationary" pupils, about whom the school team is unsure but willing to give an opportunity, provided they attend a short but intensive prep program during the summer before ninth grade.[7]

In pursuit of diversity (and communitywide support), the LASA team works hard at outreach to middle schools throughout AISD, contacting counselors, speaking to students themselves, and using current LASA pupils as part of this recruitment effort. The students are the best way to showcase the school's diversity—and its receptivity to black and Latino youngsters—particularly considering that LASA, when we visited, had no African-American teachers and just a few Hispanic faculty members (mainly teaching foreign languages). This dearth of ethnic diversity on the staff is said to be a topic of frequent conversation within the school's leadership team, but if it's a problem, that seems to be the case districtwide.[8]

In further pursuit of pupil diversity, LASA also avails itself of several nondistrict efforts such as the privately funded "Breakthrough" program designed to clear a path to college for first-generation students.[9] Yet despite all the outreach, more than two-thirds of LASA pupils come from Austin's two academically selective middle school magnets, versus about 20 percent from all other AISD middle schools. (There are about twenty.) That means much of LASA's selection process starts, de facto, when youngsters are in fifth grade, deciding where to go in sixth. This has both pluses and minuses—the clearest advantage being that able youngsters in Austin can obtain a high-quality academic education within this urban public-school system beginning at a relatively young age, and can emerge from middle school well prepared for the academic rigors of LASA and other selective high schools. On the other hand, this process plainly gives some advantage to kids whose families are savvy and motivated enough to navigate an early entry into the city's "magnet" sector.[10]

LASA itself is decently integrated in ethnic terms. As with several other schools on our list, it can legitimately call itself the "most diverse school in town," with 23 percent Hispanic, 4 percent black, 15 percent Asian, 54 percent white, and 4 percent multiracial pupils, drawn from neighborhoods throughout the city. It does not, however, have a low-income enrollment representative of Austin; just under one in five LASA pupils qualifies for the federal subsidized-lunch program, while the district regards more than 60 percent of its total student population as "economically disadvantaged." Not many LASA pupils have special-ed IEPs (Individualized Education Plans), either, and the school has no program for youngsters with limited English proficiency, although some 28 percent of the total AISD enrollment consists of English-language learners. (Most of those, however, are in elementary schools.)[11]

Finances

LASA's efforts to foster diversity are helped by the fact that AISD runs an extensive busing system that brings youngsters from across this sprawling, traffic-jammed district to the LASA/LBJ campus each morning and takes them home in the afternoon.[12] During our visit, the hottest issue at the school—and throughout AISD, but especially in the citywide magnets—was whether the severe budget cuts that the system was (and would be) struggling with would radically curtail the busing program, thus making schools like LASA markedly harder to get to and from.[13] (Eventually, the district decided to take the busing issue "off the table" for the time being, so transportation will continue as before, at least through 2011–12.)

LASA's administrative team says the school gets the lowest per-pupil funding in AISD, primarily because its demographics don't entitle it to categorical monies intended for disadvantaged kids and its strong academic performance means it doesn't quality for "turnaround" funding, either. On the other hand, AISD provides additional "magnet program" teaching positions—almost a dozen of these at LASA—and (so far) absorbs the extra transportation costs associated with busing districtwide magnet pupils farther than kids in geographically zoned schools. The systemwide budget reductions now underway will, however, mean a loss of teaching positions at LASA.

The school's lean leadership team has been in flux. Halfway through the 2010–11 year, the principal was abruptly relieved of his duties (evidently owing to personal misbehavior) and an interim principal named. In June 2011, that individual was moved out and a new permanent principal brought in from a mid-level leadership position in another Austin high school.

Academics

The school's track record is strong, judged "exemplary" by the state and ranked very high by both *Newsweek* and *U.S. News*. The class of 2010 boasted an average SAT score totaling 1877, an average ACT score of 26, scads of National Merit finalists, and a stellar college-placement track record.[14]

As in other schools we visited, the students, almost without exception, appear motivated, self-directed, eager, intellectually acute, and self-aware. "If you're the smartest person in the room," one of them remarked, explaining why he wanted to attend LASA rather than a comprehensive high school nearer home, "you're in the wrong room." An administrator described the student body as "taking geekdom to a new level"—but the kids can be a little boastful, too. When it comes time for mandatory state testing, for example, they're known to bring pillows to the room so they can ostentatiously "nap" after speeding through the test in far less than the allotted time.

Also much as in other schools we visited, the atmosphere is calm but intellectually alive, and the classes we saw were stimulating, with engaged students and knowledgeable, engaged teachers. Attendance is nearly perfect, conventional high school discipline is no problem, and the challenges that students present are likelier to arise from stress (and cheating associated with competitiveness) than from behavior issues.

Though there were hints at LASA—as at other schools—that not every instructor is at the top of his/her game ("some people are just punching the time clock"), most appeared competent and motivated. Teacher selection, we were told, is "worked out" between the principal and the central office downtown, and most of LASA's instructional staff is plainly stimulated and gratified by the opportunity to work with "these gifted, wonderful kids and colleagues." Recruiting such instructors to the premier secondary school in the alluring city of Austin is relatively easy. On the other hand, it's hard, even in Texas, to "non-renew" a teaching contract. Layoffs pose a real challenge, too, even though the district ranks "seniority" as only the third of four factors to be considered in making those decisions.[15] At the time of our visit, it was feared that LASA could end up losing as many as seven of its fifty-two teaching slots, though retirements and various personnel machinations finally meant the school had to sacrifice just two instructors that it hated to lose. Still, class sizes are definitely growing, and some courses may have to be dropped or offered less frequently.

Faculty members are especially proud of a quartet of interdisciplinary "signature" classes that they developed: Electronic Magazine (creating both a print and digital publication), SciTech (employing robotics and other sophisticated technologies), Planet Earth (geobiology), and Great Ideas. The school's other course descriptions read more like those of a college than a public high school, with subjects including medical microbiology, playwriting, constitutional law, and fifth-year Japanese.[16] Students can also get "dual enrollment" credit from the local community college. Veteran teachers enthusiastically talk of the entrepreneurialism and innovativeness of LASA's original faculty and curriculum but also complain that contemporary "accountability" pressures and the college-admissions frenzy are eroding the school's distinctiveness. "You don't have innovative curriculum unless you have innovative [student-performance] evaluations" associated with those courses, we were told, and the obligation to take lots of state tests as well as Advanced Placement exams was said to foster conformity on the part of both pupils and instructors.

Relations between LASA and the superintendent's office appeared decent, for the most part, but teachers regard some central-office demands as irrelevant, such as mandatory "in-service" programs on issues that don't apply to LASA (test prep, classroom control, etc.). Mostly, though, they just feel ignored ("We have a national reputation but they don't know us downtown"), even as they recognize that such neglect is not an altogether bad thing; they simply ignore some citywide rules and procedures—and nobody seems to mind very much.

The Future

As in other districts with similar schools, two strong rationales for the existence of LASA (and the academic-magnet middle schools that send many of their own graduates to it) are to afford a strong public-sector option for low-income families with able youngsters and to retain middle-class families in the city and its public-education system.[17]

Unlike several other communities that we visited, however, academic selectivity does not seem terribly contentious in Austin. State law allows for it, and local residents are accustomed to it. Moreover, in a city with an enormous number of university professors and high-tech firms, as well as the state capitol, and with plenty of mobility and choosiness on the part of its educated middle-class populations, there's considerable demand for academically rigorous school options for kids.

At the same time, practically nobody in the "education reform" world in Texas and beyond seems interested in the future of schools like this, and nearly all private philanthropy and government grants focus instead on troubled schools and those serving needy kids. There is also said to be lingering resentment among other AISD principals because LASA "takes all the good kids." One teacher remarked that it's "the most political school in the district."

Though there's been talk of turning LASA into a charter school, that would be costly—in both start-up funds and operating budgets—and the extra autonomy and self-government that accompany such a change don't seem quite worth it, at least not when revenues are scarce.

The school does engage in a modest amount of external fund-raising but less than in years past. When it was new, it benefited from some $800,000 in grants from industry and the National Science Foundation, which helped pay for innovative curriculum development and such. Now there is only a trickle of grant dollars, as well as some private and community support from the "parents and friends of LASA." This gives teachers a bit of spending money for classroom supplies and allows them to apply for "mini-grants." The extra funding also helps pay for textbooks and other instructional materials that aren't on the state-adoption list. ("We have to buy the books on that list but we tend not to use them.")

The LASA team dreams of someday having its own facility and campus, being able to grow beyond what its current physical plant allows, not having to engage in complicated scheduling exercises with LBJ over their joint facilities, and ending what remains of the "upstairs-downstairs" touchiness. For now, however, it seems destined to stay where it is and to continue providing a top-notch academic program for a diverse (if unrepresentative) population of very smart teenagers in the capital city of our second-largest state.

Chapter 8

Jones College Prep

● ● ● ● ● ● ● ● ●

Chicago, IL

From Commerce Prep to College Prep

Over the past fifteen years, the commercial and residential growth of Chicago's South Loop has transformed the area into a desirable place to shop and live. In that same time, a high school on the corner of South State Street was also transformed—from Jones Metropolitan High School of Business and Commerce into Jones College Prep, a high-performing selective-enrollment school with a mission to "help students develop themselves as leaders through a rigorous college prep program that focuses on educating the whole person." Lesser known than some of its Chicago Public Schools (CPS) peers (e.g., Whitney Young, Northside College Prep, Walter Payton), Jones has steadily elevated its profile and attracted higher-achieving applicants. "We used to be under the radar," said Joe Powers, an administrative veteran from outside CPS and Jones's principal for the past three years. The school has lately garnered a number of awards and appeared on lists of top high schools. In 2006, it was the first CPS high school to be named a U.S. Department of Education Blue Ribbon school.

It's hard to imagine that any CPS school beats Jones's location on the south edge of downtown, steps away from the financial district, several public and private colleges, theaters, museums, Grant and Millennium parks, and the lakefront. The mammoth Harold Washington Library sits two blocks to the north and, in fact, began doubling as Jones's library when the school library was ousted to resolve space issues. (Some students remarked that "nobody really used [the school library] anyway," and "the public library has everything we need.") Geography may also contribute to Jones being the most racially balanced of the CPS selective-enrollment high schools (table 8.1). The city's other eight selective high schools are located in places that demand difficult commutes from many parts of town. By contrast, Jones is easily accessed from the south, west, and north via public transportation. (East is, of course, Lake Michigan.)

One Hispanic student emphasized that, for him, Jones's diversity wasn't as much about race as it was about exposure to a range of *ideas*. "I know in a lot of schools you get a more homogeneous environment," he explained. "It's not like that here. There are so many clubs you can join to find out about other people. As a freshman, I joined the Jewish club, because I had no idea [what they believed]. It was cool."

In addition to location and diversity, students and parents cite Jones's relatively intimate size among its most appealing characteristics. "Every teacher knows who the kids are, even if they don't have them in class," one parent said. Safety is another advantage, especially when compared to the alternatives. Another parent said, "At [School X], they boasted that there was only one shooting this year. Our biggest problem here is a few kids smoking pot." A female student was thankful that she didn't get "picked on" at Jones, as she had been in middle school. Students recognize, too, that Jones affords them opportunities they might not otherwise have. One young man who had been accepted at Yale elaborated on the powerful impact of his involvement in various school clubs that developed his "passion for service" and opened doors to global travel.

Jones is one of five academically selective public high schools in Chicago that rank among the top performing in the state, providing viable—and, in some cases, superior—alternatives to moving to the suburbs, paying for private or parochial school, or risking a charter. One parent of a senior quipped, "We looked at [a private school], but it just didn't have a $25,000 advantage over Jones." Another parent

Table 8.1: Student Demographics, Chicago Selective-Enrollment Public High Schools, 2009–10

	Total enrollment	American Indian/Alaska Native	Asian/Pacific Islander	Black	Hispanic	White	Free/reduced-price lunch
Brooks	750	< 1%	< 1%	86%	12%	< 1%	87%
Jones	823	< 1%	14%	25%	32%	29%	55%
King	893	0%	1%	96%	2%	1%	74%
Lane	4,191	< 1%	13%	12%	43%	30%	65%
Lindblom	724	0%	< 1%	75%	21%	3%	N/A
Northside	1,067	1%	32%	5%	23%	39%	35%
Payton	903	< 1%	15%	27%	24%	34%	33%
Westinghouse[a]	278	0%	1%	77%	20%	1%	89%
Young	2,234	< 1%	19%	31%	20%	33%	39%

Source: NCES Common Core of Data, 2009–10.

[a] Westinghouse is not included on our list of 165 academically selective schools because it was opened in 2009–10 and does not yet include 12th grade.

whose older children had gone private said, "You sometimes forget that [Jones] is a *public* school. I have to catch myself to refer to it as 'public.'"

History

The original "Jones"—named after William Jones, first president of the CPS Board of Education—was an elementary school located near the current school site. In 1921, it became a high school (Jones Continuation), and then a two-year vocational business school for girls (Jones Commercial). In 1967, the school moved into a new facility intentionally designed to look like an office building and became one of the city's first magnet options for secondary students. But it maintained its focus on preparing young women for entry-level office positions as it underwent another name change in 1983 (Jones Metropolitan High School of Business and Commerce). One teacher who recalled the transition in 1998 said, "We always prepared kids for college," adding that, while the school's class offerings changed, the diversity of the student body didn't.

Before becoming a selective-enrollment high school for the 1998–99 academic year, Jones was attended largely by black and Latino students (see figure 8.1). After the school became "Jones College Prep," its demographics shifted significantly. Hispanic students are now the largest subgroup, and there are more Asian and white students than ever before. Increased competition to get into the school, changing demographics in the surrounding neighborhoods, and the city's evolving admissions process are probably among the reasons.

Jones also has three special-education programs involving 10–15 percent of enrolled students. Per CPS policy, students in "high incidence" categories (e.g., learning disabled) enter through the selective enrollment process and are fully integrated in the college prep program. The school also houses two "low incidence" cluster programs for students with more severe cognitive impairments. These students are placed at Jones in a mostly self-contained setting.

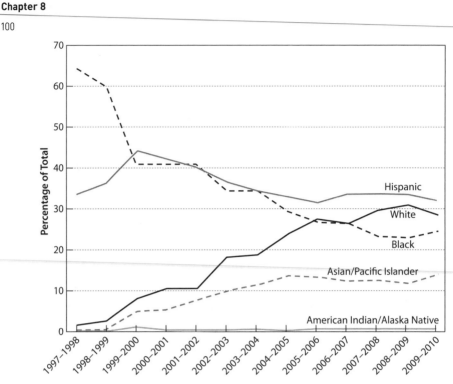

Figure 8.1: Changes in Enrollment Demographics at Jones College Prep, 1997–2010

Getting In

Admission to Jones—as to all selective-enrollment high schools in CPS—is a centralized process overseen by the district's Office of Academic Enhancement (OAE), whose job is to "make sure that the right kid is in the right seat," according to one administrator in that department, which means determining which of 15,000–16,000 applicants should be matched to approximately 3,000 available slots.

Created to help implement a 1980 desegregation consent decree, the OAE had two goals: "(1) to achieve and maintain the greatest possible number of stably desegregated schools and (2) to provide educational programs that would move toward equity of outcomes for all students, particularly those in schools that cannot be desegregated because of the demographics of the city." To help achieve these ends, CPS used a variety of magnet and selective-enrollment programs and schools under what is still called the "Options for Knowledge" program. A "racial balance" policy also dictated that a school's enrollment could not contain more than 30 percent of any one racial group. Applicants to the selective-enrollment high schools were sorted into "minority" and "non-minority" lists and admitted to schools by score according to their ethnic status.

In September 2009, a federal court vacated the three-decades-old consent decree, determining that CPS had demonstrated as much significant compliance with the mandates as was practical and that judicial oversight was no longer necessary. This returned control of the admissions process entirely to CPS. In light of the Supreme Court's 2007 decision in *Meredith v. Jefferson County*, it also meant that continuing to use race as a criterion for entry into any school would be legally risky. These developments, in addition to ongoing allegations of improprieties in the selection process (i.e., less-than-qualified children of influential individuals being granted admission to the most competitive high schools), compelled changes to the admissions process for all selective-enrollment high schools in CPS.

Today, qualified students[1] submit 7th-grade report-card grades in core subjects and standardized test scores in reading and math, and take an entrance exam. Each of these elements is worth a maximum of 300 points for 900 points total. A rubric determines how many points an applicant receives for his or her grades and test scores. All applicants' total points are then ranked from high to low citywide. Thirty percent of the seats offered in a given year are to the top scorers on this list.

The remaining 70 percent of seats are offered to applicants based on their scores relative to other students in their same socioeconomic "tier." Essentially, the district assigns each census tract in the city a score that is based on variables that correlate with educational outcomes— median family income, adult educational attainment, percentage of single-parent households, percentage of owner-occupied homes, and percentage of population speaking a language other than English—as well as achievement scores from feeder schools in the tract. This approach is, strictly speaking, racially blind, yet aimed at maintaining racial diversity. In general, for admission to the most competitive schools through this pathway, a student who lives in a part of the city in tier 3 or 4 (denoting higher socioeconomic status) needs a higher total score than a student in tier 1 or 2—a reality that has not gone unnoticed or unchallenged by parents of applicants in those tiers.

For both the rank- and tier-based admission methods, a computer considers the "best fit" between a student's top six school choices and his or her total points, and ultimately makes a single offer of admission to each applicant. (Jones was the first choice of 70 percent of students who were admitted to its entering class of 2010–11). Not all offers are accepted, so schools use additional "rounds" to fill their seats. CPS policy also permits the principals to select 5 percent of the incoming class through a separate application process that allows the applicant to submit additional evidence of academic performance or promise (e.g., personal statement, awards, letters of recommendation).

Jones's principal feels that the new admission process is "working" for his school, insofar as maintaining the diversity and quality of the student body is concerned. One OAE representative asserted that "there is no 'gaming' this process," and also noted that if they relied strictly on students' grades and test scores, the selective-enrollment schools would almost certainly "go white." Presumably, this is more a concern for the higher-achieving schools like Payton, Young, Jones, and Northside College Prep. While none of those schools (nor any of the eight) was more than 39 percent white, four were more than 75 percent black (see table 8.1).[2]

The "Prep" in College Prep

Dr. Powers described the model Jones student as committed to academics, the life of the school, and other people; able to look at peers as equals; and willing to embrace diversity. Both he and his teachers recognized that even high-performing, highly motivated students need support and encouragement to grow toward these qualities and those expressed in the school's "Profile of the Ideal Graduate of Jones College Prep at Graduation."[3] "The teacher is the first line of support," he said—and it shows. Parents and students described dedicated professionals clocking long hours before and after school to help students succeed, including some youngsters who came to Jones having been very successful in elementary school but without having had to work very hard there.

One student likened her first year at Jones to "jumping into a cold shower." Another related, "I didn't expect to be challenged so much. I'd been used to getting things right away. I came in prepared, I think. . . . I just wasn't used to the pace. And the teachers won't baby you around. They care, but you have to show initiative." Rather than blame feeder schools or the admissions process, teachers and counselors help students through these sometimes-rough transitions. One teacher explained: "We have a lot of support systems in place. We can reach out to kids who are bright but [who] might not be seen as motivated, or who might have challenges at home."

The young man on his way to Yale recounted his most challenging experience at Jones: "I was used to being great at everything, but physics was really hard. I started with a C average. I went for help every day after school, though. And the teacher helped me, which I think shows the commitment that teachers here at Jones have." (Did it work?) "I aced the final," he beamed.

Many Jones graduates are the first in their family to attend college. And as one teacher put it, "For some kids, this is their one chance to get out of the neighborhood." To provide support for that process, all students participate in a College Knowledge program taught by school counselors. Junior year, the class builds familiarity with the ACT and Work Keys exam (which also doubles as the state test in Illinois), conducting college searches, and writing mock application essays. Senior year emphasizes filling out college applications and financial aid forms and applying for scholarships. One student remarked that, during his last two years at Jones, his counselor was "like a member of my family." These relationships and explicit instruction apparently pay off. True to its name, Jones boasts nearly 100 percent college acceptance and matriculation rates. One parent noted proudly, "College isn't the exception here; it's the rule." According to Dr. Powers, a recent graduating class had collectively earned over $15 million in college scholarships.

Still, Jones administrators, counselors, and teachers insist that academic expectations and the emphasis on getting into college don't eclipse developing "balanced individuals." Toward this end, students are sometimes discouraged from taking too many of the school's twenty Advanced Placement classes at once. Some parents and students, however, mentioned "running out" of challenging course options at Jones. In previous years, CPS had funded dual-enrollment courses with nearby colleges. Budget cuts have since eliminated that option, save for students willing or able to pay out of pocket.

Autonomy in an Urban System

Jones is one of the CPS high schools designated an Autonomously Managed Performance School (AMPS). Chosen for high academic or operational performance—or for submitting an innovative plan for using autonomy to increase student achievement—AMPS schools enjoy considerable freedom in making decisions and implementing changes in their buildings. In general, they are not required to implement certain curricula and are given *suggestions* for change by central office administrators, rather than mandates. All nine selective high schools are in AMPS by virtue of their solid academic performance. A district administrator agreed that this advantages schools that choose their own students but noted, "These [selective] schools are managed by the market." Jones's principal attributed to AMPS his strong sense of autonomy in that position.

Jones's AMPS status also means that it is not subject to evaluation via administrative walk-throughs, only through data. As the competition to get into Jones becomes fiercer, so too does "proving" (if only to itself) that its students' performance is attributable to what happens *after* students are admitted. "We have to make sure our value-added is apparent," said Dr. Powers. He noted that 65–70 percent of students were making expected gains from the EXPLORE test to the ACT, "but we need to do better." An area ripe for improvement, he believes, is increased curricular alignment, both vertically (between courses in a department at different grade levels) and horizontally (across the same course taught by different teachers). Along with Lindblom and Brooks—two other selective high schools—Dr. Powers opted his school into a curriculum project for the 2011–12 school year designed to help him and his teachers achieve that goal.[4]

The Future

Jones College Prep will soon add another chapter to its history when it moves into a new, eight-floor, $100 million building just south of the current campus with the capacity to enroll 1,250 students. When that happens (in 2013, we were told), the school may transition to a dual program model of 50 percent selective enrollment and 50 percent career/tech. A CPS administrator pointed out that this would give more students access to Jones—and to the new building—and speculated that in the future the district was likely to have more dual programs than self-contained schools like Jones. But the idea of a mixed model doesn't sit well with everyone. "I don't want us to lose our identity," said the principal, referring to Jones's diversity and "culture of cooperation and respect." One parent was concerned that such a program—and any use of lottery admissions that might come with it—would eventually double enrollment and depersonalize the environment. Teachers were likewise concerned about losing Jones's "intimacy," sacrificing the culture of the school, and lowering standards. To complicate matters, the local alderman's office requested that three hundred enrollments be allotted to students who live in the South Loop.

Regardless of the direction Jones takes, in its relatively short life as a selective-enrollment high school it has given hundreds of students a better education than they might have received otherwise. "[Jones] is really one of the best decisions I've ever made," said one student in her last year. "I don't regret it at all. I'm very grateful for the kind of education I've received—especially at a public school."

Chapter 9

Benjamin Franklin High School

● ● ● ● ● ● ● ● ● ● ● ● ● ● ●

New Orleans, LA

Charter School Unlike the Rest

Located on the campus of the University of New Orleans, on the shore of Lake Pontchartrain, the Benjamin Franklin High School (BFHS) has three notable distinctions: It's the highest-achieving public high school in all of Louisiana. It's a strong contender for, and likely winner of, the title of "most integrated public high school in New Orleans." (There's really only one rival.) And it's one of the country's very few academically selective *charter* schools.

But it wasn't always a charter. Before Hurricane Katrina hit the Crescent City in 2005, Ben Franklin was a selective academic magnet within the Orleans Parish school system (known locally as NOPS). After the devastating storm, however, the school board made noises about not reopening it that year—and maybe never reopening it as a selective school. Whereupon the then-principal and agitated parents and alumni/ae, pulling strings locally and in Baton Rouge, swiftly obtained a charter for the school and, in effect, seceded from the district. Because it was a "conversion" charter rather than a start-up, the school was able to retain both its current student body and its academic selectivity. (Louisiana now has a handful of selective charters, four of them in New Orleans. Ben Franklin is one of two such high schools there.)

Independence also brought the right to clean up the school—the ground floor had been submerged and everything was a horrendous mess—without waiting for the district. This was largely done with volunteer help from parents, students, and school staff. They labored mightily, and as a result BFHS was able to reopen in January 2006, just four months after the storm.

As with every reopened school in the Big Easy, its post-Katrina enrollment was lower than before—at its prestorm peak, Ben Franklin had 936 pupils—but the school slowly grew back to 650 students by 2010–11, with further growth projected over the next few years.

BFHS recently sought renewal of its initial five-year charter, and in October 2011, after many months of contention over this and several other charter renewals, the Orleans Parish school board gave it a ten-year extension.[1] This was no simple matter, however, both because of disputes within the board over the selectivity of BFHS (and several other NOPS-sponsored charters) and because of major tensions over finance, with budgets stretched tight and the system seeking more and—from the schools' standpoint—more onerous fees and charges from "its" charters.

As a charter school, Ben Franklin has its own ten-member board, a nonprofit corporation called "Advocates for Academic Excellence in Education," and manages its own $5 million to $6 million budget as well as its personnel and student admissions. The latter are based exclusively on applicants' scores on a four-part matrix that includes middle school grades and three tests. The school established a cut-score for this matrix and admits every applicant above that line. The line hasn't moved in years, and school leaders are determined to enroll everyone who attains that score and wishes to attend. So, while admission is highly selective, it's not a zero-sum game whereby a child who is accepted means another is not.

Not surprisingly, Ben Franklin gets lots of applicants—almost 700 for the 2011–12 school year. Of these, about 280 met the school's admissions criteria.[2] This happened—and keeps happening—even though BFHS is located on the city's northern edge and provides no transportation. Students get to school and back home each day via parents, car pools, their own vehicles, the city's mediocre transit system, and in at least one case a bus that parents teamed up to hire for this purpose.

The challenge of getting there may deter some kids from coming from the more distant parts of town, but BFHS enrolls an impressively diverse student body, at least when gauged in ethnic terms. In 2010–11, 42 percent of its students were white, 30 percent black, and 22 percent Asian, along with small numbers of Hispanic and "mixed origin" youngsters.

History

New Orleans has a long tradition—a habit, one might fairly say—of private and parochial schools that cater to those who can afford them, which has mostly meant white (and, more recently, Asian) families. The city's multidecade history of dismal public schools, operating within a corrupt political environment and burdened by a powerful but retrograde teacher union, understandably led those who could swing it to send their daughters and sons to study elsewhere, either in the suburbs or in the private sector.

BFHS started as a district magnet in 1957, a manifestation of the country's Sputnik-era push to do better at educating youngsters with unusual potential. At the outset, it was both academically selective and racially segregated (i.e., a school for smart white kids). The public schools of New Orleans did not begin to desegregate until the 1960s, at which point Ben Franklin began to be viewed as a taxpayer-supported version of the private "white flight" schools or "segregation academies" that were springing up around the South. Though it started to enroll black students, it didn't have many, and its relocation during the 1980s to the historically white "lakefront" area and the campus of a historically white university deepened community suspicions that this school was still a bastion of brainy, middle-class Caucasians. That pot was further stirred by newly empowered African-American politicians who were widely viewed as anti-white, indeed desirous of transforming New Orleans into a black city.

Ben Franklin's African-American enrollment remained relatively small, however, owing, it seems, to the school's history, image, and location, as well as the plain fact that getting into it meant having done well in earlier grades, which generally meant having attended a good elementary or middle school, studying hard, getting top marks, being encouraged by family, et cetera.

The school's admissions criteria (and those of the city's other selective public schools) were scrutinized by the federal Office for Civil Rights (OCR) more than a dozen years ago after activists filed complaints. This led to a 1998 "consent decree" entered into by OCR and NOPS but didn't end the controversy, as irked magnet-school parents (some of them black) sued to prevent changes in the admissions process. After several tense and argumentative months, OCR okayed new admissions guidelines for New Orleans magnets, eliminating racial quotas and IQ tests in the selection process and instead giving greater weight to prior school grades and achievement-test scores.[3]

Ben Franklin Today

Walking around BFHS today is a bit like touring a teenage United Nations, so varied is its student body, especially within the school's sizable Asian-American population. But that doesn't mean it's "representative" of New Orleans, a city whose population is about three-fifths African-American—and only 3 percent Asian. Nor are attendees as poor as the city around them; just under 30 percent of BFHS students qualify for the federal subsidized-lunch program (though such data are notoriously understated at the high school level). The school has only a handful of disabled pupils and doesn't claim to meet all "special needs." (The NOPS district retains basic responsibility for providing special-ed services to youngsters who need them—and retains most of the federal and state funds for this purpose, too.)

Yet simply being integrated is remarkable for a New Orleans public school. The blunt reality, we were told, is that BFHS is one of just a few district or charter schools in the city that white (and Asian) parents will send their children to. And its admissions team works hard at outreach so that 7th and 8th graders throughout the Big Easy—and their parents, teachers, and counselors—are aware of it and what it has to offer. With a gleam in his eye, the BFHS principal talks of a long-range plan that would include growing its physical plant to accommodate more pupils, opening a middle school so that more young New Orleanians would be prepared to attend Ben Franklin, even creating a residential facility for teacher trainees and, perhaps, high schoolers from sorely distressed families.

In the meantime, as with so many other schools we identified, the flip side of Ben Franklin's not being fully representative of the city's demographics is that it contributes to holding middle-class families in town and in public education. Indeed, recent years have seen a growing number of kids entering BFHS from private middle schools. How significant this contribution is to community vitality, economic strength, and diversity will inevitably remain a topic for debate. Unique among American cities, post-Katrina New Orleans is amply supplied with private, parochial, and charter schools. What it doesn't have many of today is traditional district schools.

Inside the School

The visitor to Ben Franklin finds an orderly, serious, yet excited place, largely free of discipline and "classroom management" problems and full of eager, bright, motivated, high-achieving pupils and the kinds of teachers who gravitate to such instructional opportunities. As administrators of a charter school, the BFHS team, backstopped by the school's governing board, determines who gets hired to teach there—and who gets retained. The current principal, for example, who completed his third year at Ben Franklin in 2010–11, is the product of a national search carried out by the board and comes from a university and private-school background in Pennsylvania.

As expected, the school has a strong academic curriculum, and students must maintain at least a 2.0 average to return the following year.

Over four years, Ben Franklin loses about 18 percent of its entering students, winding up with a graduating class of 140 or so. It's a fast track, and not everyone who qualifies for admission wants to study and work that hard—or, perhaps, travel that far—though BFHS does offer tutoring for kids who need help with one or another subject. It also offers a (voluntary) two-week summer "camp college" for entering 9th graders that seeks to prepare them academically and attitudinally for the rigors to follow.

As at most of the schools we identified, Ben Franklin's curriculum is designed to offer students an array of rigorous classes. Ordinary courses are designated "honors," and in most subjects "gifted" and "Advanced Placement" upgrades are available. BFHS offers twenty-two AP classes and has a strong record of passing AP exams, with roughly half the students—more, if one looks only at grades 11 and 12—taking a total of about 660 exams a year and three-quarters of them scoring 3 or better. Indeed, Ben Franklin makes "successful completion of at least two AP courses" a requirement for graduation.[4] (The school does not, however, participate in the International Baccalaureate program.)

Everyone takes a full academic load—including four units each of English, math, science, and social studies, as well as three foreign-language credits. (The school offers Latin, French, Spanish, German, and Chinese.) For those with artistic leanings, in addition to its own course offerings BFHS has a relationship with the New Orleans Center for Creative Arts, located near the French Quarter, an audition-based regional center for secondary students with a particular interest in the performing and visual arts. Some sixty Ben Franklin students—about a tenth of the enrollment—take one or more courses at a time there.

To dispel "senioritis," 12th graders at BFHS must take a demanding course load, too, no matter how many graduation requirements they've already satisfied. But student life isn't all academic. The school has an impressive array of extracurricular activities, including a prize-winning literary magazine and a first-rate orchestra—and more than twenty athletic teams.[5] The building itself is available to students from early morning until mid-evening—and at least one teacher is on duty to help with homework until 6:00 p.m. (There's plenty of homework.)[6]

All of this seems to pay off. Ben Franklin's academic record and reputation are stellar. It's a federal Blue Ribbon school, large numbers of its seniors get recognized by the National Merit Scholarship program, it has a lofty rank in listings by national magazines as well as by Louisiana, and essentially all its graduates attend four-year colleges, many with generous scholarships. (The colleges range from local to Ivy League, with rising numbers going to Louisiana State, where highly qualified state residents get free tuition.)

Resources and Politics

The school's budget of $5.5 million works out to a decent but not overwhelming $8,500 or so per pupil, and the administration and board must struggle to keep it balanced. This worked badly in the first few years of charter status, when the school failed to lay off staff and cut other major expenses despite its shrunken post-Katrina enrollment and diminished revenue stream. It thereby "spent down" some $3 million in private dollars raised in the hurricane's aftermath and has essentially nothing left by way of a financial cushion.

School leaders have since right-sized the budget, which has meant a number of layoffs and positions left unfilled, and have begun to engage in "development" work in a serious way; and the school charges fees for some activities, field trips, and sports. Though Ben Franklin does not have to pay for use of its building—NOPS owns it, on land belonging to the University of New Orleans—it must pay various fees to the district for charter sponsorship and sundry services that it may or may not receive. The size and extent of those fees were major topics of dispute during the recent charter renegotiation, with the BFHS team convinced that NOPS is collecting far more from the school than can be justified by the actual services it renders, and that this is because the district needs cash to cover its enormous real-estate debts.[7] The current economic downturn, public-sector fiscal pressures, and the end of federal "bailout" dollars have naturally exacerbated the district's budgetary challenges.

Local politics remain somewhat precarious, too, though less so than in earlier years. The NOPS board now contains more supporters and fewer foes of selective schools, although those who don't like them remain vocal.[8] That's why the charter-renewal process was so lengthy and fraught.

It's taken some time to work through all the implications of being a more-or-less independent educational institution rather than a component of a large system. The school's board and staff have had to adjust in many ways—politically, fiscally, managerially. And they've had to do it pretty much on their own. Enhancing the school experience of smart, mostly middle-class kids is not a priority for the many national foundations and on-the-ground education-reforming, charter-advancing, school-turning-around, and "incubating" organizations that play major roles in post-hurricane education in New Orleans. They focus instead on schools populated by poor and minority youngsters, certainly a legitimate emphasis but one that has led to BFHS and the city's other selective charters feeling marginalized if not actually scorned. As on the NOPS board, some in the reform community are appalled by selectivity in any form, especially in the charter sector—"hugely problematic," stated a senior staff member at the National Alliance for Public Charter Schools—while others simply view these schools as places that are doing okay on their own in a city whose education system is still broken and needy in so many ways.

BFHS isn't completely isolated, however. It has joined with nine other charters in the East Bank Collaborative, which functions as a kind of lobbying organization for their interests and mutual defense, both locally and in Baton Rouge. Having the University of New Orleans as an ally doesn't hurt, either, and Ben Franklin's own board has recently expanded to broaden the school's political base and extend its reach in the New Orleans community.

While structures, governance, enrollment, and finances are only just emerging from post-Katrina complications and alterations at BFHS, what hasn't much changed are the school's solid academic emphasis, its college-prep curriculum, its strong faculty, and its students' impressive track record. Why fix something that, for more than half a century, has been working remarkably well?

Chapter 10

Townsend Harris High School

• • • • • • • • • • • • •

Queens, NY

Back from the Dead—and Thoroughly Alive

Townsend Harris High School (THHS)—which caused a stir in 2010 when the *New York Post* rated it number 1 citywide, ahead of Stuyvesant, Bronx Science, and the rest of the city's venerated public schools—re-emerged in 1984 from the ashes of what was for decades Gotham's most selective high school, albeit only for boys. The original institution, known as Townsend Harris Hall and shut down by Mayor Fiorello LaGuardia in 1942, traced its origins back to 1848. Its history was bound up with that of the City College of New York, and it boasted many distinguished alumni (multiple Nobel and Pulitzer prizewinners and more.)[1]

Some of these alums agitated for years to resurrect their beloved school but made little headway until the 1980s, when they were able to enlist the high-powered intervention of the president of Queens College and the Queens borough president. The trade-off was that the revived high school would be located there rather than Manhattan.[2] And that's what happened. After operating in temporary quarters for a decade, in 1995 the new THHS moved into its own attractive six-story building on a corner of the college campus in Flushing.

The building was designed for about 1,000 students, though the school now enrolls 1,100 and most classes nudge the 34-pupil limit in the citywide teachers' contract. Indeed, it's a bit snug. Fifty-five teachers share some forty-two classrooms (and labs, music rooms, etc.), and the closest thing to a robotics lab is located in a former boys' restroom.

Admissions Maze

Despite tight quarters in a city where space is always hard to come by, Townsend Harris is flooded with eager applicants (about 5,000 for 270 9th-grade openings), of whom many (around 1,200) meet its very demanding threshold requirements for admission.[3] It does not, however, control its own admissions—though it wields considerable influence over who ends up enrolling.

Since 2004, New York City's method for matching 8th graders with places in the system's 650-odd high school programs in almost 400 buildings has been, in its way, rational and generally fair, but it's also seriously complicated. It's intended to foster school choice on a citywide basis and to minimize "gaming" and influence peddling en route into Gotham's competitive-admission schools and programs.

Unless they want to attend one of the city's twenty-some charter high schools or its myriad private and parochial schools, every 8th grader in New York must pass through a centralized placement system before landing somewhere for 9th grade. There's no longer an automatic default into a "zoned" or neighborhood high school.

Modeled on the medical field's "match" procedure for placing newly minted doctors in residency programs in specialties of their choice, the New York system asks every 8th grader to list twelve high school programs in order of preference. Many of these are open to all comers, and listing one of them as top choice pretty much guarantees entry into it. But hundreds of programs and schools (including Townsend Harris) are "screened," meaning that those running such a school or program establish its admission prerequisites and then rank their (eligible) applicants in order of the school's preference, based on its own distinctive criteria. The school doesn't know where the applicant ranked it, and the applicant doesn't know where the "screened" school to which he/she applied ranked him/her. Then the "big computer in the sky" seeks to match students with programs in order of each's preference for the other. After all this, the student receives a single placement.[4]

This works pretty well for most kids. City data indicate that some 83 percent of applicants (for 2011–12 high school entry) got one of their top five choices and another 9 percent got one of their other choices. But, for a host of reasons, almost one-tenth of 8th graders fail to "match" anywhere during the main selection cycle and must present themselves in person to arrange individual placements—rarely into desirable screened programs—by the Education Department's Office of Student Enrollment.[5]

High-demand academic schools like THHS face a different problem—and complicating wrinkle—namely, that the city also operates what amounts to a parallel admissions process for nine of its most competitive high schools, including the illustrious original big three: Stuyvesant, Bronx Science, and Brooklyn Tech.[6] These plus five newer academic high schools have their admissions determined strictly by student scores on the Specialized High Schools Admissions Test (SHSAT), which some 28,000 youngsters take each year and for which many eager families spend serious money to "prep" their children, as if for the SAT.[7] This separate admissions system enables students to apply to *both* the test-based schools *and* the regular 600+ high school programs, and it's possible to end up being matched with one of each.

That's what happens to many THHS applicants, which is why this school's "yield"—those who actually enroll there—is about half of the 600 or so kids who are matched to it. The other half wind up attending one of the "exam" schools or a private school. The reason, of course, is that Townsend Harris's applicant pool contains many of the same kids who are applying, and often getting admitted, to Stuyvesant and the other "exam" schools.

They aren't *all* the same kids, however, not unless they live in Queens. For while admission to THHS is nominally citywide (unlike some screened schools that give priority to a specific neighborhood or region), 95 percent of the youngsters who end up studying there reside in that borough. This heavy geographic concentration turns out to be the product of several factors. Queens itself is a big place (2.3 million residents, 118 square miles). The school is not on a subway line, so getting there means bus travel, sometimes multiple buses, amid New York traffic. Moreover, unlike Manhattan and Brooklyn, Queens is minimally supplied with high-powered academic high school options. And its heavily immigrant population, while frequently keen on educational quality and rigor, is often wary of sending its children, particularly its daughters, on long journeys alone, especially into "the city," as Manhattan is commonly termed by inhabitants of the "outer boroughs."

The upshot is that Townsend Harris gets thousands of applicants from Queens residents, particularly girls and especially Asian-American youngsters, and not so many from the city's other boroughs and private schools.

There's one more wrinkle. Both to foster ethnic diversity *and* because the principals of several extant Queens high schools, particularly in upper-middle-class Bayside, fretted about their best students being "creamed" off by the new THHS, a pact was entered into when the school was reborn that obliges Townsend Harris to distribute the Queens part of its admissions evenly across the entire borough. The method by which it "ranks" applicants does precisely that, in essence using the borough's twenty or so old high school "zones" as the basis for geographic quotas. Thus THHS may find itself accepting, say, a 92nd percentile student from one zone rather than a 97th percentile applicant from another. This gets particularly hard to explain to parents when those two youngsters turn out to sit side by side in the same 8th-grade classroom, a situation that arises with increasing frequency as more Queens middle schools turn into magnets that draw their own pupils from across the borough.[8]

After all is said and done, here is a statistical profile of those who end up at Townsend Harris: two-thirds are girls, one-third boys; 51 percent are Asian (both East and South Asian); 27 percent white; 12 percent Hispanic; 6 percent black; and 4 percent multiracial. Half the kids come from homes where English is not spoken, and many are products of an earlier ELL (English Language Learners) program, though THHS itself does not have such a program. Only a handful of its pupils are disabled, but two in five qualify for subsidized lunches.

Inside the School

In many respects, today's Townsend Harris mirrors the classic image in New York and other major seaboard cities of a school for upwardly mobile immigrant families that want their children to get a first-rate education and attain careers and lifestyles that improve on those of their parents. A century ago, the original Townsend Harris was apt to enroll Jewish kids whose families came from eastern Europe. Today, they're mostly from Asia and Latin America. But their hopes and dreams are much the same.[9]

The kids are all smart high achievers, with near-perfect attendance and graduation rates. School leaders take pride in *not* being an "exam school" because, they say, the citywide high school entrance test is basically an appraisal of intellectual aptitude, not actual accomplishment. By placing heavy weight instead on middle school grades, state assessment results, and attendance, Townsend Harris feels it ends up with students who have demonstrated the capacity to be serious and successful, not just brainy.

The school retains a surprising number of "classical" elements, some pressed by alumni at the time of its reincarnation, others encouraged by founding principal Malcolm Largmann (an English teacher who selected the original teaching staff) and former Queens College president Saul B. Cohen. These include two years of mandatory Latin or Greek instruction and a required college-level "great books" course on the college campus—co-taught by college and THHS instructors—during senior year. (Seniors must also take six additional credit hours at Queens College.)

Other distinctive curricular features include a heavy, schoolwide emphasis on writing in almost every class—teachers note that many pupils enter with scant experience in serious English composition—and at least forty hours a year of mandatory community service.

Eleven hundred students is *small* by New York high school standards—Stuyvesant enrolls 3,000 pupils and Brooklyn Tech a whopping 5,000—and kids and parents alike remarked on the appeal of this relatively intimate scale. It might be seen as a trade-off for classes with as many as 34 pupils, and the large class sizes clearly burden teachers who assign lots of writing, independent-study projects, and what the school calls "collaterals" (research papers, pupil presentations, etc.).

Budget cuts and hiring freezes have shrunk the staff from a total workforce of about eighty-five a few years back to seventy-five today. School leaders have done their best to preserve teaching slots, instead taking reductions from the ranks of administrators and support staff. When reduced resources meant there was no money to pay teachers additional stipends for the school's unusual eighth period (for "enrichment," i.e., tutoring, club advising, etc.), two minutes were shaved from every other period so that the school's full program could be preserved within the thirty-four-hour (and ten minutes!) work week that the United Federation of Teachers has negotiated for all New York City instructors.[10] (Many teachers voluntarily stay later, however, to work with pupils and take part in activities, not to mention the extra time spent evaluating mountains of student work and preparing lessons.)

The teaching staff is loyal, turning over not more than two or three individuals a year, and those we met appeared exceptionally bright, well educated, and enthusiastic. Their average tenure at THHS is sixteen years; almost everyone has at least a master's degree; and more than a quarter have experience in business, science-related work, or university teaching. Several of the younger instructors are Townsend Harris alums, delighted to be back at a school that served them well.

Classroom instruction is often the traditional teacher-led kind, particularly in core courses, though students may team up briefly during the class period to work on specific topics or problems. Staff say they are trying to encourage more project-style and inquiry-based learning while offering plausible explanations as to why this happens mostly in advanced and elective classes. But "teacher-led" at THHS typically incorporates a heavy Socratic element. Though 9th graders may be reticent about speaking out in class, most veteran students appear eager to engage in lively back-and-forth discussion with instructors and classmates.

It seems to be working. The school's Advanced Placement test-taking and passing rates are impressive.[11] The class of 2010 had SAT scores averaging 1923 (out of 2400). Pretty much everyone goes on to four-year colleges, about half within the city and state university systems, the other half to a wide array of costlier (and often more prestigious) institutions, frequently with scholarship aid. The school gets top marks on the city's evaluation systems and on a host of national rating and ranking systems.

Like most of the schools we visited, Townsend Harris seems to have a distinctive culture, at once competitive and mutually helpful, in this case oriented more to the humanities than to science/technology, and (as noted earlier) more girls than boys. The climate is peaceful yet excited, hardworking yet cheerful and inquisitive. Even the security guard at the front door seemed engaged and affable. The counseling office was a buzzing, busy place—wrapping up college admissions and financial aid for the seniors during our visit.

Leadership and Bureaucratics

THHS has benefited from steady leadership. Today's young principal is only the third occupant of that chair in twenty-seven years. He appears to rule with a light hand, aided by several veteran assistant principals (most of whom also teach) and maintains close contact with parents and alums. (An active PTA raises some $70,000 a year, and the alumni/ae association maintains a multimillion-dollar endowment on the school's behalf.) Though the principal has few discretionary dollars from the city to spend—that's where the PTA and alumni/ae come in—he has near-total control over teacher and staff hiring decisions. The school's budget is, however, enhanced both by the additional weighting that New York assigns to high school students and by a special grant to Queens College to pay for the "bridge year" program with its great-books course and other college-level offerings. On the other hand, the fact that THHS is staffed primarily by senior teachers means they're relatively expensive.

It's hard to run a distinctive school within the toils of a vast bureaucracy, and even as New York has striven to empower its principals in some ways, the system is tightening up and homogenizing in others.

The city's centralized "double-blind" student admissions system curbs the school's capacity to select the kids its team feels might fare best there.[12] The embrace of statewide (and, soon, multistate) academic standards cramps the capacity of individual schools to formulate their own curricula—and curricular sequences—as does the pressure of city- and statewide testing. And of course the teachers are none too pleased with the state's plan to rest much of its new teacher evaluation system on student results on more and more tests in more and more subjects.[13]

Much of this is predictable, political, and unrelated to THHS itself. But one must at least pause to ponder the more distinctive point that proliferating tests and their widening uses are particularly ill fitted to curricula and students like those at Townsend Harris, threatening to press what has been special and advanced into something more conventional and middling.

Chapter 11

Pine View School for the Gifted

● ● ● ● ● ● ● ● ● ● ● ● ● ●

Osprey, FL

Private Education in a Public System?

Talk with anyone at Pine View School for the Gifted in Osprey, Florida, and within five minutes he or she is sure to mention what a "special" and "different" place it is. Described by one community member as "the cheapest private school parents in Sarasota County can get," Pine View is a public school of 2,170 students[1] with several distinguishing characteristics. For one, it's the only school on our list to span grades 2–12. Principal Steve Largo, now in his twenty-fourth year as the school's lead administrator, believes the range of grade levels is a "huge plus" that contributes to a strong sense of school community and makes for smoother transitions between grade levels. Teachers, parents, and students see it mostly as a plus, too. Older kids provide role models for younger ones, teachers can watch kids grow over time, parents are assured of a continuous experience through high school, and students develop relationships with intellectual peers.

Pine View is also the only school that we identified that uses *gifted* in its name. School culture leverages this identity through phrases used to characterize various fund-raising efforts, community outreach, and character education (e.g., "Gifts are for sharing" and "To whom much is given, much is expected"). Students and parents are also very conscious of the moniker. One high schooler remarked: "Pine View is a community that's available for gifted students. We are surrounded by kids who are like us." While some parents valued the descriptor ("They're different animals, different creatures, gifted kids," said one), others expressed reservations about the "for the gifted" part of the school's name. "My sons were okay with telling people they went [here], whereas my daughter won't tell anyone," said one longtime Pine View parent, adding, "For me, I guess I feel like all kids are gifted in some way."

Pine View is the only school of its kind in Florida and one of several options for gifted students in Sarasota County. Consistent with state guidelines for teaching in gifted programs, all Pine View teachers must take five graduate-level courses in gifted education. Students are enrolled in either nonhonors or honors courses at the middle school level in core subjects, and either honors or Advanced Placement courses in grades 9–12. In a given semester, about twenty AP courses are offered. Students can also take four upper-level math courses and a science course for dual-enrollment credit from the State College of Florida. Students who are exceptionally advanced in a subject area are placed in a higher grade-level course (e.g., a middle school student taking a high school math class).

Pine View's motto—"a tradition of excellence"—applies as well to the school's many high-performing academic teams and organizations. Indeed, the school is as well known for its out-of-classroom achievements as for its high test scores and acceptance rates at prestigious colleges. In April 2011, for example, a team of five students participated in Moody's Mega Math Challenge 2011, an Internet-based applied math contest, to win the $20,000 championship prize.

The recognition that individuals and teams of students receive—as well as awards bestowed on the school—predictably attract parents in search of a more academically challenging education for their children. Some move their families from other cities in Florida or from other states specifically so their kids can attend Pine View.

Current parents were impressed with the safe, nurturing environment in which students identified as gifted "get to be with each another" and experience "a lot of freedom that they wouldn't have elsewhere."

One recalled "looking for a school where my child wouldn't get beat up every day [for being smart]." Some kids—often those who have been attending Pine View since primary school—transfer to other high schools after 8th grade for various reasons, including wanting to be with friends and looking for a more "typical" American high school experience or fewer academic pressures. A parent whose child transferred from Pine View cited environmental factors ("drugs," "fighting," "rude kids"), as well as "easier [i.e., insufficiently challenging] classes," as reasons that her child returned to Pine View after leaving. A group of high school students we talked with also noted the social advantages of being at the school. One young man was convinced that he "would be an outcast at another school" and that "the social benefits [of Pine View]" had allowed him to "reap the academic benefits."

Notably, many teachers, counselors, school administrators, and central office personnel themselves have children who attend or have attended Pine View. One teacher recalled that, upon moving to the area, she heard the school characterized as "elitist." After hearing more about what the school offered, she thought to herself, "That sounds like the kind of school I want my kid to go to."

An Experiment in Gifted Education

Pine View began in 1969 as an experiment in full-time, self-contained, gifted education, opening soon after Florida added the word *gifted* to its definition of *exceptional student*. A three-year grant from the state helped founding principal John Woolever and a few teachers open the school to 128 students in grades 4–8. Classes were held in a half-dozen portable classrooms on five acres of land surrounded by pine trees; there was no cafeteria, auditorium, or gym. Students from Sarasota County were identified for the school with IQ and achievement tests.[2] An alum who attended the school in its earliest days characterized his classrooms as unlike those in other public schools at the time, explaining further: "It was like Montessori in the way class was run. There were a lot of individualized assignments, and a lot of free time. . . . no chalkboard or sitting in rows. Our desks were in a different configuration every day when we walked in." Another reflected, "We had an enviable experience." Students in the early years of the school also recalled "being studied" by observers and (ironically) taking pilot versions of standardized tests.

In 1973, when state money ran out, the district was faced with the decision to close the school or fund it directly. According to current superintendent Lori White, herself a member of Pine View's first graduating class, "It was a huge issue for the school board. It really could have gone either way."[3] Another graduate recalled the district taking over Pine View "grudgingly" amid debate over the political implications of having a separate school for gifted students. "People were always trying to shut it down."

By the early 1990s, over a hundred trailers and 1,500 students crowded the campus. In 1994, today's seventy-four-acre site opened with a design inspired by Thomas Jefferson's "academical village" at the University of Virginia. Funding for the school today comes mostly from the same sources as that of other schools in the district. Pine View's per-pupil spending is lower than in most high schools in Sarasota County, a fact that defenders consistently point to when questions are raised as to whether the school is a wise and efficient use of taxpayer money. Other sources of funding that come from Advanced Placement incentives and gifted-education programs have been severely limited or cut altogether as Florida (like many states) has slashed its education budgets.

Perhaps it's these and other contemporary economic and political pressures that prompted principal Largo to muse, "Maybe I'm naïve, but I really question whether a Pine View could be created again today."

Admissions

For many years, the Pine View admissions process was handled at the school level. As the school grew (and, one imagines, demand increased), this proved "overwhelming," according to Largo, and was moved to the district level at the school's request. The current process has been in place for about twenty years.

To be eligible for gifted services in the Sarasota County schools (including but not limited to Pine View), students must have an IQ score of 130 or higher on an approved intelligence test.[4] A district psychologist may administer the test, or parents can submit scores from private testing, provided that the district has approved the professional. Per state guidelines, scores of 130 or higher on parts of the test can be submitted for consideration, with a psychologist's explanation. If a child attains the minimum score, additional information is collected to determine his or her eligibility. The classroom teacher rates the student using a tool for assessing gifted behaviors and characteristics in children. The student must also "demonstrate a need for a special instructional program."[5]

To qualify for full-time services, either at Pine View or at one of the district's elementary or middle school "gifted cluster sites," students must also earn minimum threshold scores in reading and math on one of two academic achievement tests[6] and above-average report-card grades in reading and math. These criteria are assigned points that are then totaled and used to reach a decision about a student's eligibility. Students who do not qualify may retest after a twelve-month waiting period.

Although not explained on the school website, state guidelines call for districts to develop an alternative plan for identifying students who are typically underrepresented in programs for gifted learners, namely, English Language Learners (ELL) and students from disadvantaged backgrounds. According to district personnel, Sarasota County exercises this "Plan B" approach for students eligible for free/reduced-price lunch and English for Speakers of Other Languages (ESOL) students who don't qualify under "Plan A." The process includes using alternate identification instruments suggested by the state and closely monitoring student progress for two years. "We always try to get the kids identified under Plan A though, if we can," said an administrator.

Pine View's grade 2–12 enrollment demographics (table 11.1) suggest that the combined identification plans yield a student body that is somewhat less diverse than that of the county, with significantly fewer students eligible for free/reduced-price lunches.

Table 11.1: Student Demographics, Pine View vs. Sarasota County Schools

	Pine View	Sarasota County schools
White	81%	71%
Asian	8%	2%
Hispanic	5%	12%
Black	< 1%	9.5%
Native American	< 1%	< 1%
Eligible for free/reduced-price lunch	9%	41%
English Language Learners	0%	5.5%

Interestingly, when asked what they might change about Pine View, several students said they wished the school had "more diversity." One boy elaborated that he was a little worried that with his lack of exposure to different kinds of people in and beyond the school—namely, "African-Americans and Latinos"—he "might not be equipped to deal with the outside world."

Pine View Pressures

Talk of admissions inevitably leads some staff members to raise the issue of whether all students at Pine View "belong" there. Perhaps alluding to the submission of IQ scores generated via private testing, one staff member remarked, "this school isn't for everyone." For others, it isn't so much a question of whether all students are correctly identified as whether the school's implied (and applied) definition of "being gifted" is realistic. Speaking to the requirement for high school students to take advanced courses in every subject, regardless of aptitude or interest, a counselor reflected: "Our concept of gifted education is so different here. It's like kids have to be gifted in everything."

Perhaps because of this expectation, some staff members felt the school could use more supports for students when they struggle academically, and for students with special needs. Others felt there was enough in place already, including extensive one-on-one teacher assistance when students demonstrate a need (or seek help) as well as peer tutoring. Counselors monitor pupil grades closely, as students must maintain a minimum 2.5 GPA to stay at Pine View. "We want them to be successful," said one. However challenging a course load of AP and honors classes might be, weighting the course grades seems to help ensure that many students meet or exceed the GPA requirement.[7] According to data for the Pine View class of 2010, on a 4.0 weighted scale, 69 percent of students had a 4.0, 29 percent between 3.5 and 3.99, and 2 percent from 3.00 to 3.49.

Although a few students talked about feeling pressured to get perfect grades ("My parents pushed me to get As and only As."), in general grades seemed to be lower on the list of academic pressures that Pine View high schoolers said they felt. On the other hand, getting into a top college—not just any college—is clearly an expectation that weighs heavily on some students. While counselors and teachers attributed this pressure to parents, students were split as to whether their parents or the school was the primary source. One senior who attributed it to the school said: "It's not enough here to do your best. You have to go to the best, too." One math classroom illustrated his point well. Apparently an aspect of a statistics project, we saw the names of roughly eighty of the country's most prestigious universities handwritten on a whiteboard, some with students' names next to them to indicate where seniors had been accepted.

Likely due to the late-spring timing of our visit, students also talked about feeling the stress of taking and acing multiple AP exams. One senior taking seven of the tests—and attending an Ivy League school in the fall—said, "I feel like I have to get a 5 on all of them."

Value Added?

In an age of accountability, Pine View's mission statement to provide a "qualitatively different learning environment" begs the question of what outcomes—qualitative and quantitative—such an environment produces. Principal Largo astutely recognized that there was a time when many instructional and curricular approaches advocated for use with gifted students were not similarly recommended for use with all students. "But the rest of education has caught up with us."

The school is certainly successful by traditional measures, with an average ACT composite score of 29.1, nineteen National Merit Scholars and twenty-two semifinalists, 100 percent of graduates going to college and 87 percent of the 1,024 AP tests that students took in 2010 earning scores of 3 or higher. Largo cited additional evidence such as the accomplishments of academic teams, number of college scholarships, and student anecdotes. "Kids come back and say how well prepared they were for college," he said. "We take some credit for that, but the truth is they are prepared very early on." Other stakeholders also alluded to whether the environment and classrooms of Pine View are largely responsible for what students accomplish—or if it's mostly a function of the admissions process. "The kids are our biggest asset here," said one staff member. "Of course, they come to us amazing." One parent was more direct, saying bluntly, "This school is what it is because of the kids."

Because the same criteria and standards are used to identify students who choose to attend Pine View and those who opt to attend schools with other gifted-student programs, within-district comparisons of student performance should be possible, as should comparisons between students who stay at Pine View for high school and those who leave to attend another high school in the district. Along these lines, a local businessman (and Pine View parent) had recently brought to administrators' attention the Florida Comprehensive Assessment Test (FCAT) and SAT scores of Pine View students alongside the scores of other students identified as gifted, both in Sarasota County and across Florida, to raise questions about whether the school is performing as well as it could be when comparing "apples with apples."[8]

But before standards and testing and lists of top high schools, Pine View was an idea that a full-time public school for gifted students could make a difference for kids whose parents took a chance in sending them there. Looking back forty-two years later, one of those kids said, "I believe that if I would not have had Pine View, I would not have achieved what I did in life." And chances are good that he would agree with a list of adjectives that present-day Pine View students generated when asked to characterize their school: "synergistic," "competitive," "community-oriented," "inspired," and, of course, "unique."

Chapter 12

Oxford Academy

● ● ● ● ● ● ● ●

Cypress, CA

Rigor on a Shoestring

Serving over 1,100 students in grades 7–12—and often mistaken for a private school by people in the area—Oxford Academy in Cypress, California (pop. 47,800), is one of twenty-two schools in the Anaheim Union High School District (AUHSD). Located on the more affluent west side of the thirty-five-square-mile district in Orange County, the academy occupies a campus of nine small buildings built in 1966 within striking distance of Cypress High School, a comprehensive high school in the same district.

In recent years, Oxford has enjoyed high rankings on lists of top high schools in *U.S. News*, *Newsweek*, and the *Washington Post*, and boasts one of the highest Academic Performance Index (API) scores in California. Kathy Scott, principal for six years—and by all accounts a strong curricular and instructional leader—says with cautious pride, "We're a great school, but not a perfect school."

Oxford's academic program is designed around its mission to "prepare students to be ethically and academically focused for entrance into college or university post-secondary education." Students participate in "a comprehensive honors curriculum" with all core classes designated honors or Advanced Placement. During their sophomore year, students also select one of two "career pathways"—Biotechnology &

Table 12.1: Student Demographics, Oxford Academy vs. Anaheim Union High School District

	Oxford Academy[a]	Anaheim Union High School District
White	12%	15%
Black	1%	3%
Asian/Pacific Islander/ Filipino	69%	17%
Hispanic	14%	64%
Native American	0%	< 1%
Eligible for free/ reduced-price lunch	28%	73%

[a] School Accountability Report Card (2009–10), retrieved via http://www.auhsd.k12 .ca.us/.

Medical Research or Business—through which they take additional elective courses and experiences geared toward real-world applications. The school uses a block schedule, with classes meeting on alternate days to mimic what students will encounter in college.

Like many academically selective public high schools, Oxford has more girls than boys (54 percent to 46 percent). Compared with AUHSD as a whole (table 12.1), it also has more Asian students, fewer Hispanic, black and white students, and fewer youngsters eligible for free/ reduced price lunch. But it's far from a bastion of privilege. "People think our kids are wealthy," says Ms. Scott. "That's a misperception.... There are a lot of 'regular' kids here—kids who work and kids who take care of siblings."

The makeup of the student body is influenced in part by the school's location, which entails a long commute for many students. The idea of building another Oxford on the district's east side is floated periodically, but no plans are in the works.

Parent motivation is also a significant influence on who attends Oxford. "I applied because my mom wanted me to," one student recalled without a hint of contempt or regret. "Her co-worker's niece was applying, too." Another reflected: "My parents didn't want me to go to [another high school]. I would've been a minority. They also wanted better for me than they had for themselves."

The opportunity for academic challenge, the school's small size, a sense of safety, accessibility of teachers, and prestige ("a brag factor," one parent called it) are among the reasons parents gave for wanting their children to go to Oxford. Administrators try to emphasize to parents, however, that ultimately their child has to *want* to be at Oxford. "I wish we had a screener or test for *student* motivation," said one counselor. "This isn't a school for everyone."

History

Oxford's physical plant had two lives before emerging as an academically selective public school in 1998. Initially a junior high that closed because of declining enrollment, the district had been leasing the property to a Christian school when that school fell behind in the rent. Faced with a decision about what to do with the property, the AUHSD school board held a series of discussions that generated different ideas for creating a "focused" school open to students across the attendance area. One such idea was a proposal to serve a population that some felt was "flying under the radar": students who were earning Bs and Cs and could use an extra push to realize their full potential. Referring to a national college-readiness program for underserved pupils, a teacher recalled that Oxford was originally "supposed to be like the AVID [Advancement Via Individual Determination] model."[1]

A team of school board members, administrators, community members, and teachers worked on a more detailed vision. The process proved somewhat controversial, with some parents and board members favoring a school for academically elite students similar to the high-profile (and also academically selective) Gretchen Whitney High School in nearby Cerritos.[2] According to one board member, "We [had] put so much money into children who hadn't functioned well academically. [We] needed a school with outstanding academics that could be offered to students throughout the district."

Although our questions about the original target population and mission of the school—and how (even whether) these changed—elicited differing accounts, all parties agreed that the focus was always on college-prep academics. Underscoring this emphasis, Oxford did not initially offer music, arts, or sports programs. That quickly changed, however, and the school now offers students an array of opportunities in music, the arts, and sports, albeit fewer than other high schools in the district.

Staff members recalled a difficult early relationship with other high schools in the district, arising from resentment that Oxford was "stealing" their students. "It was extremely negative in the beginning," said one, "but we're not perceived as being as threatening we once were." A veteran teacher remembered similar sentiments, especially at district-wide departmental meetings, but didn't think things had changed as much as they could. "They perceived us as a threat—and still do."

Admissions

In its first years, Oxford did not use a competitive admissions process. Students entered via lottery after undergoing an initial screening with the Iowa Test of Basic Skills (ITBS). This approach faced several challenges. School leaders felt that some applicants were unfairly advantaged because parents could (and did) have their children tutored or drilled with practice tests. A staff member presented compelling evidence from his graduate thesis that showed a low correlation between ITBS scores and students' academic performance. A further factor in changing the process was the perception that many students could not handle or were not prepared for the coursework. One counselor who recalled the shift to greater selectivity said, "It's better not to be lottery. It wasn't humane." A parent who had several children at the school provided a different perspective: "I think those first kids admitted with the lottery did fine. It's really the small size of this school that makes the difference." Others recalled what they felt was a more varied student body under the original arrangement. "We had more diversity with the lottery," said a parent. "It seems like the school sees one kind of kid

[now]." A teacher concurred: "With the lottery, our population looked different," later adding, "the kids had more personality; they were more multidimensional."

In any case, the lottery was abandoned for a blind two-step process open to rising 7th through 9th graders, in effect shifting the school's focus from B and C students to high achievers—and likely yielding a more homogeneous enrollment. Applicants are now "screened" by their grades, citizenship and effort behaviors, scores on the California Standards Test, and previous math coursework. The standards are generally followed closely, though with flexibility afforded for cases of students with high standardized test scores but low grades. Applicants are not asked to provide ethnicity or economic-status information.

Approximately eight hundred applicants who meet the minimum guidelines then take a four-hour entrance exam written by Oxford teachers and based on content suggested by the California State Standards that includes language arts and math sections plus an essay. That exam is a high-pressure event. A parent reflected: "It was stressful for my 6th grader. We had him in test prep classes to get him ready." Indeed, a veritable cottage industry has arisen in the community that purports to prepare students for Oxford's entrance exam.

To draw equally from both sides of the district, students' scores are then grouped according to which of eight junior high schools they attend. The top 25 scores from each are rank-ordered to match 200–210 openings in 7th grade. This allows for an "education-alike" comparison of applicants from the same schools. If a student decides not to come to Oxford, the slot is offered to the next-highest-scoring student from that junior high. (The number of spots available to incoming 8th and 9th graders varies yearly, based on enrollment.)

Because it is ultimately students' relative scores on the entrance exam that determine their admission, administrators cite the process as evidence that Oxford is *not* contributing to a "brain drain." They note that many high-achieving students do not make the "top 25" cutoff at their respective schools, while a number of comparatively lower-achieving students do. Leaders also note that some strong student-athletes and students with specialized extracurricular interests and talents choose to attend other district or private high schools.

For 2011–12 applications, Oxford decided not to admit any student scoring below 60 on the entrance exam, regardless of whether the student was in the top 25 for his or her school. This decision was based on evidence that students scoring in that range do not end up performing well at Oxford. "We don't want kids to come here and be unsuccessful," one counselor said. (As it turned out, just three [of 699] applicants were turned down because of scores below 60. All were from the same middle school.)

Retention and Curriculum

Five to 10 percent of students who enter Oxford do not graduate from it, principally because of the school's rigorous academic curriculum and norms. Asked to describe the kind of student who succeeds at Oxford, faculty members used terms and phrases like "works hard," "complacent," "follows directions," "motivated by external rewards and pressure." They described students who struggle at the school as "less confident" with "significant skill gaps." Several teachers remarked on cultural differences as well. One noted that, for many Asian families, school is a student's job; whereas some students from Hispanic families are expected to take on a job outside school or work at home.

School policy requires freshmen and sophomores to maintain a 2.7 GPA, and juniors and seniors a 3.0. In practice, these minimums serve as guidelines that instigate months-long monitoring and support processes, rather than establish hard-and-fast rules that threaten students with immediate dismissal. Overall, school leaders, teachers, parents, and students seem to think the minimum GPA policy is a positive one that contributes to the school's reputation and atmosphere as an academically challenging place—and helps keeps everyone on their toes. One staff member pointed out that, in contrast to many high schools, the GPA policy is a proactive approach that puts kids who are struggling "on the radar," rather than simply saying "Just don't fail."

All Oxford students in grades 7–9 are given additional academic support in a course called Learning Skills, scheduled toward the end of the day. Essentially a structured study hall, students use common forms to maintain a weekly log of their assignments. They eventually compile a portfolio of their best work and reflect on it with their Learning Skills teacher. Students we spoke with said they appreciated the time in the second half of the day to do homework.

Despite the many available supports to boost academic success, a recurring theme in conversations with parents, teachers, and students was Oxford's implicit expectation that all students would perform at a high level (and with a high degree of interest) in all subject areas. Some wondered whether the graduation requirement of at least five AP courses (English Language, English Literature, U.S. Government & Politics, U.S. History, and one science course) benefited all students. One instructor felt that the school could stand to provide more "safety nets" to youngsters from disadvantaged backgrounds, especially those with longer commute times or home obligations that prevented them from being able to take advantage of the after-school tutoring program and individualized teacher attention.

Because many students come to Oxford having been at the top of their class at another school, they often need to get used being a relatively small fish in a bigger pond. "Kids don't stand out here anymore, like they did in elementary [school]," one teacher said. The transition can also prove challenging for parents, especially those who are troubled by the realization that their child might be able to put in less work and perform better relative to peers at a comprehensive high school. One parent of a 9th grader worried, "I don't think everybody gets us, especially colleges. They don't understand how tough Oxford is. . . . I think the attention from national media has helped, though."

Resource Challenges

Some of Oxford's biggest challenges relate to resources. With what one faculty member called limited "manpower" to meet the demands of the kids, Oxford has an overall pupil/teacher ratio of almost 26 to 1. We observed classes ranging from 25 to a whopping 40 students. Although teachers know they are being stretched; several years ago, when the district eliminated all block schedules owing to budget cuts, they voted to teach an extra period each day to retain the schedule. This required a waiver from the union-negotiated contract.

Some teachers devote even more of their own time to extended learning opportunities. For example, in 2009–10 AUHSD provided each school, Oxford included, with an in-house lesson design specialist. That person coaches and mentors colleagues and leads some of the school's Monday morning professional sessions on using research-based instructional strategies. At Oxford, the specialist has also been facilitating a cohort of willing colleagues who meet during lunch once a month; their activities have included book study, model lessons, and student shadowing.

Because of its status as a choice school, however, Oxford does not qualify for some kinds of funding that might be used to support additional professional learning activities, teachers, or other resources. The Oxford Academy Foundation (OFA)—a nonprofit organization that provides supplemental private funding for the school—makes potential donors aware of this reality via its website:

> as a school of choice, Oxford does not get some categorical funds like EIA [Economic Impact Aid] and ELAP [English Language Acquisition Program] that other schools get. In fact, some schools in our district get almost $2 million more than Oxford per year. This is why the foundation works so hard to raise money to provide a quality learning environment.

The OFA also challenges any suppositions that the school is patronized mainly by families with deep pockets and therefore doesn't need additional resources:

> Many [Oxford Academy students] come from disadvantaged backgrounds, both cultural and economic. More than 20% receive some form of government aid. They continue to achieve academic excellence while overcoming hardships. . . . [But] the current [school] facilities

are not sufficiently comprehensive to support a complete high school program. Our physical plant was built in 1966 and is in need of modernization. The students need your support to help correct these deficiencies to continue to grow and learn.

Fiscal stress was an issue that surfaced across conversations with faculty and parents. Even students seemed aware of it. In one classroom where students' research questions were posted, a 7th grader wrote among her five examples, "Why do we get such a small amount of money from the district?"

Based on student achievement and school performance, however, Oxford Academy is plainly doing well with what it has. Perhaps better than any high-profile accolade is the testimony of one student who was just weeks away from graduation when we visited: "I love this school, really . . . it's a like a family. . . . I hope I've lived up to [its] expectations."

Chapter 13

Bergen County Academies

● ● ● ● ● ● ● ● ● ● ● ●

Hackensack, NJ

Voc Ed for the Gifted in Twenty-First Century Suburbia

It isn't easy to wrap one's mind around the Bergen County Academies, where this unusual school came from, and how it operates. But the effort pays off. For it's one of the best secondary schools in New Jersey, and its distinctive (if somewhat cumbersome) structure is worth understanding. It may also be the oddest "vocational school" in America.

Bergen County Academies (BCA) is a single public magnet high school, located in Hackensack, a smallish (43,000 people) city within the densely populated northern New Jersey suburbs of New York City. But the school houses seven semidistinct "academies" and serves all of Bergen County (900,000 people, largest in the Garden State), a sprawling (247 square mile), mostly prosperous (median family income around $100,000) jurisdiction containing more than *seventy* separate public-school districts, most with high schools of their own.

Complicated, yes. A bit of history and orientation may help. New Jersey is well known for its enormous number of local school systems—six hundred of them, averaging just four schools apiece—serving every city, town, suburb, and hamlet.[1] Superimposed on these are twenty-one county-level "executive superintendents"[2] with certain administrative responsibilities on behalf of the state, as well as twenty-one countywide "technical-vocational" districts, each with *its own* superintendent and governing board (separate from the "executive superintendents," who are really extensions of the state Department of Education).[3]

Originally, those parallel, county-level tech-voc systems provided old-fashioned, career-oriented, secondary-school programs (auto mechanics, carpentry, printing, etc.) for young people who did not want—or perhaps could not succeed in—a conventional "academic" curriculum and who were not, for the most part, bound for college. Over time, however, most of these systems have evolved. They now offer a host of adult-education programs, akin to those ordinarily found in community colleges.[4] Many also operate special-education programs and schools for the county's disabled youngsters (sometimes just the most severely impaired). And half a dozen of them have developed countywide high schools that anywhere else in America would be called selective-admission academic magnets.

That's what happened in Bergen County, beginning in the late 1980s under the leadership of a visionary superintendent named John Grieco, who saw the need to bring high-tech "enrichment" classes to youngsters wanting to pursue work in electronics, computers, et cetera.[5] As the school district's literature puts it, this program—originally with just be-fore- and after-school science and tech-ed classes—"opened the world of modern vocational education to gifted and talented students." The old-style technical-vocational high school building gradually acquired all manner of state-of-the-art technology, and by 1992 two schools were cohabiting in it, one of them the new Academy for the Advancement of Science and Technology, which produced its first graduating class in 1996.[6]

The schools shared the space for almost another decade as the new, academically oriented magnet programs for ambitious, college-bound youngsters gradually displaced the older vocational-technical programs. By 2004, however, the school's conversion was complete—including its participation in the late Theodore Sizer's Coalition of Essential Schools and that organization's demanding process of school-by-school reinvention.

Today, the same old building (with a spiffy new annex), now named the Dr. John Grieco Campus, houses 1,050 high school pupils divided among BCA's seven academies.[7] Unable and unwilling to shed entirely the "voc-tech" veneer (which helps retain a lot of money for the school's budget), each of these appears on paper to be a career-oriented, job-readying program with a definite "applied" orientation. The academies' names carry phrases like "engineering and design technology," "medical science technology," "visual and performing arts," even "culinary arts and hotel administration."

What's really going on under that roof, however, is both a lot of curricular commonality across academies and a rigorous, advanced, and intellectually challenging program that sends essentially everyone on to four-year colleges and universities, albeit some to campuses with "career" orientations of their own (e.g., Cornell's School of Hotel Administration).

Admissions

Attending BCA entails a lot of hard work. The school day is unusually long (eight hours). Innumerable extracurricular activities, athletics, performances, tutoring, and suchlike keep many kids on campus until dark. And there's plenty of homework.

These are brainy, motivated kids who pass through a tough admissions process that screens some 1,450 applicants for 275 slots. They come from all over the county—and bring about $9,000 each from their home school districts with them. That's how it works in New Jersey's county voc-tech schools: the young people who attend them carry quasi vouchers from the districts where they would otherwise attend high school.[8]

But this money comprises just a fraction of BCA's budget and the budgets of kindred schools in other Garden State counties, for the "freeholders" (i.e., county councils) kick in millions of dollars as well. So does Uncle Sam under the Perkins Act and other legacies of the old federal "voc ed" programs.

The "sending" districts understandably hate to part with the money. In Bergen County, as we also found in several other "magnet" situations, they're also loath to lose some of their brightest and most driven youngsters, kids who could boost their home high schools' standing on various metrics. So (as we also observed in several other settings) BCA entered into a "gentlemen's agreement"—worked out under Dr. Grieco—not to enroll more than a specified number of students from each of the county's teeming districts, with those maximums varying from five to twenty-two (per entering class) according to district size.

This ensures geographic breadth and a measure of ethnic and socioeconomic diversity as well, though as with all quota-type systems it brings unfairnesses of its own. Occasionally a district has fewer BCA applicants, or fewer qualified applicants, than its quota, meaning that some slots go unused, even as other districts within the county brim with eager applicants. The degree of competitiveness thus also varies dramatically as one traverses the county.[9]

Then there's the challenge of meeting the school's criteria for entrance. Though these vary a bit by academy (as do the admissions processes and numbers of 9th-grade openings), they're all demanding. BCA weighs applicants' 7th- and 8th-grade report cards, their scores on state achievement tests in middle school, plus three recommendations from teachers and the school's own customized entrance exams. Two exams, that is: an essay (to be written in forty minutes) to appraise one's prowess in English composition and a forty-question multiple-choice math test.[10]

After all that, about 500 youngsters—a bit more than one-third of the applicant pool—are invited to come for interviews. Depending on the academy, some are group interviews, some individual (and the arts academy requires portfolios and auditions).

Thus the entering class—students are admitted into 9th grade only—is the product of a rigorous, multifaceted, and highly competitive process *as well as* geographic quotas within the county and somewhat different criteria for each academy within BCA. Further complicating the picture: the school has room to enroll only about 275 new students a year—

and almost everyone it admits does in fact enroll. But the district-level quotas total about 380 countywide. Put all these elements together, and one may fairly conclude that the BCA admissions process is as complex as that of any educational institution in America.

The school is ethnically diverse in a North Jersey suburban sort of way. About half its students are white; about 8 percent are black or Hispanic; and a whopping 42 percent are Asian. That does not, however, mean that its pupil population mirrors the surrounding community, as Bergen County's overall high school demographics are 25 percent black/Hispanic and just 16 percent Asian.

Girls slightly outnumber boys (eleven to nine) at BCA—and just 4 or 5 percent of the students qualify for the federal subsidized-lunch program. About 35 youngsters have some sort of disability entitling them to either an Individualized Education Plan or a "504" plan.

Once enrolled, few pupils leave. The school graduates 97 or 98 percent of those it admits. And everybody goes on to four-year colleges.

BCA's college-placement record is strong—and correlates only modestly with the school's voc-tech heritage. Among the institutions entered by the class of 2010 were Carnegie-Mellon (13 students), Cornell (19), MIT (10), Princeton (7), Chicago (5), and Yale (4). The students' SAT combined-score average in recent years has been around 2200 out of a possible 2400, impressive by any standard. BCA has also accumulated its share of honors and accolades, including a federal Blue Ribbon School designation, recognition by *Newsweek*, *Business Week*, Intel, and various other listings of top high schools.

As we have found in other communities with academically strong selective-admission high schools, BCA is hugely popular with the county's Asian immigrants, particularly with Bergen County's large Korean-American population. They seem as bent on getting their sons and daughters into competitive schools (and universities) as many Koreans are in their families' places of origin, and they take pains to get them into BCA, including specialized "cram schools" to ready them for the BCA admissions tests—akin to the *hagwon* programs one might find in Seoul or Pusan.

Academics

We were surprised to learn that students cannot transfer out of the academies into which they are admitted, even if their interests or career goals change during high school.[11] Many youngsters to whom we spoke indicated that they had indeed altered their priorities while at BCA. The school deals with this fairly well, however, by offering many elective courses that cut across its academies as well as numerous schoolwide courses that New Jersey requires for graduation plus a mandatory one-day-a-week off-campus "senior experience"—a sort of internship with mentor—for every 12th grader, largely designed and organized by the students themselves. (A plethora of extracurricular activities are also schoolwide.)

Still, each academy has its own flavor, curricular specialties, and core-course requirements, and they're not always quite what one would expect. For example, all 11th and 12th graders in the Academy for Business and Finance take the full (and humanities-centric) International Baccalaureate program, preparing them for IB exams and the IB diploma. (Individual IB courses may also be taken by students in the other academies.)

The International Baccalaureate isn't the only supercharged educational opportunity available to BCA students. The Advanced Placement program also looms large here, especially in science and math, with about eight hundred AP exams taken annually—that's about two each per year for juniors and seniors not in the IB program. (And seven out of eight of these yield a score of 3 or higher.)

This is not, however, an unmitigated plus, at least from the teachers' perspective. As at other schools we visited, BCA instructors lament that the pressure to take and pass AP exams, plus all the state (and federal) testing, combined with the college-admissions competition force a sameness upon the school, its curriculum, and its pedagogy that dampens their ability to innovate and tailor their instruction to the singularities of their pupils.

Each academy has some teachers of its own and some special facilities, too. BCA is extraordinarily well endowed in this realm with, for example, an elaborate teaching kitchen for youngsters studying culinary arts and an awesome nanotechnology lab containing several electron microscopes—almost unheard of in American high schools. Also on hand are faculty and staff who appear proficient in handling such sophisticated gear and using it to create high-quality learning experiences.

Teaching at BCA

Though budget cuts in recent years have shrunk their numbers a bit, in 2010–11 BCA employed one hundred teachers and some twenty other staff members, making for an unusually generous teacher-student ratio, an average class size of eighteen (and none larger than twenty-four), and specialized staff for some labs and technology centers. More than a quarter of the teachers have significant prior experience in college teaching or work experience in business or science and technology. Almost everyone has at least a master's degree, and there's a smattering of doctorates on staff, too, especially in the sciences. About a third of the instructors passed through New Jersey's many "alternate routes" to certification rather than ordinary college-of-education programs.

Once employed at BCA, they tend to stick around. The average teacher has been there eight years, and seldom do more than five positions turn over in a year—with hiring decisions made by the school team itself, not a distant "central office." Dismissing anyone is hard, though. After three years in the school, teachers have tenure—and all belong to the local union.

Their work is demanding, too. Because the kids are smart, they can be challenging to teach. The day is long (for which teachers are paid an additional $8,000 per year); there are lots of student papers and independent research projects to review, comment on, and grade. Plenty of class preparation is needed to keep ahead of (or just keep up with) the kids. For those who thrive amid such challenges, BCA appears to be a stimulating, gratifying place to teach. It helps that there are virtually no discipline problems, though kids complain of stress and the guidance staff must deal with the consequences of academic pressure and competitiveness.

Resources

Fortunately, the school can afford a big guidance team. New Jersey is known for generously funding its public schools—and for correspondingly high taxes. Governor Chris Christie made news in May 2011 when his education team recalculated just how much was being spent on public schooling in the Garden State and determined that (in 2009–10) the average exceeded $17,000 per pupil.[12] A similar calculation for the Bergen County Vocational District, which includes BCA (but also high-cost special education), yielded an astounding $33,000 per student.[13]

About 35 percent of that money comes with individual students from their home districts but more (about 42 percent) comes from countywide tax levies. (The Bergen County budget is almost half a billion dollars.) Most of the rest is state and federal aid, including the aforementioned federal Perkins Act dollars, which further explains why BCA clings to its voc-tech heritage and facade even as it prepares bright kids for competitive colleges.

All these resources notwithstanding, the school does not feel like an institution awash in extra dollars. There have been cutbacks in practically every one of its funding sources, and today there is much budgetary uncertainty. When we visited in May 2011, the school did not yet have a budget for the upcoming year, because the county had not finalized its own budget. The principal was developing multiple scenarios, but even the rosiest of these contemplated laying off two or three more staff members. He's grateful that the parents' association raises some $40,000–50,000 a year to supplement the budget, particularly to help pay for things like field trips for kids whose parents cannot afford to send them.[14]

One nontrivial cost that BCA doesn't have to cover is transporting pupils to and from school. That's the responsibility of their home districts, which dispatch a remarkable fifty-three buses a day to move these kids across the county. Students remarked that the bus ride is a good time to bond with other pupils from their hometowns, who may or may not be in their classes—or even the same academy—within BCA.

Though less famous (at least beyond the borders of its eponymous county), BCA legitimately regards itself as a peer (and friendly rival) of Bronx Science, Thomas Jefferson, and other acclaimed high schools atop the academic-status heap of American public education. It's a school in which almost anyone with an able, energized, and high-achieving child might happily picture enrolling him or her. Plainly, there are more such youngsters in Bergen County (and far beyond) than this school can accommodate. One wonders, once again, about the wisdom of the political and policy constraints that keep more such institutions from being established to serve more kids throughout the area.

Chapter 14

Thomas Jefferson High
School for Science and Technology

● ● ● ● ● ● ● ● ● ● ● ● ● ● ● ●

Annandale, VA

Best High School in the Land?

Few people associated with TJ, as the Thomas Jefferson School for Science and Technology is known throughout the metro Washington area and much of the education world, have come down from the thrill of being designated by *U.S. News* as America's best high school. That first happened in 2007 but is an ongoing pleasure, as TJ's top ranking continues in the magazine's annual rankings.[1]

Operated by the sprawling Fairfax County Public Schools system (FCPS), the nation's eleventh-largest district, which educates some 175,000 youngsters across a sizable—and mostly prosperous—chunk of Washington's northern-Virginia suburbs, TJ also serves smaller numbers of students from four other county (and two city) school systems. But four-fifths of its 1,800 pupils live in Fairfax.

The main reason TJ enrolls several hundred kids from other jurisdictions—not all of which are unfailingly keen to dispatch their ablest pupils to this Fairfax school—is that it's one of nineteen "Governor's Schools" in Virginia, a program that began in 1973 to provide some of the commonwealth's ablest young people with academically (and artistically) challenging programs that go beyond the offerings of their home schools. Fairfax operates TJ, but all Governor's Schools are "regional magnets" in scope and mission and, in return, receive extra state funding, enhanced access to other state resources (including the university system), and a measure of operational autonomy. Most are part-time programs, however. TJ is one of just three that are full-time, full-fledged high schools.[2]

TJ dates to 1985 and to the impulse—which we've seen in several other cities—to respond to *A Nation at Risk* by creating a top-notch school in defiance of the gloomy assertions that American K–12 education was awash in mediocrity. The initial impulse within FCPS was to devise a straightforward, employment-oriented school that would do a solid job of preparing young people to work for local firms, essentially an updated vocational school. But leaders of Northern Virginia's burgeoning high-tech sector made clear that they needed scientists more than technicians—people who could create technology, not just apply it. School founders also understood that success in today's demanding leadership positions requires more than knowledge of science, math, and technology; it calls as well for understanding the humanities, building powerful communication skills, learning how to work as part of teams, and becoming adept at meeting complex systemic challenges involving multiple disciplines, variables, and perspectives. So the school plan was reworked into a more complex and sophisticated education strategy.

The building, however, didn't get reworked much. FCPS took an extant high school and (over a couple of years of cohabitation) moved its original students out to other schools while installing the new magnet program in the two-decades-old structure. Though geographically well situated (midcounty), the building was ill equipped to house the modern labs and state-of-the-art technologies that it gradually accumulated, often with the help of the same high-tech firms that had pushed for TJ's creation. Plenty of small-scale retrofitting followed, but today's school still occupies a nondescript and crowded building supplemented by a couple of dozen trailers ("learning cottages") out back. Some of the labs are cramped, maze-like warrens of rooms and little corridors, though the equipment and courses and student projects housed within are often stunning.

At this writing, a major buildingwide makeover, to last several years and cost many millions, will soon get underway. But the current facility, inadequate as it is, accommodates some remarkable stuff. For example, we entered a biotechnology laboratory (one of TJ's thirteen specialized research labs) and found therein a DNA sequencer, a gas spectrometer, a cell counter, and innumerable other costly, complex devices that one might expect to see in a research university preparing doctoral students, not in a public high school.

The courses are impressive, too. That particular lab is home to a two-part "DNA science" sequence as well as ambitious senior-year research projects. But throughout TJ one finds demanding classes, often college level, many of them going well beyond the Advanced Placement standard in their respective fields, particularly (as one might expect) in math, science, and technology. Examples include Relativity, Electrodynamics, and Quantum Mechanics; Neurobiology; Computational Physics; Introductory Organic Chemistry; Advanced Microprocessor System Design; and Introduction to Engineering. These often meet just two or three times a week for lengthy periods, a "block schedule" that resembles most university courses. Besides classroom time, however, these courses prescribe tons of homework and plenty of laboratory and writing work for students.

But the school's curricular capstone doesn't take the form of courses. It's the "senior research" requirement, carried out either in TJ's own labs or via an outside mentorship, and done either solo or teamed with other students. Such projects typically build on exacting prerequisites, often AP-level study completed before 12th grade. As the school describes this culminating educational experience, "All students are expected to complete a major science or engineering research project, either by working in one of the science and technology research laboratories, or by working in a commercial, government or university research lab or technical facility through our mentorship program."

Recent examples of senior projects include "A Search for Exosolar Planets Using Radio Images," "A Hexapod All-Terrain Walking Robot," "Petite Mutation Induction In *Saccharomyces Cerevisiae* [a yeast]," "The Cultivation of Algae for Oil Generation and Biodiesel Synthesis," and "The Effect of Background Sound on Viewer Memory."

Some of these projects go on for years, passing unfinished from one cohort of TJ seniors to the next, with each taking the progress achieved to the next level.[3] Other projects mimic "real science" in that they fail to produce the hoped-for results or encounter glitches that prevent them from being completed as designed.[4] Such setbacks don't get in the way of earning credit so long as students are able to analyze what went wrong—and many of them manage to devise alternative courses of action with little or no teacher assistance. Indeed, the kids note that the usual instructor response to a student research quandary is "well, you'd better figure out what to do."

This push to become independent learners and thinkers is one reason that TJ alums coming back to visit frequently comment on how well prepared they were for college, compared with classmates from other high schools. They had already internalized time management, college-style course structures (as well as college-level intellectual mastery), clear written and oral expression, teamwork, and an understanding of how to do their own research.

Demographics and Admissions

In 2010–11, 94 percent of TJ pupils were white (44 percent) or Asian (50 percent); black and Hispanic youngsters comprised just 4 percent of its enrollment, and fewer than 3 percent were economically disadvantaged. (Boys slightly outnumbered girls—about eleven to nine.)[5] These blunt facts give rise to a host of issues.

In recent years, TJ has had about 3,300 applicants annually for 480 9th-grade openings. (A small number of students are admitted in grades 10 and 11 to fill vacancies resulting from attrition.)[6] All must reside in one of the participating jurisdictions and must have completed Algebra 1 (or something more advanced) in 8th grade.[7] Initial applicants fill out a form—including mandatory racial-classification information—and pay a $90 "processing fee."[8] In December, all must take the Thomas Jefferson Admissions Test, consisting of a two-hour multiple choice exam and two thirty-minute essays.[9] Custom-designed for FCPS by Pearson, the TJ test resembles the College Board's SAT in format, timing, and intellectual content.

Test scores and middle school grades are then weighed to determine the semifinalist pool—ordinarily about half of all applicants, which means more than three times what the school can accommodate. Then begins a challenging second-round cycle that mimics the admissions process at an elite college. Test scores and grades are re-examined— particularly in math and science—as are students' essays (from the December exam). Two middle school teacher recommendations are required at this stage, and kids must fill out a probing information sheet about themselves.

All this material is closely reviewed by two-person teams of teachers and administrators from Fairfax and other participating systems— with a third reader available to resolve discrepancies. Though TJ makes public almost everything else related to the admissions process, it protects the rubrics by which these appraisals are done. And admissions are handled by a separate office for that purpose within FCPS, not by TJ itself, meaning that school leaders don't themselves decide which kids will turn up in 9th grade—and cannot be pressured or cajoled by the thousands of eager (and sometimes wealthy, influential, politically connected) families that are keen to enroll their sons and daughters.

While TJ and FCPS engage in many energetic outreach activities meant to foster racial and ethnic diversity in the applicant pool (and, especially during summer, to provide some of the benefits of TJ to schools and kids who don't attend it during the regular year), the screening process itself does not engage in "affirmative action." The applicant pool for the class of 2015 was 13.5 percent black and Hispanic, but those groups comprised just 4 percent of those admitted. By contrast, 57 percent of admittees were Asian, compared with 41 percent of applicants.[10] Merit—as defined by what the school deems important and measured by the metrics that it and FCPS have chosen to use—appears to rule the day.

This is partly the outcome of a series of federal court rulings that made it increasingly difficult, then (in 2007) totally verboten, to consider race explicitly in public-school admissions.[11] Along the way, Fairfax County had tried several approaches to boosting the minority (i.e., black and Latino) enrollment at TJ, especially by giving greater weight to teacher recommendations and less to test scores. For a time, that enrollment was up to about 14 percent—and, report those who were around at the time, the youngsters entering via such forms of "soft affirmative action" did fine once at TJ. Eventually, however, the FCPS attorney advised the superintendent that admissions considerations tied to race had to cease. Recent superintendents sought to deal with this situation—and TJ's worsening "diversity profile"—by developing geographic attendance zones and admitting the most qualified applicants from within each of these. But former Fairfax superintendent Dan Domenech, now executive director of the American Association of School Administrators, recalls being rebuffed by the board when he suggested using such zones—he had opted for county "judicial districts"—as the organizing structure for TJ admissions.

Today, there's plenty of outreach but not a lot of black or Hispanic (or low-income) students. There is, however, a steadily rising Asian-American presence within TJ. That portion of the school's enrollment climbed from 38 to 46 percent in just two years—2009–10 was apparently the first year that Asian kids outnumbered whites—and, as noted above, close to three-fifths of those admitted into the class of 2015 self-identify as Asian.[12]

Within that population, the largest groups are youngsters of Korean, Chinese, and Indian descent and, according to almost everyone we spoke with, Korean-American families are the keenest to enroll their kids in TJ and the most apt to pay for tutors, "cram courses," and test-prep centers designed to boost scores on the school's entrance exam. Teachers allege that some families send their children from Korea to northern Virginia to live with relatives (or occasionally maybe even on their own) in order to establish residency and thereby qualify for TJ.[13]

Demand and Supply

It's possible that changes on the Fairfax County school board (which saw much turnover in November 2011) and in district leadership (veteran superintendent Jack Dale concludes his eight-year tenure in that role in 2012), or perhaps on the U.S. Supreme Court, will alter TJ's current countywide, merit-based admissions process and, perhaps, produce a student body a bit more representative of the area. (The 2010 census found the Fairfax population to be 18 percent Asian and 25 percent black and Latino.) It's also possible that ongoing efforts to boost academic performance in other local schools, beginning with younger children, as well as outreach programs to familiarize more kids and families with the TJ option, will yield a different student profile. On the other hand, there is absolutely no reason to expect the demand from Asian-American families to slacken—to the contrary—and it seems extremely unlikely that the school itself is going to grow or be replicated. TJ is undoubtedly a scarce commodity in education. As it is already unable to enroll five in six of those who want to attend—and not even a third of those who meet its threshold entry requirements get in—expanding the number of qualified applicants would serve mainly to reduce the percentage of students who actually matriculate.

Rather than enlarge or clone TJ, Fairfax County has opened specialized "academies" in many of its two dozen other high schools—for example, science and engineering at Chantilly, international studies at Edison and Marshall, "communications and the arts" at West Potomac, and the International Baccalaureate program in eight schools. Advanced Placement courses are offered everywhere, and many FCPS high schools make available an "AP Diploma" to students who "pass" at least five AP exams. Such moves ease the pain of being turned down at TJ, make the other high schools more appealing to district residents (and taxpayers, voters, etc.), and calm the agitation among those schools' leaders that their best students will be "creamed" by TJ.[14]

The Advanced Placement Cudgel

The Advanced Placement program is ubiquitous across FCPS, but nowhere does it dominate a school to the extent it does at TJ. Indeed, a major issue facing this school's leaders and instructors is the intense emphasis that its students and parents place on AP courses and tests—and on the bonus GPA points that accrue from those courses.[15] It's true that TJ pupils excel at passing them. They take an average of seven

AP tests apiece during their time in the school—four are all but universal[16]—and do extremely well, earning scores of 3 or better on a mind-blowing 98 percent of the 3,357 AP exams that they sat for in 2010.

The problem with racking up a bunch of AP achievements is that this doesn't always make for an optimal high school education. Teachers and school leaders say this focus can discourage students from experimenting with interesting, possibly life-changing electives and from pursuing a sequence of courses in a field of interest that may well go *beyond* the Advanced Placement level. A perceptive student commented that kids "miss out on other electives and extracurriculars that don't count for AP." The required senior-year course in "geosystems," for example, is an intellectually demanding effort to integrate what students previously studied in physics, chemistry, and biology, but it doesn't lead to an AP exam. Students (and parents) constantly ask why the school doesn't instead offer "environmental science," which *does* lead to an AP exam. The geosystems course description cogently explains the school's rationale but also comes across as rather defensive on this point.[17]

Instructors at TJ view the AP program as narrowing their curriculum (not unlike an intellectually more rigorous version of No Child Left Behind or Virginia's "Standards of Learning"), cramping their pedagogical freedom, and placing greater emphasis on passing the test than on widening intellectual horizons and deepening understanding. "The type of teaching we do," one commented, "is things that don't get standardized on exams." They seek to teach "inquisitiveness," for example, but "how to gauge it?" And they're frustrated by bright young people "who only want the right answer and the A and don't end up with tools for 'knowing what to do when they don't know what to do.'"

The GPA-grubbing also gives rise to TJ's only real discipline problem. It's not cutting classes, fighting in the corridors, bringing weapons to school, or threatening teachers, but violating the norms of academic integrity. The temptation is strong to cheat, plagiarize, "borrow" from classmates, and let teammates do the heavy lifting on group projects. These are clever kids, not all of whom are adept at resisting such temptations.

Nobody seems to have a good alternative, though. Any suggestion that Advanced Placement scores, course grades, and GPAs might be de-emphasized at TJ would, we were assured, meet with instant rejection by students and parents alike, not least because AP credits can really save time and money in college. And the colleges add to the clamor by signaling to applicants that 4s and 5s on a lot of AP tests will boost their admission prospects.

Bureaucracy and Budgets

TJ's young principal, just completing his third year there when we visited, says his goal is for the school to supply the "frosting and decoration atop a test-based cake." He doesn't see much flexibility with the test-based part but believes that TJ teachers should have "fifteen percent curricular freedom" and does his best to assure that, which means occasional tussles with the district when he requests exceptions and waivers from rules and practices that don't make much sense when applied to this high school.

It was clear from the outset that TJ would need the flexibility to do some things differently, whether it be the length and configuration of the day, the sequencing of the curriculum, letting seniors go off on self-designed projects and internships, or simply giving them the freedom to leave school at lunchtime. (That privilege was recently revoked by FCPS.) A former principal recalls that ex-superintendent Robert ("Bud") Spillane, who led FCPS for twelve years, was his "hero" for sheltering TJ from many of the system's bureaucratic and conformist pressures.

There's less sheltering-from-above today, and more depends on the political and bureaucratic skills of the principal himself. "We play nice in the sandbox," insists the incumbent, and don't seek special favors or resources for TJ. This seems to work okay so long as the FCPS bureaucracy is reasonable—and the TJ team strives for reasonableness in return. When it comes to filling the occasional empty teacher slot, for instance, "the system works with us." The FCPS personnel people know enough to send TJ "candidates who won't get eaten alive by our students." And the school's department heads (here called "division managers") insist that they and their fellow teachers are the main deciders of who gets brought on board. On the other hand, notes the principal, TJ must occasionally accept an instructor who has been "de-staffed" elsewhere in the system. There are seniority and tenure systems in Fairfax County, and in this respect TJ is definitely part of FCPS.[18]

The school is not overflowing with money. Two and three years ago, TJ was losing several faculty positions a year, though that has since stabilized. But the school has long been able to muster additional resources. Indeed, it has always needed to supplement its regular FCPS allocation with a million or two of top-up funds. By being designated a Governor's School, it gets some extra money from the state and, as an advanced magnet school, it receives additional dollars from Fairfax to reduce the average class by 1.8 students below the countywide average. The administration struggles to keep all core courses and science classes at no more than 25 pupils—there are issues of lab safety and having enough microscopes, et cetera—but some electives have more than 30 students in them, which teachers find both burdensome (all those papers to mark up) and ill suited to the types of classroom interactions they think are best for these kids and the material they're studying.

The principal estimates that TJ spends, on average, about $1,000 per pupil more than other high schools in the area, but that number is also associated with a longer school day, eight periods instead of seven, and teachers who get paid a 7 percent premium for handling six assignments instead of the five that is the norm under their contract.

In addition to the public dollars in TJ's budget (about $23 million), the school musters a nontrivial amount of private funding. The parents' association raises about $25,000 per year; many teams and activities have their own "booster" groups; and a separate nonprofit organization called the Thomas Jefferson Partnership Fund makes available some $650,000–700,000 per annum in resources (both cash and in-kind) raised from corporations, parents, and alumni/ae. Many of those dollars are used to purchase sophisticated lab equipment.[19]

Far be it from us to either affirm or challenge the *U.S. News* gold-star rating for the Thomas Jefferson High School for Science and Technology. But it's a most impressive educational institution serving high-performing youngsters who are fortunate to study there.

Chapter 15

Similarities and Differences

• • • • • • • • • • • • •

Judging from our eleven site visits, there's no such thing as "the" academically selective American public high school. Each of them is distinctive—but they have important likenesses, too.

Certainly their varied histories and current demographics challenge allegations that these are bastions of privilege or tools of social stratification and racial segregation. Only five of them (Pine View, Ben Franklin, IMSA, Townsend Harris, and TJ) were even designed at the outset to serve a selected group of highly talented students. The other six began for different reasons and became academically focused and selective, gradually or quickly, in response to political forces or evolving community needs.

The five policy objectives outlined in chapter 1 (pp. 11–12) intersect with these schools' diverse origins. The histories of Jones College Prep, LASA, and Central were all tied in some way to racial desegregation. Developing talent in STEM-related fields drove the creation of IMSA, Thomas Jefferson (TJ), and Bergen County Academies. Four schools— Jones, School Without Walls (SWW), Central, and Oxford—initially served populations of students or purposes that weren't being satisfactorily addressed before becoming academically selective. Although only Oxford and Ben Franklin began as within-district efforts spurred by board and community members, nearly all of the schools were sustained or championed by local advocates.

In this chapter, we flag additional patterns among the schools we visited. While not every generalization applies to each school, their similarities are at least as notable as their differences.

Teaching and Learning Environment

By and large, all the schools we visited were serious, purposeful places: competitive yet supportive, energized yet calm. Behavior problems (save for cheating and plagiarism) were minimal, and students attended regularly. The kids wanted to be there—and were motivated to succeed. (That's scarcely surprising, considering how many of the schools screen for those qualities among their applicants.) Most classrooms we observed were similarly alive, engaged places in which teachers appeared to have uniformly high expectations for their pupils and planned instruction around the assumption that students can and want to learn.

We also noticed across schools that the use of time—by day and by week—was structured in ways that facilitate in-depth learning and prepare students for a college schedule. These included staggered start times, eight-hour days, class periods of varying lengths, fewer class meeting days within the week, and dedicated time for collaborative and independent research projects.

The schools' curricula and course offerings, however, reflected differing philosophies about what and how academically talented students should learn. All had taken a position regarding the role of Advanced Placement courses, making them (and prerequisite honors courses) the heart of the curriculum (e.g., Pine View, Oxford), or sprinkling in a few APs to augment the curriculum for some students (e.g., Central), or offering them alongside a more general curriculum (e.g., SWW, Jones), or making them major adjuncts to a more advanced or specialized curriculum (LASA, TJ), or even eschewing them altogether (IMSA).

The schools' principals hailed from various backgrounds, not just from within the school or district. As a group, however, they exhibited traits that one would expect of leaders of successful high schools that in some cases are the pride of their communities and in every case are closely watched: all were extraordinarily dedicated and hardworking individuals who were also politically astute. They had wrested (or inherited) a moderate degree of freedom for their buildings and those inside them, despite often operating within systems that had a fair share of bureaucratic oversight. Their teachers didn't have many formal waivers from union contracts, yet principals said that they could usually "work things out."

These leaders oversaw instructional staffs that were similarly capable, consisting mostly of intelligent, dedicated individuals, well grounded in their fields, many with unconventional backgrounds and ample teaching experience. Turnover was reportedly low. Most teachers belonged to unions and were paid on the "contract scale" but many received additional compensation for longer days and extra duties. Regardless, they tended to come early, stay late, and design complex assignments and lesson plans that may have taken as much time to formulate and grade as for their students to complete.

Teachers in all the schools also acknowledged that working with eager and talented kids—often backstopped by engaged and supportive parents—was a kind of professional luxury. Yet they felt that their jobs weren't easier because they were teaching such students. Indeed, many remarked on how hard they had to work to "keep up" with kids who were mostly smart but far from alike. In fact, when we asked teachers in different schools to respond to two statements about the nature of their jobs (*It must be so easy teaching at that school—all the kids are smart, motivated, and have parent support* and *Teaching 25 of the same kind of kid in every class must be pretty nice*), they all pushed back. One said: "The best and the brightest are here. But there are also many kids who struggle. I've got to challenge everyone and provide support at the same time." Consistent with that view, few teachers evinced a "sink or swim" mentality about academics—and all of their schools provided "life preservers" for flailing students.

Several instructors at schools with more ethnically homogeneous populations also mentioned that having so many students from the same cultural background actually made some aspects of teaching more difficult, such as eliciting diverse perspectives during a classroom discussion.

Getting In

All the schools we visited attracted scads of qualified applicants, thanks in part to local and national media coverage of their students' and graduates' accomplishments and, in some cases, to districtwide choice programs that either required all students to apply to high school or simply increased awareness of the range of alternatives within the system. Even the lowest-performing of the schools we visited (Central) had more applicants than it could accommodate. Given the demand, potentially the most controversial aspect of this kind of school isn't *that* it selects its students but *how* it selects them.

Familiar indicators of academic performance or potential, notably grades, test scores, and teacher recommendations, were the primary criteria for admissions. All eleven schools used these, and some employed additional variables (e.g., behavior records) to screen applicants or set minimal requirements for considering them.

They differed, however, as did schools on our wider survey, in the emphases they placed on conventional academic criteria and on additional evidence such as interviews and essays—when these were weighed at all.

Four schools (Oxford, Jones, TJ, SWW) fit within the traditional definition of an "exam school," that is, they developed or adapted their own admission test and required all of their eligible applicants to sit for it.[1] These assessments ranged from professionally designed to teacher created. Whatever their construction, neither parents nor school staff seemed to question their use, even though it wasn't clear whether the schools and districts gathered validity and reliability data on them, or whether and how often they changed.

Each school's admissions process tended either to rely primarily "on the numbers" or to emphasize a more holistic, student-by-student approach. Schools employing the former method stressed trying to make "objective" decisions—via committee or computer—about applicants by using combinations of minimum GPAs and test-score cutoffs, ranking applicants, assigning numerical values to nonacademic criteria, and the like. Oxford, Pine View, and Ben Franklin took this tack. Schools within vast urban systems with centrally controlled application-and-selection procedures (e.g., Jones, Townsend Harris) also crunched numbers while weighing such factors as applicants' addresses and rank-ordered preferences. Schools with a more holistic approach (e.g., IMSA, TJ, SWW) appeared to have the time, resources, philosophy, or political mandate to consider applicants more subjectively and as individuals—though not until they met threshold eligibility requirements. Among the techniques they employed were complex (and sometimes secret) scoring rubrics, individual interviews, essays, and committee discussions akin to those used by selective colleges.

Given the high rejection rates across schools, we were somewhat surprised that few appeared to undertake (nor, so far as we could make out, did their districts undertake) regular internal or external evaluation of their admissions criteria and procedures. Indeed, in many cases, the process (and its results) seemed to go unquestioned. Those that did evaluate and continue to do so (e.g., IMSA, TJ) had at some point been prodded in this direction by outside forces (e.g., pressure to increase student diversity, challenges from parents whose children were denied admission). Schools without such data were hard pressed to answer fundamental questions about whether their system "worked," that is, whether it could actually distinguish applicants likely to benefit from the school from those who would not, and whether it might be unintentionally biased against certain applicant groups.

Who Goes There

In part because these kinds of schools are oversubscribed, the questions of who ends up in them and whether their pupil populations "look" anything like the communities from which they draw students provoke significant interest, especially for those who level charges of elitism.

Though some of the eleven schools we visited enrolled students predominantly of one race, more had students from multiple racial and ethnic groups, and several were more diverse than any other high school in their area (e.g., LASA, SWW, Jones, Ben Franklin). None, however, was a demographic or socioeconomic miniature of the place it served. In addition to such obvious explanations as uneven preparation at the elementary and middle school level, we discovered that a school's location can affect its diversity (by deterring would-be applicants) because of longer days that don't fit district bus schedules, because the school draws pupils from a wide area (e.g., a sprawling city, several counties), or because attending it means living there (IMSA). Few students actually reside close to these schools—and getting there on foot is uncommon. (Every morning and afternoon, more than fifty buses pull up to Bergen County Academies to transport the school's 1,050 pupils around a big chunk of northern New Jersey.) Although leaders and teachers in all the schools were aware (if not concerned) that certain groups were over- or underrepresented in the student body, few questioned the admissions criteria or process. Rather, the responsibility for increasing ethnic, socioeconomic, and geographic diversity was placed squarely on recruitment. As one administrator put it, "We can only consider kids who apply."

Toward that end—and to enhance the quality of their applicant pools—most of the schools engaged in multifaceted outreach efforts in their communities, regions or states, seeking to inform potential students (and parents, teachers, counselors, donors, etc.) about the educational opportunity that they offer. Like most high schools, these institutions have little influence over their feeder schools. This makes outreach efforts both more important and more challenging as they (or their districts) strive to ensure that their applicant pools are demographically diverse, reasonably representative of their communities, *and* academically qualified.

Not surprisingly, the recruitment efforts of schools that drew applicants from multiple districts (e.g., Bergen County, TJ, IMSA) were especially vigorous, even exhaustive. In schools serving just one district, the central office was more likely to assume primary responsibility for recruitment. In the very large districts (e.g., New York, Chicago, Jefferson County), this was usually part of a broader outreach effort that involved educating parents and kids about a host of high school options.

Success and Sustainability

Townsend Harris excepted, the schools we visited were relatively young, at least in their academically selective form. They had passed the public-image and public-acceptability tests with flying colors, and most had sunk fairly deep roots in their communities, but none seemed entirely immune from pressures that could eventually alter them, perhaps even threaten their existence.

Ironically, some of those pressures related to gauging their success with the students they selected. As of 2010–11, their effectiveness was evaluated mainly by the same measures that were used to judge the success of nonselective schools. Staff in our schools tended to dismiss these metrics and the prevailing "standards-testing-accountability" regime as irksome distractions with little meaning for their schools or pupils. In most cases, the curricula implicit in statewide assessments and kindred tests were more limited than those of the schools, and the cut-scores for passing them were too low to be meaningful. Leaders and teachers at several schools (e.g., Oxford, Pine View, LASA) were acutely aware, however, that enrolling some of the district's highest-performing students came at the cost of ongoing tension with other high schools, some of which were not making "adequate yearly progress" and suspected that they would have fared better had they not surrendered those pupils to the selective schools.

While few of our schools were seriously concerned about (or evaluated their own success by) state assessment results, none had developed its own metrics for gauging how much or how well its students learned in its classrooms. More often, the schools (and the proliferating ratings and rankings by media outlets) counted Advanced Placement tests taken and passed, or the number of seniors gaining admission to top colleges, as evidence of their success. Perhaps even more than the typical high school, our schools felt pressure from students, parents, and colleges to maximize AP credits—sometimes in ways that seemed to foster a "just pass the test" mentality and discouraged unconventional courses and instructional methods. Some also felt heavy pressure to ensure that their graduates attend not just any college but the best colleges.

The communities and political contexts in which many of these schools operate created pressure, too. Intermittent controversy over perceived elitism fed some apprehension about their futures as selective institutions. More immediate were budget cuts, which are painful for a school at any time but more so when major reductions are occurring in state and district revenues. Leaders of the schools we visited felt doubly vulnerable as attention—and resources—were concentrated on low-performing schools and students. ("Smart kids will do fine, regardless, and in any case are not today's priority" was the undertone they picked up.) Many had become accustomed to having at least some extra resources, often for transportation or smaller classes. While some schools benefited from certain categorical funds (e.g., magnet dollars, STEM or tech-voc dollars), many didn't qualify for other state and federal programs such as Title I, bilingual education, and special education. Most engaged in supplementary private fund-raising to sustain resources for transportation, smaller classes, or other school features to which they and their students, parents, and teachers were habituated.

Despite such strains and challenges, the eleven schools we visited seemed to enjoy multiple sources of support that mitigated the budgetary distress and bolstered their resilience for the foreseeable future. Most, for example, benefited—politically and in other ways, such as fund-raising—from exceptionally devoted friends, sometimes in high places, including alums, local politicians, business and university leaders, even journalists. Many had ties with outside organizations, including universities, labs, and businesses, which brought expertise and some resources into the schools, afforded them some political protection, and supplied them with venues for student internships and independent projects.

Some schools were also viewed as magnets for economic development and talent recruitment, or otherwise boasted reputations as assets to their community or state. School board members and district leaders believed that their school's presence encouraged middle- and upper-middle-class families to stay in town and stick with public education.

Perhaps most importantly, these schools were blessed with overwhelming advocacy from the parents of their students, many of whom felt that their children were receiving a kind of private-school education at public expense. As long as parents strongly believe the schools provide safety (physical, emotional, intellectual), short- and long-term academic and career opportunities, and social benefits for their children, they will likely go a long way toward ensuring these schools' survival, if not their expansion or replication.

Part III

• • • • •

Summing Up

Chapter 16

Dilemmas and Challenges

• • • • • • • • • • • •

Seeing a subset of these schools close up, observing them in action, and talking with those most involved with them deepened our understanding of what makes them tick and the roles they play in their communities. But these visits and conversations also highlighted some perplexing issues that the schools embody and that bear on American education more generally. In this chapter we reflect on several of the knottiest of these.

Selectivity and Choice in Public Education

Americans have generally come to accept the principle and practice of students and parents choosing schools. But public schools that select their pupils raise eyebrows in a country that has long associated public education with classrooms open to all comers, at least from designated neighborhoods. The eyebrows go higher when the basis for such student selection involves judgments about youngsters' academic prowess and potential. And the situation grows dicier still when such schools are beset by hundreds or thousands more kids than they can accommodate, many of them with plenty of potential. Practically all are girls and boys whose parents ardently seek their admission to these selective schools—and more than a few will pull every string within reach to attain that goal. Shouldn't they all be able to enroll where they want to?

Two decades ago, the eminent sociologist James S. Coleman concluded that education choice should work in both directions: students selecting their schools and schools choosing their pupils. This, he insisted, would help to "get the incentives right" and thereby improve everybody's education. "The incentives for schools," he wrote, "would include an interest in attracting and keeping the best students they could. The incentives for parents and students would include the ability to get into schools they find attractive and to remain in those schools."[1]

Coleman predicted that two-way choice would reduce stratification by race and income and replace it with stratification "based on students' performance and behavior." When families cannot marshal the latter resources to get their children a good education, he observed, they resort to "money or racial exclusion."

To what extent, if at all, do the selective schools on our list bear out Coleman's proposition?

Two-way choice has long been the norm in private schools and higher education, including public colleges and universities. The highest-status among the latter (e.g., Virginia, Berkeley, North Carolina, Michigan, Wisconsin) have been selective forever, much like their private-sector counterparts (Stanford, Amherst, Duke et al.). We take for granted that they review test scores, high school grades, essays, and more in determining whom to admit.

Elements of two-way choice have crept into public education at the K–12 level, too. Various schools, programs, and courses impose prerequisites of many sorts, and it's not unusual for such criteria to include students' academic promise or prior achievement. As "tracking" emerged within the comprehensive high school, the school was more likely than pupils or parents to decide who belonged in its college-prep track.[2] Even today, honors and AP classes and IB programs in many high schools are open to some students but not others.[3] A teacher or administrator determines whether one is qualified for such coursework, largely on the basis of one's prior academic record—and space is frequently limited. Nor can students take calculus until they've passed algebra 2, or French 3 without French 2.

Indeed, as we extend such lists, we see that prerequisites, preconditions, and screening procedures, including but not limited to the academic kind, are not so unusual in American public education after all. Sometimes, of course, they're just arbitrary barriers, such as the municipal boundaries of Beverly Hills, Winnetka, or Scarsdale. (Thus the stratification by income that Coleman rued.) In other circumstances, however, they're the only way to produce a viable instructional situation. (To have students in calculus class who have not mastered algebra would make little sense—and produce an unmanageable teaching challenge.) Selectivity is also a rational response to the tough reality that resources are finite, that kids differ in their needs, interests, strengths, and accomplishments, and that no system can realistically offer everything to everybody all the time. Individual student differences never go away—but even when the will to accommodate them is present, institutional capacities often have limits.

Of course we want everyone to have equal access to every opportunity. Yet honoring that goal is hard when access to scarce or desirable opportunities must be restricted, whether the rationing occurs via selectivity, lottery, or first-come, first-served. We're wary, too, lest proscribed characteristics such as race, religion, and gender enter into the rationing process, violating moral principles, civil rights statutes, constitutional doctrines, and court orders. At bottom, we fret that *selective* is somehow incompatible with *fair*—and we're mindful of times and places when selectivity has served as a way of keeping some kids (or kinds of kids) outside the sanctum, especially when those who get selected then receive (or are perceived to receive) a better education than those left outside. Private schools can generally get away with that sort of thing. Public schools can't.

All these considerations and more enter into the admissions processes in the schools we have been examining, into the political and regulatory frameworks within which they operate, into periodic interventions by activists and civil rights enforcers, into countless "outreach" efforts to widen and diversify their applicant pools, and into high-level policy decisions about whether to open more such schools, expand them, or do away with them (or alter their selection methods).

Local culture and history matter, too. Why does Cincinnati have such a school but not Columbus? Philadelphia but not Pittsburgh? New Jersey but not New Mexico? Selective public high schools are a long-standing practice in some places, unheard of in others. And after a city (or state) has lived with such schools for a while, it is apt to grow accustomed to them and their admissions processes. Sometimes—as in New York City under the leadership of schools chancellors Harold Levy and Joel Klein—it decides that it needs more of them.

If they're terrific schools that select fairly and do a fine job for kids who cannot otherwise access a first-rate education, then opening more of them almost certainly enhances equity and opportunity. Indeed, some of the schools on our list are veritable oases for youngsters whose only other educational alternatives are dangerous high schools and "dropout factories." But that's not the only consideration facing elected officials and education policy makers. Other worthy goals may be advanced, as well, such as building intellectual leadership and economic competitiveness, responding to new demands for human capital locally and nationally, attracting employers (and scientists, labs, etc.) to a state or community, accommodating persnickety parents and voters, retaining the middle class in the city (and within the orbit of public education), and more. While selective public high schools are by no means the only way to pursue such objectives, they are undeniably one way.

The number of such schools has remained tiny, however, alongside the behemoth of public education. We found just 165 of them in a universe of more than 22,000 U.S. public high schools.[4] By contrast, American *private* education boasts almost 12,000 high schools, most of them selective to some degree.[5] That's because public education has seldom opted for the "whole school" approach to address the distinctive needs of high-performing and high-potential youngsters, insofar as it has taken those needs seriously at all. Far more often, it has opted for programs, courses, and tracks—often just as selective, but less overt about it—within schools that, at least on the surface, are accessible to everyone.

One way to gain a sense of proportion is to note that the high school graduating class of 2010 contained more than half a million seniors who took and passed—with a score of 3 or higher—at least one Advanced Placement exam during their high school careers, while the total number of seniors in selective high schools (as we've defined them) is no more than 35,000. More vividly: for every graduate of a selective high school, at least ten students in other high schools successfully carried out some of their coursework at the AP level.

Elitism, Equity, and Diversity

John Gardner's 1961 query, "Can we be equal and excellent, too?" still resonates across the land. The schools on our list generally strive to embody excellence, but they also worry about equality, both because they don't want to get into political, reputational, or legal trouble and because those running them generally share the American commitment to opportunity and nondiscrimination.

Purposeful diversity in enrollment is complicated, though, the more so in a time when explicit consideration of race in school placement decisions is taboo. Student differences aside, not all middle schools are equally effective at—or serious about—preparing their students for rigorous academic challenges in high school, and not all families are equally keen on, adept at, or even aware of such educational opportunities for their children.

Mindful of this, the schools on our list engage in outreach of various kinds. And as a group they've done a good job of it, as can be observed in the national demographic data (see, in particular, tables 3.1 and 3.10.) Though Latino pupils are underrepresented in relation to their share of the nation's high school enrollment (13 percent versus 20), African-American youngsters are significantly *over* represented (30 percent versus 17). Black and Hispanic together comprise a slightly larger portion of these schools' pupils than in the general high school population (43 percent versus 37). White youngsters turn out to be significantly *under*-represented (35 percent versus 56).

The most striking demographic fact, however, is that Asian pupils are found in these selective schools at *four times* their share of the larger high school population (21 percent versus 5).

Should one be surprised by this? The United States now contains millions of immigrant families from lands, particularly in South and East Asia, where admission to "good" secondary schools is both highly prized and indisputably competitive. Many such families are strongly education-minded—but many are far from wealthy—and lots of them live in cities where the nearby public high school has little to offer high-achieving youngsters (and may not be safe or welcoming for them). These families want good schools for their daughters and sons on this side of the ocean, too, and they're ready to compete—fiercely if necessary—to obtain it.

As for African-American and Latino youngsters, recall that most of the schools on our list engage in energetic outreach to these families and their middle schools. Recall, too, that many of the schools are urban, that the most widely used term by which principals characterized their schools is "magnet"—and that most magnet schools began as ways to foster voluntary integration in city school systems.

Focus on individual communities, however, and the demographics look somewhat different (tables 3.2 and 3.5). In almost all of the districts where we carried out this analysis, we found smaller percentages of poor and black (as well as Latino) students in the selective schools than in the surrounding system, and in most cases a larger percentage of white (as well as Asian) youngsters. These discrepancies are not trivial, although neither are they enormous, save for the "over representation" of Asian pupils. As for income levels, it's noteworthy that, judged by participation in the federal subsidized-lunch program, the students in schools on our list, taken as a whole, are only slightly less poor than the national high school population (table 3.4). We don't know whether this is a result of their mostly urban location, of purposeful recruitment, or simply a product of the yearning by motivated low-income families for good options for their daughters and sons. Most likely, all these factors converge. But it's striking, especially since, as noted in chapter 1, poor families often find it challenging to access—and ensure that their children are prepared for—selective-admission schools. Yet the near-equal participation of low-income youngsters in these schools suggests that, when all is said and done, this part of "the system" is working pretty well. Selective these schools are, but "elitist" is not a fair or accurate term for them.

We're reminded, however, that "racial imbalance" continues to characterize American public education writ large, that poverty is more concentrated in some communities than others, and that few individual schools mirror the demographics of the country as a whole or even a state or city within it. Indeed, it would be remarkable if the pupil population of any one school, particularly a "school of choice," turned out to be a microcosm of the entire community from which it draws, much less the nation. Looking again at our list, the individual high schools on it mostly commence in 9th grade and, despite their earnest outreach efforts, wield no control over who dives into their applicant pool or the quality of their feeder schools. There is no reason to expect that those seeking admission to an academically selective school will mirror the community's demographics —and many such schools draw applicants from multiple communities, even the whole state. So long as a school has volitional applications from across a wide area and then employs a merit-based selection process that relies heavily on prior educational achievement, its own demographics may resemble nothing but its own demographics.

Consider, also, the likelihood that, particularly in urban America, these schools serve as a sort of refuge for education-minded families of every race, many of them immigrants, ambitious families with high-achieving youngsters but not much money. Although enrollments in the urban schools on our list are not *as* poor as the high school populations of their communities, they are attended by nontrivial numbers of low-income youngsters. (See table 3.4.) Even in Jefferson County, Kentucky, which came up lowest in this analysis, more than one-third of students in the selective-admission high schools qualify for subsidized lunches. (See table 3.5.) These are kids whose families probably could not manage private-school attendance or a move to serene suburbs with academically strong (and safe) general high schools of the Great Neck–Newton–Haverford genre.

Nor are low-income youngsters confined to a handful of "lesser" schools on our list. For example, in what is probably the single most selective public high school in America, New York City's Stuyvesant, some 37 percent of the students are poor.[6]

Yes, some prosperous families also take advantage of selective-admission schools as bargain equivalents of private schools or just because they like city amenities and would rather not live in suburbia. Yet it's no bad thing to retain as many as possible of such families "in town" and in the public-education system. Their daughters and sons also benefit from having classmates who look more "like America" than would likely be the case in many private or suburban high schools.

Most of the low-income kids in these schools are also benefiting from a racially (and socioeconomically) diverse experience, as well as a solid education in a safe environment. Most will make their way to college—and be prepared to succeed there, which might not otherwise be possible for them. It's a sad but inescapable fact that urban America affords few really satisfactory education options for motivated high achievers from disadvantaged circumstances—and for many other kinds of kids. Selective-admission high schools are a beacon of hope and possibility for thousands of such young people.

Yet that welcome reality raises additional perplexing questions. Are these schools' recruitment and selection procedures fair to all who might benefit? How ought we define and deploy "fairness" in selective schools within a society that is both egalitarian and meritocratic? Should individual schools that predominantly serve families of one or two races (table 3.2) try even harder to enroll a cross section of their communities, or is there merit in the diversity of these 165 schools as a group? Should their admissions criteria give less weight to test scores and more to student motivation and teacher judgments?[7]

To be sure, short of instituting quotas, even the best of admissions policies and the most energetic and far-reaching recruitment efforts won't guarantee that all high-potential students of all backgrounds have a fair (or equal) shot of getting into a selective public high school, if only because there aren't enough spaces. Indeed, the best strategy for making the enrollments of selective high schools look more like the communities they serve may be to open more of them.

School Effectiveness: The Great Unknown

A hoary quip about universities like Stanford and Harvard, highly selective institutions with gold-plated reputations and many successful alumni/ae, says, "Sure, the faculty and curriculum are good, but the admissions office is really terrific." Can the same be said for America's selective high schools?

Social scientists worry about "selection effects" wherein the outcome of an experiment, intervention, program, or institution is heavily influenced, even predetermined, by characteristics of those who sign up for it. That's why rigorous methodologists in many fields plead for "random assignment" of individuals to various programs and treatments, so as to tease out the actual impact of the intervention rather than factors inherent in its participants that may make it look more (or less) effective than it actually is.

Though random trials are no longer unusual in educational research, random selection of students for attendance at a school or participation in a school program is rare, save in the charter sector, where lotteries are normally used to determine which among too many applicants will enter.

With a few partial exceptions, the schools on our list do *not* use lotteries in determining who enrolls. (If they did, they wouldn't be on our list!) By and large, they evaluate their applicants and admit those they find best qualified for the school or most apt to succeed there (and beyond). Some take just a tiny percentage of their applicants, not unlike Harvard and Stanford (figure 3.1). We would expect, therefore, to find a "selection effect" on their students' and the school's performance.

Though not all our schools are high achieving—note the middling Great Schools ratings associated with some of them—most produce admirable outcomes when gauged by college admission, prizes and accolades, as well as scores on AP exams and kindred measures. They rank near the top of everyone's "best high schools" lists.

The big question we cannot definitively answer is the extent to which their impressive outcomes are *caused* by what happens inside them—their standards, curricula, teachers, homework, et cetera—or are manifestations of "what the kids brought with them." We're mindful, too, that some of what happens to youngsters within these schools reflects what *other* kids bring into class. This speaks to potential environmental influences of all sorts, ranging from the diminished anxiety of a youngster who need no longer fear being thought a "nerd" or "acting white," to the heightened anxiety of an adolescent accustomed to being at the top of his class who now finds himself outgunned intellectually by classmates, to the stimulating environment of classrooms in which teachers are more comfortable with the span of pupil abilities, prior knowledge, behaviors, and motivations. The school's peer culture likely has some influence on its pupils, but it's hard to say which elements have how much.

Nor can we be certain how much difference teacher expectations make in what students learn—and how they develop—in these schools. Their administrators and instructors start with the assumption that essentially all their pupils can think at high levels and have records of strong prior achievement. The school year opens with everyone taking for granted—if only because so many others were turned away—that this is a special place that must be effective or it wouldn't be in such demand. This may be circular reasoning, but it also contributes to an attitude or climate within the school—different from what one finds at the typical "comprehensive" high school—that could influence its teacher expectations and have a powerful effect on its students' actual results. Again, though, we cannot be certain.

We accumulated plenty of anecdotes and testimonials by students, parents, teachers, and alumni/ae, often in the vein of "how much better prepared I was for college than my classmates" from other high schools. We observed awesome individual research projects, heard sophisticated presentations by students, and listened to rarefied classroom discussions. (We also sat in on some mundane classes consisting of so-so teachers and at least a few sleepy or distracted kids.) But we have no real "value-added" data for these schools, and few of them do, either. As one mystified but curious principal put it, "Do the kids do well *because of* us or *in spite of* us? We're not sure."

Much like private schools, which are more apt to trade on their reputations and college-placement records than on hard evidence of what students learn in their classrooms, the schools on our list generally don't know—in any rigorous, formal sense—how much their students learn or how much difference the school itself makes in their post-high-school careers. Few even try hard to track their graduates beyond the college gates.[8] This is, obviously, a major data gap that schools, school systems, government statisticians, and education analysts should strive to close.

The schools themselves are only partly culpable, however. They have rarely been asked to justify themselves in terms of pupil learning gains. On the contrary, they're flooded with eager applicants, media attention, and accolades. They can proudly demonstrate intricate research projects, display cases full of academic prizes, science-fair and robotics-competition ribbons, National Merit lists, and messages from grateful alums. But they have access to little "value-added" data. Nearly all the tests their pupils take are of the "mastery" kind—like earning a 5 on an AP exam or racking up a lofty SAT score—rather than before-and-after assessments. And insofar as their states impose graduation tests as prerequisites for receiving diplomas, the passing score is generally a cinch for kids like these.

The research community has mostly ignored these schools, too. One recent study by economists at Duke and MIT—the first of its kind, say the authors—set out to explore this territory. They used a sophisticated methodology to look for value-added effects (gauged by scores on state tests, the SAT, and AP exams) in six prominent "exam schools" in Boston and New York City. And they didn't find much to applaud:

> Our results offer little evidence of an achievement gain for those admitted to an exam school. . . . In spite of their exposure to much higher-achieving peers and a more challenging curriculum, marginal students admitted to exam schools generally do no better on a variety of standardized tests.[9]

A similar study by Harvard's Roland Fryer and Will Dobbie was confined to the three oldest and most famous of New York's "exam schools" and used similar analytic methods to gauge school effects. It found that "attending an exam school increases the rigor of high school courses taken and the probability that a student graduates with an advanced high school degree" but "has little impact on Scholastic Aptitude Test scores, college enrollment, or college graduation."[10]

These pioneering studies are sobering, although limited both by their focus on "marginal" students (those barely over and just under the schools' entry-score cutoffs) and by their reliance on short-term measures of effectiveness. The schools' effects on other kinds of gauges and over the longer haul are simply unknown, as are their effects on the higher scorers among their entering pupils. This is obviously a ripe area for further investigation and analysis—but today it's legitimate to observe, even on the basis of this limited research, that the burden is shifting to the schools and their supporters to measure and make public whatever academic benefit they do bestow on their students versus what the same young people might have learned in other settings.[11]

The marketplace signals, however, are undeniable: far more youngsters want to attend these schools than they can accommodate. We know that many applicants go to exceptional lengths to prepare for the admissions gantlet—which may well lead to more learning in earlier grades than the same youngsters might have absorbed without this incentive. And we also know that most of those who are admitted stick with it through graduation—an average of 91 percent across the fifty-five schools responding to our survey.[12]

What's Really Different about These Schools?

In both survey results and site visits, some of what we found by way of curriculum, instruction, and other programmatic elements was foreordained by how we selected the schools. It's no surprise that their curricular focus is "academic," that they work hard at college preparation, or that their standards are high and many of their courses are "advanced." That's pretty much what we went looking for.

A number of schools boasted at least a few courses or course sequences of their own devising, sometimes proudly terming these "signatures" of their curricula. Such courses seemed mostly to be the work of the school's own faculty, sometimes developed with outside help (and occasional grant assistance).

Somewhat more surprising was the extent of college-level work that their students engage in, sometimes carried out on university campuses or co-taught by college faculty, sometimes through the familiar AP route, but often in the form of independent study and research projects. These often yield formal college credit even as they help prepare students for collegiate modes of study and inquiry.

Many of the schools on our list try not only to equip their pupils for the academic rigors of what follows but also to help them develop the personal attributes needed to flourish in college and beyond. These include individual initiative and responsibility, time management, balancing competing demands, working on teams, solving problems and confronting roadblocks (and knowing when to seek help), treating others with respect (even while competing with them), behaving properly without constant supervision, and demonstrating personal integrity.

Some schools are true "open campuses" whose pupils come and go on their own initiative. Most are stricter about attendance but relaxed about where students are within the school and how they're spending their time. We often observed kids sprawled in the hall, reading or conferring; studying—or chatting—in the library or lunchroom, and not just at lunchtime; coming in and out of class without a blizzard of permission slips; and arriving early or staying late to work on something or meet with someone. Save for instances of cheating or plagiarism, discipline problems are rare in these corridors and classrooms. When there are security guards and locked doors, it's more to keep the outside world at bay than to control those within the school. That's not to say everyone always acts maturely, much less that they eschew teenage behavior outside school. But the school itself is a serious, purposeful—yet often laid-back and friendly—place, and the kids are generally responsible about arriving with their homework done and their independent projects under control.

Resources, Relationships, and Bureaucratics

Despite an earnest effort via our survey, we were unable to obtain systematic information about these schools' finances in forms that can readily be compared with each other or with the universe of American public secondary education.[13] As noted in chapter 3, the overall teacher-student ratio suggests that these schools are slightly underresourced in this realm. Since so many of their instructors are classroom veterans, however, it's likely that the money spent on teacher salaries is no less per pupil.

Nearly all of the schools we visited were facing budget crunches in 2010–11 and expecting the same or worse for 2011–12. That was true for nearly all of public education, to be sure, but most of our schools felt unjustly victimized—that is, subjected to deeper cuts than other schools in the area—and were pulling all available strings to contain the damage. Several offered credible evidence that the system was harder on them than on other high schools, but some also acknowledged that this was a consequence of district efforts to concentrate available resources on troubled schools and disadvantaged pupils—a reminder that the simultaneous pursuit of excellence and equity often deteriorates into a resource competition between those goals.

Some of the schools we visited had large classes, nudging the district limit (thirty-four pupils in New York City). On the other hand, some benefited from special "magnet" funding meant to keep class sizes smaller than usual, though administrators are struggling harder than before to decide *which* classes should benefit from that modest bounty. (Should it be the core courses, the most advanced electives, the lab-science classes, etc.?) Others are subsidized in part through higher-education budgets, special lines in state budgets, countywide levies or taxes, federal vocational-ed dollars, and more.

We visited some extraordinarily well-resourced schools with, for example, an overall ratio of one staff member to ten pupils as well as facilities brimming with state-of-the-art equipment. But we also visited schools that barely make ends meet on per-pupil allocations less than the typical high school in their area. And we learned that a number of schools, whether relatively prosperous or sorely strapped, engage in fund-raising of their own, sometimes modest parent-association efforts, sometimes much larger sums from alumni/ae, local industry, even endowed funds.

The quality of personnel in a school is, of course, another key resource, if even harder to gauge than bodies or dollars. It's clear from our survey data (some of it shown in tables 3.12 and 3.13), as well as from site visits, that the schools on our list have teaching staffs with somewhat deeper academic credentials (including earned doctorates) than do U.S. high schools generally.[14] They also bring to class a diversity of backgrounds in higher education, science, and business. And we found in their classrooms a great many experienced teachers, few rookies, and minimal staff turnover. It's not that salaries are better—though some schools pay more than the regular "schedule" for longer days, extra periods, or additional duties—but that, by and large, one's students and colleagues are stimulating, motivated, well behaved, and results oriented. That isn't an environment in which all teachers thrive, but those who do would seem to have few reasons to give it up. The satisfaction that comes from teaching such kids in schools like these is not the same as additional cash income but can be its own valuable psychic reward and may yield a heightened sense of return on one's investment of hard work and sacrifice.

Sometimes the teachers voluntarily add to that sacrifice. In two of the schools we visited, the faculty had voted to extend or rearrange their school day, including extra duties without additional compensation, in order to preserve curricula or schedules that they valued but that the district was eliminating for budgetary reasons.

Leadership matters, too, of course, and while every principal we met was intelligent, enthusiastic, hardworking, politically adept, and affable, several were relatively new to their front-office roles. We detected no career pattern among them, though the principals who responded to our survey averaged six years in this post.[15]

Particularly for schools operating within large districts—as opposed to freestanding magnets, statewide schools, university affiliates, and such—political, bureaucratic, and contractual challenges can be a major part of the principal's job. The schools on our list appear to enjoy few formal waivers or exemptions from general rules and contractual provisions and, when they do, it's not because they're selective. It's more often because they're not district-operated or have embraced options that are generally available for any school that seeks them, such as New York's provision (in its teachers' contract) that schools where a majority of the faculty votes in favor can obtain substantial site-based authority over staffing, scheduling, and such.

Very few of these are charter schools, and few have any contractual right or statutory exemption to do things differently.[16] What generally seems to happen when one of them needs to deviate from a district norm is that the principal "works it out" with the central office—or sometimes just goes ahead and does it on the time-tested belief that it's easier to seek forgiveness than to obtain permission. Astute principals are not diffident about quietly enlisting influential alumni/ae, local politicians, business leaders, parents, and others to help achieve their ends. But they have to pick their targets and accept trade-offs. Thomas Jefferson High School, for example, forfeited (as part of a countywide policy) the right of its seniors to leave campus at lunchtime—but it's getting a costly and much-needed building renovation.

All but the newest of these schools have "friends in high places," whether their own alums, the parents of current students, university presidents and business folk, or elected officials for whose district, city, or state the school is a valued asset. That may not yield more resources, formal exemptions, or other special treatment, but it can create a protected zone within which the school is freer to pursue its mission, even if what it does—educate smart, motivated, high-scoring kids—is not currently high on the education priority list at the superintendent's office, the state education department, or the White House.

The Advanced Placement Conundrum

Those who live by the sword. . . . We've flagged this issue previously, but it bears repeating: today's scramble for entry into top-tier colleges plus the premium being placed (by multiple players) on taking and passing AP exams plus standardized-test-based accountability pressures emanating from government do not add up to an optimal environment for academically selective high schools, whatever good such practices may do in other realms of K–12 education. In these schools, they don't raise standards so much as standardize. They press on students, parents, teachers, and entire schools in ways that are plausibly said to discourage experimentation, risk taking, unconventional thinking, unique courses, individualized research, and independent study, as well as pedagogical creativity and curricular innovation.

Moreover, insofar as these schools allow (or are forced to allow) their curricula and standards to be fitted into external norms and programs at the same time that other public high schools are embracing (or being forced into) those same norms and programs, it underscores the question of what is qualitatively distinctive about their educational offerings.

One frequent rejoinder is that, if U.S. school-accountability systems relied more on "value-added" measures that account for academic gains by students across the spectrum rather than a single pass-fail/proficiency-or-not cut-point, even the most selective schools and their high-scoring pupils would be suitably challenged and prodded by the assessment regime. We're not persuaded. Moving to value-added analyses of student, teacher, and school performance has much to be said for it, but it's not apt to solve the version of this problem faced by most of the high schools on our list. Neither would the statewide "end of course" exams that have become a popular alternative in some jurisdictions. For few of the tests in widespread use even capture student gains (or differences) at the top of the psychometric spectrum. If you administer a 100-question exam aimed at the average student or the middle of the achievement range, and you use the results of this exam to gauge learning progress, the average student may well go from, say, 40 at the end of fourth grade to 50 at the end of fifth, or from 65 at the beginning of the year to 72 at the end. But many of the teenagers in our schools will score in the 90s on such a test even before they take the course, and whatever gains they make will barely register.[17] To be sure, assessments could be devised to track gains and differentiate among students at the upper end of the spectrum, but such tests wouldn't do much good farther down. Solving both problems calls either for enormously long tests or for computer-adaptive assessments that contain hundreds, even thousands of items but expose individual pupils to just a small subset of these.

In any case, the major test-centered problem facing *our* schools today isn't the state assessment or the federally dictated "proficiency" standard. It's the Advanced Placement exam and others like it, tests that are already "high end" and able to differentiate (even within a scoring range from 1 to 5) among students in the upper part of the achievement spectrum. The exams themselves are generally fine for the intended purpose, which is to determine whether a student at the conclusion of a course deserves "college credit" for what he/she now knows about that subject. But the ways that such exams are being used and the roles they have come to play in the college admissions process, in parental aspirations, in student competitiveness and GPA-grubbing, and in any number of high-school rating systems are indeed confining, even distorting, for schools that take pride in their differentness and in the flexible ways they handle youngsters with exceptional academic prowess.

We spoke with frustrated teachers and exasperated administrators well aware that they're riding the back of an AP tiger from which it's truly hard to dismount, especially for a public school that must weigh the priorities of its parents, taxpayers, and voters. We talked with highly motivated students, too, who were (as one young man put it) "exhausted" from carrying course loads that included as many as six AP classes in a semester in pursuit of a high school transcript that would wow the admissions committees of elite universities.

Some school leaders are pushing back, encouraging their teachers to develop challenging courses that don't fit the AP mold, or offering college-level courses shorn of the AP brand. Others, we sensed, would love to emulate Scarsdale High School, an upscale (but comprehensive) public institution in a prosperous New York suburb with more than its share of ambitious parents and bright youngsters. Five years back, Scarsdale opted to join a handful of private schools and spurn the Advanced Placement program in favor of its own teacher-developed courses called "Advanced Topics." There's been some public pushback, however, and today the Scarsdale system carefully notes that "Advanced Topics courses will prepare students to sit for Advanced Placement Examinations."[18] District leaders now seem to want to have it both ways, and one supposes that some Scarsdale teachers are again chafing under the pressure to prepare their pupils for AP exams. Still, that school's declaration of independence gave them somewhat greater curricular flexibility than before—and the number of AP exams actually taken by Scarsdale high school pupils is dramatically down from earlier years. Whether that's a good thing or not we leave for others to debate.

Our site visits came at a time of year when many teachers and pupils were deep into AP exam prep. By and large, what we observed in their classrooms did not leave us confident that these youngsters were receiving a better, more rigorous, or significantly different version of the AP course than they would have experienced in an "ordinary" high school. What's the payoff to teaching the same courses to "selected" students in a separate building?

Yet classes with the same label may contain very different educational experiences, even if this was not always visible during our visits. It's one thing simply to teach an Advanced Placement course and quite another to have one's students learn enough to take and do well on the exam. The nation's recent push to open up access to AP courses is certainly succeeding on the surface: the number of pupils participating in such courses grew 149 percent between 1998 and 2008. As these rates have increased, however, so has the proportion of students who take the course without passing the AP exam. Many don't even take it and, among those who did in 2009, according to calculations by *USA Today*, 41.5 percent received failing marks (i.e., scores of 1 or 2 out of 5), up from 36.5 percent a decade earlier.[19] It's reasonable to expect that, over the course of a school year, the teaching-and-learning experience in AP classrooms in which few students end up taking or passing the exam will differ from what happens in analogous courses in schools where essentially every student will sit for the exam and nearly all will pass it, many with top marks.

That distinction doesn't ease the Advanced Placement pressure on our schools or their teachers and pupils. But it does hark back to the original AP vision, which was to create opportunities for motivated or high-achieving students to master college-level work—not just go through the motions—while still enrolled in high school. At the schools on our list, a great deal of that kind of mastery appears to be occurring. It may be, however, that something else is being sacrificed.

Chapter 17

Conclusions

• • • • • •

The Goldilocks Question

Should America have more or fewer academically selective high schools, or do we have about the right number today? Would it be a good thing if additional communities and states had such schools and more young people attended them? As noted above, the schools on our list comprise fewer than one percent of all U.S. public high schools—and their students about the same.

Does that make them simply an eccentric corner of American secondary education that some places like and others shun, or are they a distinctively valuable element of the country's K–12 policies and practices that should be seriously considered for expansion? Recall that almost all the schools on our list are oversubscribed, with far more qualified candidates than they can accommodate. Recall, too, that half the schools for which we have start dates are creations of the past two decades, so we are not dealing only with aging holdovers from prior policy eras. For dozens of American communities, the establishment of such a school was a recent decision.

What about places that don't have any today or don't have enough to meet popular demand? Should they start some? Expand? Replicate? Should states, philanthropists, and possibly the federal government encourage this?

The answers depend greatly on the value one assigns to "whole schools" for smart kids versus AP courses and specialized programs such as the International Baccalaureate within comprehensive high schools. We're persuaded that there's much to be said for the whole-school version, but we're also mindful of some drawbacks.

The benefits and drawbacks change, however, from the viewpoints of different constituents within the education system. Here we consider six such perspectives.

If you are governor of a state with no selective high schools and are being urged by leaders of the high-tech business sector to launch some, how should you respond?

First, note that such schools can take several forms, including a state-wide residential institution (like IMSA) or network of regional schools and part-time programs (like the Virginia Governor's Schools), as well as schools that serve individual cities, counties, or metro areas. State offi-cials are best positioned to bring the first or second of these into being.

You might, of course, favor an online alternative (akin to the Florida Virtual School, now enrolling some 130,000 full- and part-time stu-dents) to bring advanced courses in a variety of subjects within reach of more youngsters around the state, or you could try to persuade existing high schools and districts to join forces to beef up their course offerings. You could also emulate several states (including Virginia and Michi-gan) and develop regional centers that offer part-day, summer, or after-school options of an advanced sort to students across sizable swaths of territory without removing them entirely from their local high schools. But your business leaders probably favor the "whole school" version of advanced secondary education, whether statewide or regional. Such schools have the advantages of critical mass and total immersion, and readily lend themselves to partnerships with and direct support by those same firms. They may help turn your state into a talent magnet and make it a more appealing place for companies and families that want advanced educational options for their own or their employees' children. This could boost economic development and, properly struc-tured, could also benefit other children and educators on a part-time basis. Your universities may also welcome the arrival of more students with top-notch secondary-school preparation and the personal attributes to fare well in college. Many families are apt to respond favorably, too, especially those with bright kids who are otherwise stuck in rural, small-town, and troubled urban schools with few advanced offerings.

On the other hand, dollar costs accompany the creation of new schools, not to mention their continued operation—and this kind of school is apt to need additional investment in labs, equipment, and such. There will be governance issues—who, exactly, is responsible for operating these schools, which probably don't belong to traditional districts? There will surely be pushback from existing high schools, fretful about losing their strongest pupils and, perhaps, the enrollment that enables them to offer their own advanced courses. (If, for example, half the calculus-level math students in an existing high school leave for the new regional option, there might not be enough left to justify a calculus teacher in the old school.) Though the parents of kids who gain admission to the new school(s) will be appreciative, others may be embittered by rejection—and if you open still more selective schools to oblige them, you will incur further costs and objections from your established schools.

If you are a school board member in a sizable city with, say, five or more high schools but none that is selective, and you are petitioned by parents seeking such a school for their kids, what should you do?

The parents of gifted-and-talented youngsters—and other parents who have high hopes for their kids or simply crave an edge in the college-admission race—are determined folks who may well have reason to be dissatisfied with the advanced course offerings of existing high schools. They may also be dismayed by other aspects of those schools, such as safety, climate, dubious peer influences, or inadequate college counseling. Such concerns are often justified. High schools are the hardest to reform of our public-education institutions, and their graduation rates and 12th-grade scores have been flat or nearly so for decades. Some deserve the designation "dropout factories."

Devising school options that satisfy and placate such parents—probably including influential community residents—is not bad politics, and it has other pluses, too. It may make one's city more appealing to sophisticated employers and middle-class families, while strengthening their ties to its public-education system. It may foster racial, ethnic, and socioeconomic diversity by drawing students of dissimilar backgrounds out of their neighborhoods into a shared school experience. It's apt to appeal to certain kinds of intellectually keen teachers. It may invite partnerships with local firms, especially the high-tech and scientifically oriented kind, as well as with cultural institutions and area colleges and universities.

But there are downsides, too. If other local high schools suffer from significant curricular and environmental shortcomings, opening a new school won't likely solve those problems. If your district has a stable (or declining) enrollment, opening a new school also means shrinking others. The principals (and some teachers, PTAs, etc.) of existing high schools will be loath to lose able pupils and education-minded parents. The status of other schools may slip on rankings such as those by *U.S. News* and the *Washington Post*. Colleges may focus their admissions on students from the selective high school. The pressure to improve—and offer more advanced courses at—existing schools may ease. There may be backlash from families whose daughters and sons do *not* gain entry to the new school. And there are sure to be costs and complexities associated with facilities, equipment, staffing, pupil transportation, admissions policies, and more. There may also be union issues if, for example, the new school seeks to operate on a longer day, to compensate its faculty in unconventional ways, or to reject teachers who assert a seniority-based right to fill its classroom openings. When all is said and done, you also face the risk that, after going through ample expense and hassle, the graduates of your selective high school may end up taking their knowledge and skills elsewhere after completing college. Your investment may well yield a public good for the country but not necessarily for your own community.

If you are a current or aspiring principal, and the superintendent gives you a choice between leading a selective or a comprehensive high school, what factors should influence your decision?

On the positive side, the selective high school is probably among the most visible and respected educational institutions in town, and leading it is apt to be a high-profile, high-status job and very possibly a career booster for you. On the other hand, running that school may be mostly a matter of preserving it as is, along with its resources and (limited) privileges, its track record, friends, and community supporters, all at a time when few states or districts are putting great emphasis on students and schools like these. You may end up feeling that "there's no place to go but down." A comprehensive high school, by contrast, is more likely to require a tune-up if not a makeover, and the kids attending it are apt to be needier in multiple ways. What kind of challenge puts a glint in your eye?

Selective high schools are under the microscope, too, not so much to see whether they're improving as to see whether they're maintaining their reputations. Are they still at the top of the media rankings? Getting lots of graduates into high-status colleges? Still boasting a high pass rate on AP exams? Maintaining their active parent and alumni/ae bodies—and their private benefactors? Their sufficiently diverse student bodies? At the very least, you'll likely face many (and sometimes competing) demands to prove your school's worth.

Your school may be the object of envy and political pressure, too: from other schools that want to hold on to those pupils, from parents whose kids fail to get in, from resource-strapped budget directors seeking places to save money or ways to redirect it to broken schools and low-achieving youngsters, and from minority and civil rights groups fretful about diversity. Do you have the political acumen (and backbone) to withstand these forces?

Many selective schools also have strong-willed teachers, often veterans accustomed to doing things their own way and perhaps selecting their own colleagues. They may welcome compliant stewardship and resource management in the front office but may balk at other forms of leadership.

No high school principal's job is easy, but this one may be really hard.

If you are a teacher considering a career move and you learn that a selective high school in your area has a classroom opening in your field, should you apply for that position?

Teaching in an academically selective school is an appealing prospect for obvious reasons. Most of its students are smart, motivated to learn, reasonably well behaved, and supported by their parents. If you're coming from a school that has struggled with accountability challenges, chances are excellent that you'll step into a place where "proficiency" is no big deal. You probably won't be teaching courses below the honors level. Your pay may include extra dollars for longer days or additional preparations (although the basic salary scale is the same as you'll find in other district schools).

Teaching any group of adolescents well is challenging, however, and academically able students are no exception. They will not necessarily be "easier" to teach, in that the job will call for much preparation, background knowledge, commitment, and, very often, extra time for longer days, independent projects, after-school conversations, and much individualized feedback and coaching on drafts, models, experiments, prototypes, and such. Despite the kids' obvious similarities—all were selected for admission and presumably met the threshold criteria—you should still expect to encounter students who vary significantly across many dimensions: academic background, interest in your subject, family situation, cultural heritage, and preferred ways of learning.

You'll also need the skills and resolve to address the social and emotional needs of young people who may, for the first time in their lives, face truly challenging courses, a fast-paced academic environment, peers who actually surpass them, or (in the case of residential schools) living away from home. And while most kids will have strong intellects and work ethics, they are also likely to be more concerned with their grades, AP scores, and college prospects than with the Platonic ideal of education for the sake of learning. What's more, their parents may be just as driven. (Watch what happens when you give these youngsters B grades!)

Some teachers thrive amid such challenges while others regard them as not worth the hassle—or as an invitation to stress and burnout. Do you know which kind you are? And do you have the background, preparation, prior experience, and principal and peer recommendations that will qualify you for a position in these schools? Openings are rare and, unless you have seniority rights within your school system (and sometimes even if you do), you may find the teacher-selection process quite competitive, indeed persnickety.

If you are the parent of an able middle schooler and your community has an academically selective public high school, should you encourage your daughter or son to seek admission to it?

The ultimate decision to apply to one of these schools hinges on a comparison of its quality and potential "fit" for your youngster with those of other public options from which you might realistically choose. Let's say you live in Chicago and have a high-achieving child with a keen interest in math and science. A neighborhood high school now offers a decent array of AP courses in those subjects. A charter school that's been getting good press for the colleges its seniors are admitted to is not far away. Your daughter's grades and test scores suggest that she has a good chance of getting into one of the district's top selective-admission schools, but there's no guarantee (and it's on the other side of town). Another possibility—again, she'd have to be admitted—is the state-sponsored residential school (IMSA). Still another option, if you can swing it financially, is to move into the attendance area of a top-notch suburban high school (e.g., New Trier, Stevenson). What should you do? Many practical considerations are obviously involved in this scenario, including the value you place on your child attending a demographically diverse school. All things being equal, here are some questions that might help you decide in favor of, or against, an academically selective school:

Is your child more apt to thrive in a high-powered, hard-charging environment full of other smart, motivated youngsters (some of them likely smarter than she is) or in a setting with all kinds of kids and perhaps greater opportunity to distinguish herself as an outstanding pupil? Is your child unusually able across the curricular board or just in one or two subjects? Is she willing to work really hard in an intense, competitive setting, very likely involving long hours, tons of homework, and perhaps a lengthy commute? (Have you checked out your transportation options to and from the selective high school?) If the school has a particular focus (in the STEM realm, in the humanities, et cetera), does this match your daughter's own interests and aptitudes? If she has special needs—not an unusual companion to high ability—you owe it to her to find out whether the selective high school is set up to address them. You should also consider whether she is apt to miss some of the curricular or extracurricular opportunities that may be lacking at the selective school, such as a strong sports program or career-related offerings (e.g., journalism, photography, medical technology). Finally, you should gauge the odds of getting in and consider whether your child will deal successfully with rejection if she fails to win admission.

If you are a thirteen-year-old in a town with multiple high school options, including an academically selective school, how should you decide whether to apply?

First, think whether you have strong grades and test scores that will give you a decent chance of gaining admission to the selective school should you and your parents decide to apply there. Make sure you're taking (or have taken) any courses that the school requires of all applicants. (Sometimes this means algebra or an advanced science class.) Consider the logistics of attending the school, such as where it is and how you will get to and fro. Would you rather go to school closer to home and perhaps with more kids you already know? (Of course, plenty of your friends and classmates may also be considering the selective high school.)

You definitely ought to find out what your teachers and middle school counselors think about the "fit" between you and that school, as well as your other high school options. (Many communities have special programs, emphases, and opportunities of different kinds in a number of high schools. Be aware, too, that the selective high school may have an academic focus—such as science and math, or humanities and arts—that doesn't align with your own interests.) It wouldn't hurt to ask your parents, also. They probably know you better than you think—and going to the selective high school may also place some extra burdens on the family.

If none of those inquiries points you in a different direction, ask yourself whether you enjoy being in fast-moving classes with lots of smart kids—some of them maybe quicker or better prepared than you are—or whether you do better (or are more comfortable) with a more deliberate pace and the opportunity to shine. Some selective high schools require students to take all or most classes at the honors or Advanced Placement level. Does that appeal to you, or would you prefer the *option* of taking advanced courses in some subjects but not others? Think about college admissions, too. Though good colleges likely know and appreciate the selective high school and its well-prepared graduates, they might value even more an outstanding pupil from a more ordinary school. (Keep in mind, too, that 50 percent of the kids in the selective high school are in the bottom half of their class!)

Finally, you will want to determine if any of the things that the selective high school de-emphasizes are important to you, whether that's a winning football team or the chance to take more career-oriented classes. Your interests and priorities are apt to change during high school, and you can change schools later if necessary, but you might not want to start off as a round peg in a square hole.

Back to 30,000 Feet

We return, finally, to the four big-picture questions with which we began.

Is the United States providing *all* of its young people the education that they need in order to make the most of their capacities, both for their own sake and for that of the larger society?

Have we neglected to raise the ceiling while we've struggled to lift the floor? As the country strives to toughen its academic standards, close its wide achievement gaps, repair its bad schools, and "leave no child behind," is it also challenging its high-achieving and highly motivated students—and those who may not yet be high achievers but can learn substantially more than the minimum?[1] Are we as determined to build more great schools as to repair those that have collapsed?

Is America making wise investments in its own future prosperity and security by ensuring that its high-potential children are well prepared to break new ground and assume leadership roles on multiple fronts?

And at a time when we're creating new school choices and individual learning opportunities of many kinds, as well as the means for many more families to avail themselves of those options, are we paying sufficient attention to *this* kind of choice: the academically selective high school, and the learning opportunities it offers to youngsters with the capacity and inclination to benefit from them?

Our investigation doesn't yield definitive answers to these tough questions, but we emerged from it with strong impressions. It's clear that the supply of academically selective high schools doesn't come close to meeting the demand in most communities that have them, and we presume that there's plenty of latent demand in many places that currently have none. At a time when American education is striving to customize its offerings to students' interests and needs, and to afford families more choices among schools and education programs, the market is pointing to the skimpy supply of schools of this kind. Moreover, if the best of such schools are hothouses for incubating a disproportionate share of tomorrow's leaders in science, technology, entrepreneurship, and other sectors that bear on society's long-term prosperity and well-being, we'd be better off as a country if we had more of them.

This challenge, however, goes far beyond the singular world of selective high schools. It's evident from multiple studies that our K–12 education system overall is doing a mediocre job of serving its "gifted and talented" youngsters—as well as many others. It is paying far too little attention to creating appealing and viable opportunities for advanced learning—and to helping students climb as high on those ladders as they can. What policy makers have seen as more urgent needs (for basic literacy, adequate teachers, sufficient skills to earn a living, etc.) have generally prevailed. The argument for across-the-board talent development has been trumped by "closing the achievement gap" and focusing on test scores at the low end. Nobody *wants* to retard the growth of high achievers or squash excellence for the sake of equity. Yet gains by those at the upper end have, on various measures, been weaker than those of youngsters below the "proficient" bar.[2] Absent a clear policy priority or mandate (as in special education or No Child Left Behind), many very bright students are failing to realize their full potential. So are many youngsters who might not be described as very bright but who are capable of jumping higher academically than today's proficiency bars have been set for them.

American education could and should be doing much more to help every youngster achieve all that he or she is capable of. It should do this not only at the high school level and not just inside selective schools. But a major push to strengthen the cultivation of future leaders is overdue, and any such push should include careful attention to the "whole school" model. We see compelling reasons to include ample development of that model within the country's broader strategies for addressing the dual challenges of advanced learning and learners, reasons that become even more compelling if selective schools can model what all high schools should one day be.

We've known for decades that effective schools (of every kind) benefit when the entire team pulls in the same direction.[3] They are apt to be more successful than multipurpose schools that host a number of separate programs and plural education missions tailored for diverse populations and monitored by rival constituencies.[4] Nearly every one of the schools on our list is organized around a single coherent purpose.

It's also evident—and not just from our study—that "whole schools" can develop a critical mass of instructional tools and equipment, financial resources, reputations, alumni/ae, and outside supporters that is hard to assemble for a smallish program within a comprehensive school, particularly where the latter is itself small. (Thirty percent of U.S. high school pupils have fewer than nine hundred schoolmates.) And the critical-mass effect is visible in the curriculum (and extracurriculum), too. Instead of isolated honors and Advanced Placement classes, single-purpose schools can amass entire sequences at that level. They have enough students to teach multiple languages at the college level, to layer AP physics atop AP chemistry, biology, and calculus, and to offer both writing and literature. They can also develop their own courses and sequences that go beyond conventional AP offerings, do more with individual student projects, concentrate their counseling efforts on college placement, and muster teams of eager students (and teachers) for science competitions and suchlike.

There are benefits on the faculty side, too. Judging from what we observed (or were told) in the schools we visited, the teaching team that can be assembled by such a school is apt to consist almost completely of instructors well matched to such students, able to project high expectations to them without hypocrisy, and with no grounds to quarrel over who "gets the honors classes" and who is "stuck" with average or remedial assignments.

Insofar as students benefit from peer effects in classrooms, corridors, and clubs, and insofar as being surrounded by other smart kids challenges them (and wards off allegations of "nerdiness"), schools with overall cultures of high academic attainment are apt to yield more such benefits.

Finally, a distinct, "whole" school that is high achieving can be viewed as a community asset. Having an entire school of this sort to show parents, colleges, employers, firms looking to relocate, real estate agents, and others can bring a kind of élan or appeal to a place that may also help with economic development, the retention of middle-class families, and more.

We're not naïve. Especially at a time when resources are tight, we don't expect hundreds more communities and dozens more states to rush to create many more academically selective high schools, even where the reasons for doing so may be compelling. Some may be loath to invest in education programs the eventual fruits of which get harvested by jurisdictions thousands of miles away. Some may already have a balanced array of options for high-achieving, high-potential kids. Some may be wary of "creaming" the ablest pupils from other high schools. Moreover, if attention focuses exclusively on the high school program without also addressing what happens to such kids in the "feeder" schools, it may amount to redistributing the current population of high achievers rather than cultivating more of them.

These are not trivial considerations. And of course it's essential to pay attention not only to how many such schools there are and how many students enroll in them but also to what happens inside, that is, how well they serve their pupils beyond the admissions office. It's possible (alas) to have a school that is plenty selective at the front door but doesn't do a great job of teaching its students more or differently than they would encounter elsewhere. Actually *doing* a great job requires more than a choosy screening process. It also demands internal alignment of mission, philosophy, curriculum, personnel, and resources, as well as student identification, recruitment and selection. And it requires recognition that, even when all the kids are smart, they aren't identical. Batch-processed education doesn't work so well at this level, either. Part of nurturing talent is recognizing and addressing individual differences, strengths, needs, and shortcomings.

Yes, we visited some schools that America would benefit from cloning. We also saw some that perhaps should just stick to their current missions—and maybe even get better at them. (Fortunately, we didn't see any that left us wishing they would close on grounds that they're bad for kids.)

Whether we deploy many more "whole schools" of this kind or opt mainly for specialized courses and programs within ordinary schools, the kinds of rigorous and advanced education that selective-admission schools seek to provide and the youngsters that they serve need to rise higher in our national consciousness and our policy priorities. These kids and tens of thousands more like them are the seedlings of tomorrow's intellectual crops. They will—or could—fill tens of thousands of positions of leadership in science, technology, academe, business, communications, education, government, and public service. They need to be educated to the max and, for the many that aren't wealthy, they need to be educated at public expense in classes, courses, and schools designed to meet their needs and rise to the challenges that they present.

The United States has done a noble and necessary thing in pushing for a minimum standard of academic proficiency for every youngster in the land. But we downplay excellence at great cost, not only to our economic competitiveness but also perhaps to reform of the education system itself. Consider, once again, James Coleman writing twenty years ago:

Policies that focus on high levels of achievement and rewards for high levels reverberate downward through the system, providing an incentive for students at lower levels to improve. Policies that focus on the lowest levels of achievement imply that incentives for improvement among those at the lowest levels cannot arise endogenously from within the system, but must be introduced from the outside. Meanwhile, those at higher levels of achievement dangle in the wind, without being seriously challenged to improve their performance.[5]

A dynamic education system, in other words, doesn't just set minimum standards but builds in incentives for students at every level. Selective-admission schools aren't the only way to incentivize or educate high-ability youngsters in the K–12 world, but they're a valuable part of a comprehensive strategy that the United States neglects at its peril.

Appendix I

Selection Process and School List

• • • • • • • • • • • • • • • •

The sources and methods noted below provided us with leads. We then sought to confirm each candidate-school's fit via information on district and school websites or by contacting knowledgeable individuals (e.g., district administrators, school principals).

- Lists of "top" or "best" American high schools

  U.S. News, Newsweek, the *Wall Street Journal,* the *Washington Post,* and other media outlets publish lists, sometimes refreshed annually, that attempt to rank the "best" high schools in the United States using various methods and criteria. Such lists provided efficient starting points for seeking out academically selective public high schools.

- SAT and ACT scores

  We obtained confidential data on the mean and median SAT and ACT scores for every high school in the country. We used these data in two ways to identify schools for our list. First, we sorted schools by student scores (highest to lowest), which pointed us to many of the same schools featured on lists that appear in media rankings but also yielded others. Then we sorted schools by district in search of "outliers"—high schools that did not have SAT or ACT scores that would place them in the top five hundred or so nationally but whose scores were notably higher than those of other high schools in their districts. This method was particularly useful in identifying candidate schools in rural areas and some cities.

- Professional organizations

  Resources from several professional organizations also pointed to potential schools. The National Consortium for Specialized Secondary Schools of Science, Mathematics, and Technology (NCSSSMT) includes more than one hundred secondary schools across the country, most with a STEM focus. Not all are public schools or have academically selective admissions processes, but the list was a useful resource. We also consulted the websites of the National Association for Gifted Children (NAGC), Magnet Schools of America, and various state associations for gifted-and-talented education.

- State/District websites and personnel

  We referred to websites and contacted individuals in some state-level and large urban (e.g., New York, Chicago), mid-sized urban (e.g., Louisville, Milwaukee), and large suburban districts (e.g., Montgomery County, MD), regardless of whether we had already identified any of the district's schools from other sources. In some cases, we turned to knowledgeable informants on the local education scene.

The complete list appears below and comprises the universe of public high schools that use an academically selective admissions process. While this list is probably neither exhaustive (despite the pains we took, we surely missed some) nor absolutely accurate (as "verification" proved quite challenging, we likely have a few schools here that don't belong), it is, to the best of our present ability and knowledge, reflective of the locations and kinds of public high schools that are academically selective. We earnestly invite others to refine and update it.

Academically Selective Public High Schools in the United States (2010–11)

State	City	School name	Enrollment (2009–10)	Grade levels	Great Schools rating
AL	Huntsville	New Century Technology High School	306	9–12	10
AL	Mobile	Alabama School of Math and Science	255	10–12	N/A
AL	Mobile	John L. Leflore Preparatory Academy	947	9–12	9
AL	Montgomery	Booker T. Washington Magnet High School	474	9–12	10
AL	Montgomery	Loveless Academic Magnet Program High School	445	9–12	10
AR	Hot Springs	Arkansas School for Mathematics, Science, & the Arts	216	11–12	N/A
AZ	Tucson	University High School	796	9–12	10
CA	Carson	California Academy of Mathematics and Science	625	9–12	10
CA	Cerritos	Gretchen Whitney High School	1,022	7–12	10
CA	Costa Mesa	Early College High School	251	9–12	10
CA	Cypress	Oxford Academy	1,135	7–12	10
CA	Gilroy	Dr. T. J. Owens Gilroy Early College Academy	203	9–12	10
CA	Irvine	University High School	2,447	9–12	10
CA	Rohnert Park	Technology High School	220	9–12	10
CA	San Francisco	Lowell High School	2597	9–12	10

(continued)

State	City	School name	Enrollment (2009–10)	Grade levels	Great Schools rating
CA	Visalia	University Preparatory High School	68	9–12	8
DC	Washington	Benjamin Banneker Academic High School	393	9–12	10
DC	Washington	McKinley Technology High School	705	9–12	10
DC	Washington	Phelps Architecture, Construction, and Engineering High School	239	9–12	8
DC	Washington	School Without Walls High School	441	9–12	10
DE	Wilmington	The Charter School of Wilmington	987	9–12	N/A
FL	Davie	William T. McFatter Technical Center	561	9–12	10
FL	Key Biscayne	Mast Academy	550	9–12	10
FL	Miami	Design and Architecture Senior High	508	9–12	10
FL	Miami	School for Advanced Studies	505	9–12	10
FL	Osprey	Pine View School for the Gifted	2,170	2–12	10
FL	Riviera Beach	Suncoast Community High School	1,391	9–12	10
GA	Augusta	A. R. Johnson Health Science and Engineering Magnet	645	7–12	10
IL	Aurora	Illinois Mathematics & Science Academy (IMSA)	638	10–12	N/A
IL	Chicago	Brooks College Prep Academy	750	9–12	9

(continued)

State	City	School name	Enrollment (2009–10)	Grade levels	Great Schools rating
IL	Chicago	Jones College Prep High School	823	9–12	10
IL	Chicago	King College Prep High School	893	9–12	6
IL	Chicago	Lane Technical High School	4,192	9–12	10
IL	Chicago	Lindblom Math & Science Academy	724	7–12	9
IL	Chicago	Northside College Preparatory High School	1067	9–12	10
IL	Chicago	Walter Payton College Preparatory High School	903	9–12	10
IL	Chicago	Whitney Young Magnet High School	2,234	9–12	10
IL	Forest Park	Proviso Math and Science Academy	663	9–12	9
IL	Normal	University High School	611	9–12	N/A
IL	Urbana	University of Illinois Laboratory High School	307	8–12	N/A
IN	Muncie	Indiana Academy for Science, Mathematics & Humanities	298	11–12	N/A
KS	Kansas City	Sumner Academy of Arts & Science	861	8–12	7
KY	Bowling Green	Gatton Academy	120	11–12	N/A
KY	Louisville	Butler Traditional High School	1,655	9–12	8
KY	Louisville	Central High School	1,036	9–12	4
KY	Louisville	Dupont Manual High School	1,856	9–12	10

(continued)

State	City	School name	Enrollment (2009–10)	Grade levels	Great Schools rating
KY	Louisville	The J. Graham Brown School	635	K–12	9
KY	Louisville	Louisville Male High School	1,782	9–12	10
LA	Baton Rouge	Baton Rouge Magnet High School	1,224	9–12	10
LA	Baton Rouge	LSU Laboratory School	1,359	K–12	N/A
LA	Gretna	Thomas Jefferson High School for Advanced Studies	290	9–12	10
LA	Jefferson	Patrick F. Taylor Science & Technology Academy	311	6–12	10
LA	Metairie	Haynes Academy School for Advanced Studies	652	6–12	10
LA	Natchitoches	Louisiana School for Math Science & the Arts	338	10–12	10
LA	New Orleans	Benjamin Franklin High School	609	9–12	10
LA	New Orleans	Lusher Charter School	1,520	K–12	10
LA	Shreveport	Caddo Parish Magnet High School	1,002	9–12	10
MA	Boston	Boston Latin School	2,395	7–12	9
MA	Boston	Boston Latin Academy	1,759	7–12	9
MA	Boston	John D. O'Bryant School Math & Science	1,212	7–12	8
MA	Worcester	Massachusetts Academy of Math and Science	91	11–12	N/A

(continued)

State	City	School name	Enrollment (2009–10)	Grade levels	Great Schools rating
MD	Baltimore	The Baltimore City College	1,331	9–12	7
MD	Baltimore	Baltimore Polytechnic Institute	1,615	9–12	10
MD	Baltimore	Eastern Technical High School	1,283	9–12	10
MD	Baltimore	Paul Laurence Dunbar High School	553	9–12	6
MD	Baltimore	Western High School	855	9–12	10
ME	Limestone	The Maine School of Science & Mathematics	132	9–12	10
MI	Bloomfield Hills	International Academy Central	163	9–12	10
MI	Detroit	Cass Technical High School	2,195	9–12	8
MI	Detroit	Davis Aerospace High School	206	9–12	3
MI	Detroit	Renaissance High School	1,038	9–12	10
MI	Flint	Classical Academy	253	7–12	8
MO	Kansas City	Lincoln College Preparatory Academy	1,002	6–12	10
MO	Maryville	Missouri Academy of Science, Mathematics, and Computing	199	11–12	N/A
MO	Saint Louis	Metro High School	297	9–12	9
MS	Columbus	Mississippi School for Mathematics and Science	237	11–12	10
NC	Durham	North Carolina School of Science and Mathematics	673	11–12	N/A

(continued)

State	City	School name	Enrollment (2009–10)	Grade levels	Great Schools rating
NC	Greensboro	Early College at Guilford	201	9–12	10
NC	Raleigh	William G. Enloe High School	2,657	9–12	4
NJ	Camden	Brimm Medical Arts High School	248	9–12	10
NJ	Freehold	Biotechnology High School	301	9–12	10
NJ	Hackensack	Bergen County Academies	1,049	9–12	10
NJ	Jersey City	Dr. Ronald McNair Academic High School	683	9–12	10
NJ	Lincroft	High Technology High School	258	9–12	10
NJ	Manahawkin	Marine Academy of Technology & Environmental Sciences (MATES)	207	9–12	10
NJ	Neptune	Academy of Allied Health & Science	288	9–12	N/A
NJ	Newark	Science High	902	7–12	10
NJ	Newark	University High School of Humanities	521	7–12	6
NJ	North Bergen	High Tech High School	591	9–12	N/A
NJ	Rockaway	The Academy for Math, Science, & Engineering	81	9–12	10
NJ	Sandy Hook	Marine Academy of Science and Technology	276	9–12	10
NJ	Scotch Plains	Union County Academy for Allied Health Sciences	252	9–12	10

(continued)

State	City	School name	Enrollment (2009–10)	Grade levels	Great Schools rating
NJ	Scotch Plains	Union County Magnet High School	274	9–12	10
NJ	Teterboro	Bergen County Technical High School	631	9–12	10
NJ	Wall	Communications High School	283	9–12	5
NV	Henderson	College of Southern Nevada High School South	121	11–12	N/A
NV	Las Vegas	College of Southern Nevada High School West	205	11–12	N/A
NV	North Las Vegas	College of Southern Nevada High School East	107	11–12	N/A
NV	Reno	The Davidson Academy of Nevada	91	4–12	10
NY	Buffalo	City Honors School at Fosdick Masten Park	853	5–12	9
NY	NYC (Bronx)	Bronx High School of Science	2,941	9–12	10
NY	NYC (Bronx)	High School of American Studies at Lehman College	352	9–12	9
NY	NYC (Brooklyn)	The Brooklyn Latin School	281	9–12	9
NY	NYC (Brooklyn)	Brooklyn Technical High School	4,947	9–12	9
NY	NYC (Brooklyn)	Leon M. Goldstein High School for the Sciences	1,049	9–12	8
NY	NYC (Manhattan)	Bard High School Early College	584	9–12	8

(continued)

State	City	School name	Enrollment (2009–10)	Grade levels	Great Schools rating
NY	NYC (Manhattan)	Baruch College Campus High School	440	9–12	7
NY	NYC (Manhattan)	Beacon High School	1,144	9–12	10
NY	NYC (Manhattan)	Eleanor Roosevelt High School	498	9–12	9
NY	NYC (Manhattan)	Frederick Douglass Academy	1,597	6–12	5
NY	NYC (Manhattan)	High School Math Science and Engineering at CCNY	424	9–12	10
NY	NYC (Manhattan)	Hunter College High School	1,215	7–12	N/A
NY	NYC (Manhattan)	Millennium High School	619	9–12	7
NY	NYC (Manhattan)	New Explorations into Science, Technology, and Math School	1,480	K–12	9
NY	NYC (Manhattan)	NYC Lab High School for Collaborative Studies	520	9–12	7
NY	NYC (Manhattan)	School of the Future High School	689	6–12	8
NY	NYC (Manhattan)	Stuyvesant High School	3,277	9–12	10
NY	NYC (Manhattan)	Young Women's Leadership School	437	6–12	6
NY	NYC (Queens)	Baccalaureate School for Global Education	424	7–12	9
NY	NYC (Queens)	Bard High School Early College II	456	9–12	7
NY	NYC (Queens)	Queens High School for the Sciences at York College	415	9–12	10

(continued)

State	City	School name	Enrollment (2009–10)	Grade levels	Great Schools rating
NY	NYC (Queens)	Townsend Harris High School	1,108	9–12	10
NY	NYC (Staten Island)	Staten Island Technical High School	1,015	9–12	10
OH	Cincinnati	Walnut Hills High School	2,208	7–12	10
OH	Cleveland	John Hay Early College High School	247	9–12	9
OH	Cleveland	John Hay School of Architecture & Design	267	9–12	8
OH	Cleveland	John Hay School of Science & Medicine	336	9–12	9
OK	Oklahoma City	Oklahoma School of Science & Mathematics	140	11–12	N/A
PA	Erie	Northwest Pennsylvania Collegiate Academy	862	9–12	10
PA	Philadelphia	Academy at Palumbo	494	9–12	8
PA	Philadelphia	Carver High School	637	9–12	9
PA	Philadelphia	Central High School	2,331	9–12	10
PA	Philadelphia	Franklin Learning Center	643	9–12	7
PA	Philadelphia	J. R. Masterman Secondary School	1,205	5–12	3
PA	Philadelphia	Lankenau High School	297	9–12	8
PA	Philadelphia	Parkway–Center City High School	375	9–12	5
PA	Philadelphia	Parkway Northwest High School	275	9–12	10
PA	Philadelphia	Parkway West High School	312	9–12	6

(continued)

State	City	School name	Enrollment (2009–10)	Grade levels	Great Schools rating
PA	Philadelphia	Philadelphia High School for Girls	1,103	9–12	6
PA	Philadelphia	Saul Agricultural School	552	9–12	3
PA	Philadelphia	Science Leadership Academy	485	9–12	9
PA	Philadelphia	William Bodine High School	533	9–12	8
RI	Providence	Classical High School	1,031	9–12	10
SC	Darlington	Mayo High School for Math, Science, and Technology	348	9–12	10
SC	Hartsville	South Carolina Governor's School for Science and Mathematics	128	11–12	N/A
SC	North Charleston	Academic Magnet High School	603	9–12	10
TN	Henderson–Ville	Merrol Hyde Magnet School	662	K–12	10
TN	Nashville	Hume-Fogg Academic Magnet High School	914	9–12	10
TN	Nashville	Martin Luther King Jr. Academic Magnet for Health Sciences and Engineering	1,190	7–12	10
TX	Austin	Liberal Arts and Science Academy (LASA) High School	883	9–12	10
TX	Dallas	School for the Talented and Gifted	229	9–12	10
TX	Dallas	School of Business and Management	528	9–12	10

(continued)

State	City	School name	Enrollment (2009–10)	Grade levels	Great Schools rating
TX	Dallas	School of Health Professions	542	9–12	10
TX	Dallas	School of Science and Engineering	407	9–12	10
TX	Denton	Texas Academy of Mathematics & Science	370	11–12	N/A
TX	Houston	Carnegie Vanguard High School	426	9–12	10
TX	Houston	Challenge Early College High School	445	9–12	10
TX	Houston	Debakey High School for Health Professions	887	9–12	10
VA	Alexandria	Thomas Jefferson High School for Science and Technology	1,792	9–12	10
VA	Richmond	Maggie L. Walker Governor's School for Government & International Studies	713	9–12	N/A
WI	Milwaukee	Marshall High School	137	9–12	6
WI	Milwaukee	Milwaukee School of Languages	1120	6–12	4
WI	Milwaukee	Riverside High School	1580	9–12	1
WI	Milwaukee	Ronald Reagan College Preparatory High School	994	9–12	2
WI	Milwaukee	Rufus King International Baccalaureate High School	1,533	9–12	5

Appendix II

Survey Questions

• • • • • • • •

About this survey

Thank you for participating in the Survey of Academically-Competitive Admission Public High Schools being conducted by the Thomas B. Fordham Institute and Stanford University's Hoover Institution.

The study's purpose is to map and illumine the landscape of public high schools in the United States with academically-competitive admissions. It will document the characteristics and role of such schools through this survey and (later in the spring) case studies of a small number of these schools. When completed, it will provide guidance for education leaders, policymakers, school board members, philanthropists, and others who seek to enhance the quality of public education for all students, including those with high academic performance or potential.

We have obtained some of the data for this study from federal, state, or district sources (e.g., databases, websites). However, some of the most essential information can only come directly from the school's administrator.

This survey contains about 50 questions that are divided among 8 topics. Principals who have completed the pilot version of the survey reported that it took approximately 45 minutes, with some additional time for looking up information.

Some of the questions may request information that you need to look up or obtain from others, and some are "open response" questions that may take a bit of time to answer. To make this easier, you are able to exit the survey and return to it at any time through the link provided in the survey email. Once you have completed the survey, you will NOT be able to return to it to modify your responses.

Please note that survey-generated information about individual schools will NOT be made public. We will not report survey data by individual school, nor will we report survey data so that individual schools are identifiable. Your responses are confidential.

If you have any questions about this survey, please contact [the authors].

In gratitude for your participation, when the survey is completed, we will send you a $50 Amazon.com gift card. These gift cards will be emailed to all respondents after data collection has ended in March [2011].

The survey will close on Friday, March 4th. Please submit your responses by that time.

Thanks very much in advance for taking the time to help with this important research.

Respondent Information

1. Please enter your name & position, school name, and contact information.
   (REQUIRED QUESTION)
   Name/Position:
   School:
   Address:
   Address 2:
   City/Town:
   State:
   ZIP:
   Email address:
   Phone number:

2. Is your school a public school? *Survey exits respondent if "no."*
   ☐ Yes
   ☐ No

3. Does your school include 12th grade? *Survey exits respondent if "no."*
   - ☐ Yes
   - ☐ No

4. Is admission to your school *academically competitive* (i.e., more students apply than can be admitted)? *Survey exits respondent if "no."*
   - ☐ Yes
   - ☐ No

5. Is admission to your school *academically selective* (i.e., significant attention is given to an applicant's academic performance or potential)? *Survey exits respondent if "no."*
   - ☐ Yes
   - ☐ No

6. Do your students attend your school IN ADDITION TO another school (e.g., a private/parochial school, another public school, homeschool)?
   - ☐ Yes
   - ☐ No

School Characteristics

7. Which of the following terms can be used legitimately to describe your school? (Check all that apply.)
   - ☐ Magnet
   - ☐ Regional center
   - ☐ Governor's school
   - ☐ State-sponsored
   - ☐ District-sponsored
   - ☐ Residential
   - ☐ Charter
   - ☐ STEM school
   - ☐ University lab school
   - ☐ Other (please specify):

8. How long (in hours) is your typical school day during the 2010–2011 school year?

9. What is the total number of student attendance days at your school for the 2010–2011 school year?

School History & Mission

10. In what year was your school founded?

11. Briefly explain why and how your school began.

12. What is your school's mission statement? (You may copy and paste the statement below, or provide a link to a web page.)

13. Describe any significant changes to the school's mission, goals, or role that have occurred within *the past 10 years*.

Student Enrollment

14. What PERCENTAGE of students in your school have Individualized Education Plans (IEPs)? (Use the most recent available data.)

15. What PERCENTAGE of students in your school have 504 plans (but not IEPs)? Use the most recent available data.)

16. Over the past 10 years, approximately what PERCENTAGE of students entering your school did NOT graduate from it?

17. Of those students who enter your school but do not graduate, what is the primary reason given for leaving your school? (Exclude geographic mobility such as a family move.)

18. Approximately what percentage of your **MOST RECENT** graduating class did **NOT** plan to enter a four-year college/ university immediately following graduation?

Governance, Regulation, & Finance

19. What district-, state-, or federally-mandated tests are your students required to take for accountability or graduation

purposes? Do not include college-entrance exams or AP exams or others that are voluntary on the part of students.

20. What is your school's total annual operating budget? Please use the most recent year for which reasonably complete information is available. Indicate the year you are reporting, and include funds from all sources.

21. Approximately what percentage of your school's annual operating budget comes from each of the following sources?
    District sources_____
    State sources_____
    Federal sources_____
    Philanthropic sources_____
    Parent/student fees_____
    Other sources_____

22. How long has your school's current principal (head of school, CEO) been in his/her position?

23. Are the teachers in your school covered by a collectively-bargained employment contract?
    ☐ Yes
    ☐ No

24. Is this collective bargaining unit specific to the teachers in your school or is it part of a larger bargaining unit?
    ☐ It is specific to our school.
    ☐ It is part of a larger bargaining unit.

25. Indicate whether your school has exemptions or waivers (full or partial) from the provisions of the collective bargaining contract in any of the following areas:

	Yes	No
Seniority-based staffing decisions		
Standard salary schedules		
Length of work day		
Number of preparation periods		
Non-classroom duties		

26. Briefly explain any other exemptions or waivers (full or partial) from the provisions of the collective bargaining contract that apply to your school.

27. Indicate whether the following types of exemptions or waivers (full or partial) from standard state or district regulations and requirements apply to your school.

	Yes	No
Teacher certification		
Teaching assignments		
Other duties or responsibilities for teachers		
Individualized or differentiated teacher compensation		
Tenure		
Seniority		

28. Briefly explain any other exemptions or waivers (full or partial) from standard state or distinct regulations that apply to your school.

29. Which of the following statements comes CLOSEST to describing how hiring decisions about teachers at your school are made?
    ☐ These decisions are made largely by the principal, school head, and/or others within the school.
    ☐ These decisions are made largely by the school system's central office.
    ☐ These decisions are made jointly by a school team and the central office.

Teaching Faculty

30. How many teachers (full-time AND part-time) does your school employ?

31. How many of your teachers are FULL-TIME?

32. What is the average number of years of experience teaching AT YOUR SCHOOL among ALL of your teachers?

33. Enter the NUMBER of teachers in your school in each category.

Teachers who have a teaching certificate that is valid in your state	
Teachers who have an earned doctoral degree (e.g., Ph.D., Ed.D., MD)	
Teachers who have an earned Masters Degree (but not doctoral degree)	
Teachers who are Male	
Teachers who are Female	
Teachers who are White/ Caucasian	
Teachers who are African American	
Teachers who are Latino/Latina	
Teachers who are Asian American	
Teachers who are Bi/Multi-Racial	
Teachers who are Other Minority	
Teachers whose Ethnicity is Not Known	

34. We are interested in how many teachers in your school (full- or part-time) may have non-traditional teaching backgrounds. Please indicate the NUMBER of current teachers in your school in the following categories. Some teachers may fit more than one category.

Current or former college/university instructor	
Current or former private school instructor	
Extensive background in business or industry	
Extensive background in science or technical fields	
Extensive background in nonprofit organizations	
Extensive background in the military	
Extensive background in other public-sector careers	
Teach for America corps member or alumnus/a	
Did not attend a traditional teacher-preparation program	

35. Please indicate the DEGREE OF EMPHASIS that the teacher selection process for your school places on each of the possible criteria listed below.

	Strongly emphasized in the teacher selection process	Moderately emphasized in the teacher selection process	Slightly emphasized in the teacher selection process	Not a criterion in the teacher selection process
Years of teaching experience				
Type of teaching experience				
Reputation of previous places of employment				
Education level				
Subject-matter knowledge				
Pedagogical knowledge/ expertise				
Portfolio (e.g., sample unit/ lesson plans)				
Recommendations from previous administrators or supervisors				
Recommendations from previous teaching colleagues				
Recommendations from college/ university instructors or advisors				
Ability to relate to, understand, and/or engage adolescent learners				

36. Briefly explain any other criteria that are STRONGLY EM-PHASIZED in the teacher selection process for your school.

Curriculum & Instruction

37. Briefly describe any courses or programs that your school offers that are distinctively different from those offered at the public schools your students would otherwise attend. Examples may include specialized electives, before/after school programs, schools-within-your-school, virtual courses, mentorships, internships, university partnerships, etc.

38. What was the total number of AP exams that students in your school took in the 2009–2010 school year?

39. What was the total number of AP exams on which students in your school earned a score of 3 or higher in the 2009–2010 school year?

40. How many of your students were enrolled in the International Baccalaureate (IB) Program during the 2009–2010 school year?

41. Which term BEST describes the pedagogical approaches or strategies that guide MOST of the instruction at your school? (If none of the terms are good descriptions—or a combination of terms applies—please select OTHER and briefly explain.)
    - ☐ Didactic instruction
    - ☐ Problem-based learning
    - ☐ Inquiry-based learning
    - ☐ Project-based learning
    - ☐ Differentiated instruction
    - ☐ Experiential learning
    - ☐ Cooperative learning
    - ☐ Other (please specify):

Recruitment & Admissions

The questions in this final section of the survey ask for information about your school's Recruitment & Admissions processes. Some of the questions are complicated or seek information that may be considered sensitive.

Your complete and candid responses are crucial to gaining the most accurate perspective on the schools in this study.

Please be assured that all of your responses to questions in this section—as with all questions in this survey—are confidential and will not be reported by individual school.

42. Where do students who are eligible to apply to your school live?
    - ☐ Within a neighborhood or subdivision of a single city or school district
    - ☐ Within the boundaries of a single city or school district
    - ☐ Within multiple school districts in the same county or region
    - ☐ Within the boundaries of the state
    - ☐ Other (please specify):

43. Which of the following *recruitment techniques* does your school use? (Check all that apply.)
    - ☐ Having school staff visit elementary/middle/high school campuses
    - ☐ Using students, parents, or alumni to communicate with prospective applicants
    - ☐ Placing brochures, flyers, or pamphlets in schools, community centers, libraries, or other public or private facilities
    - ☐ Using email blasts
    - ☐ Sending out recruitment materials directly to prospective students' homes or schools
    - ☐ Developing and using recruitment materials in languages other than English
    - ☐ Developing recruitment techniques in partnership with local organizations

☐ Hosting school-visit days for prospective students and parents

☐ Other (please specify):

44. Please indicate the DEGREE OF EMPHASIS that your school's admissions process places on each of the possible criteria listed below.

	Strongly empha-sized in the admissions process	Moderately empha-sized in the admissions process	Slightly empha-sized in the admissions process	Not a crite-rion in the admissions process
SAT/ACT scores				
IQ test scores				
Scores from state/district tests administered in prior grades				
Other standardized achievement test scores (e.g., California Achievement Test, Iowa Test of Basic Skills)				
Scores from an entrance exam customized for your school or district				
Students' prior academic record (e.g., grades)				
Application essay responses				
Interview				
Portfolio or other work submission				
Teacher recommendation(s)				
Other recommendation(s)				
Sibling(s) attend school				

45. Briefly explain any other criteria that are STRONGLY EM-PHASIZED in your school's admissions process.

46. Provide a description of your school's admissions process, with an emphasis on the decision-making process (i.e., how it's decided which applicants will be offered admission). If your school uses a lottery at **ANY** point in the process, please explain when and how it is used. You may also note if the admissions process is centrally organized and controlled.

47. Briefly explain any strategies or preferences that your school or district uses in the admissions process to foster diversity (racial, ethnic, socio-economic, geographic, gender, etc.) in its student enrollment.

48. Please enter the NUMBER of applicants to your school in each category for the 2010–2011 school year. DO NOT USE PERCENTAGES. Use **N/A** if the information is not made available to you.

Total number of applicants to your school	
Applicants to your school who were White/Caucasian	
Applicants to your school who were African American	
Applicants to your school who were Latino/Latina	
Applicants to your school who were Asian American	
Applicants to your school who were Other Minority	
Applicants to your school who were Bi-/Multi-Racial	
Applicants to your school whose Ethnicity is Not Known	
Applicants to your school who qualified for Free/Reduced Lunch	

49. Describe any significant changes to your school's applicant pool over the past 5–10 years.

50. To what percentage of applicants for the 2010–2011 school year did your school OFFER admission?
    - ☐ 10% or less of applicants
    - ☐ Between 10% and 20% of applicants

☐ Between 20% and 30% of applicants
☐ Between 30% and 40% of applicants
☐ Between 40% and 50% of applicants
☐ Between 50% and 60% of applicants
☐ Between 60% and 70% of applicants
☐ Between 70% and 80% of applicants
☐ Between 80% and 90% of applicants
☐ 90% or more of applicants
☐ Unknown

51. What percentage of those applicants for the 2010–2011 school who were offered admission ACCEPTED admission and ACTUALLY ENROLLED?
☐ 10% or less of applicants
☐ Between 10% and 20% of applicants
☐ Between 20% and 30% of applicants
☐ Between 30% and 40% of applicants
☐ Between 40% and 50% of applicants
☐ Between 50% and 60% of applicants
☐ Between 60% and 70% of applicants
☐ Between 70% and 80% of applicants
☐ Between 80% and 90% of applicants
☐ 90% or more of applicants
☐ Unknown

Comments

52. You may use this space to clarify your responses, note any technical difficulties you encountered, provide feedback on the survey itself, or request that we contact you directly.
    [Comment box]

Notes

• • • •

Introduction

1.   Throughout this book, we use a number of terms to refer to adolescents who are either high performing in school (as gauged, for example, by test scores, grades, specific talents) or who have high potential. In general, we refrain from using the term "gifted" (unless it is historically relevant, or used by a survey respondent, school, or site visit participant), as there is significant disagreement among gifted-education experts about what it means and whether the term itself is useful. See R. J. Sternberg and J. E. Davidson, *Conceptions of Giftedness*, 2nd ed. (Cambridge: Cambridge University Press, 2005).

Chapter 1: History and Context

1.   How to reconcile such a high percentage of high school graduates in the adult population when we know that the national high school graduation rate hovers around 75 percent? Because the Census Bureau counts GED certificates and other "equivalency" credentials; because some people get their high school diplomas late; and because not everybody is truthful and precise when answering these census questions about their level of education.

2.   Besides several such schools in Louisiana, we found one in Delaware and one in Michigan.

3.   One of the interesting exceptions, Louisville's Central High School, is profiled in chapter 6. Other "academic" high schools aimed at African-American youngsters, such as the District of Columbia's famous Dunbar High School, gave up their exclusivity—both academic and racial—as desegregation and Conant-style comprehensiveness arrived at approximately the same time.

4.   Data on the growth (and intermittent shrinkage) of the Advanced Placement program also speak to diminished emphasis on "excellence" during this period. In *AP: A Critical Examination of the Advanced Placement Program* (Cambridge, MA: Harvard Education Press, 2010), Philip Sadler notes that the 1960s saw a steady increase in AP participation rates, while the 1970s saw a decrease.

5.   The "setaside" ended in 1997 in the aftermath of other litigation charging that it caused "reverse discrimination."

6.   http://www.city-journal.org/html/9_2_how_gothams_elite.html.

7.   The lack of congressional urgency on this front is indicated by the fact that sixteen years elapsed (before enactment of the Javits Act) after a major 1972 report by then-commissioner of education Sidney Marland declaring that gifted students needed special consideration within the K–12 system. The lack of current federal attention to this need is evidenced by the facts that Congress zero-funded the Javits program in 2011 and the program's remnants are now housed deep and invisibly within the Education Department.

8.   A recent illustration of the perils facing "gifted education" programs in times of fiscal stress or ascendant egalitarianism: early in 2009, the California legislature agreed to let the state's public schools divert dollars previously earmarked for gifted children (and a number of other categorical programs) into "any educational purpose." The amounts involved weren't large, only $44 million in state funding for gifted education. But just a year later, the state's legislative analyst found that more than two-thirds of the districts he surveyed had indeed shifted resources away from the education of gifted children. http://www.lao.ca.gov/reports/2010/edu/educ_survey/educ_survey_050410.pdf.

9.   Available at http://www2.ed.gov/pubs/DevTalent/toc.html.

Chapter 2: Searching for Needles in the High School Haystack

1.   A few of the statewide residential schools, such as the Illinois Mathematics and Science Academy and the Texas Academy of Mathematics and Science, ask students and their families to pay for room and board, not for instruction, but also make available financial aid to those who cannot afford to pay this.

2.   Several "conversion" charters in Louisiana, including Benjamin Franklin High School, profiled in chapter 9, are also included on our list because they are academically selective—and do *not* use a lottery.

3. We're mindful that we may have been more "rigorous" with the New York City schools than in winnowing the selective-admission schools in several other cities such as Milwaukee. Unless we found information to the contrary regarding its admissions process, or a reasonable basis on which to form our own judgments, we often had to defer to school or district personnel to confirm a school's suitability for the list—even if its academic performance suggested otherwise. That's one reason we include the Great Schools ratings shown in appendix I.

4. Based on lists maintained by the National Center for Education Statistics (NCES), this number includes all virtual, alternative, charter, regular, and special-education schools that include grade 12 and may offer, at the lowest, grade 6. Limiting the national list to the country's 17,000+ "regular" public high schools as defined by NCES would have led to a slightly misleading comparison, since several schools on our list fit into the categories that NCES has termed "alternative," "charter," and even special ed.

5. A few schools on our list have not been rated by Great Schools. For the most part, these are university-sponsored schools, distinct state agencies, charter schools, and others whose students are exempt from the state's accountability testing.

6. Great Schools assesses the percentage of students tested at each school that meet or exceed proficiency standards for each grade and subject, as defined by the state. These performance results are sorted from low to high and divided into deciles. Schools in the bottom 10 percent are assigned a rating of 1, in the next highest decile a rating of 2, and so on. Individual schools are assigned ratings for each grade/subject combination with performance data. Those grade/subject ratings are then averaged to create "By Grade" ratings. The school's overall rating is calculated by averaging the ratings for all grade/subject combinations in which the school participates and for which data are available. This methodology is further explained on the Great Schools website at http://www.greatschools.org/find-a-school/defining-your-ideal/2423-ratings.gs.

Chapter 3: Exploring a New Constellation

1. One source of national "racial isolation" data is Gary Orfield and Chungmei Lee, "Historic Reversals, Accelerating Resegregation, and the Need for New Integration Strategies," Civil Rights Project, UCLA, August 2007.

2. There are several possible explanations for the high concentration of minority students in the urban schools on our list. As one urban education

expert said to us, "White parents with smart kids would likely think of private schools or maybe moving. Black parents, many of them without a lot of education options, would look at available public schools and try to determine the best fit for their children."

3.   Readers should be aware that there is some doubt as to how enthusiastic high school students are in seeking—and how accurate in reporting their eligibility for—subsidized meals.

4.   Twenty-one schools reported having 50 or more students with IEPs (Individualized Education Plans), with some urban schools (none larger than 1,600 pupils total) reporting between 100 and 275 students with IEPs. One possible explanation for these higher numbers is that several schools may resemble Jones College Prep High School in Chicago (see chapter 8). Here's how a Chicago Public Schools administrator described that arrangement: "We have three special education programs at Jones. Our 'high incidence' students (LD and other common categories) enter through the selective enrollment process and are fully integrated in the college prep program. We also have two 'low incidence' cluster programs (severe/profound and moderate cognitive) in which the students are placed at Jones and are mostly self-contained. Some of the moderate cognitive (TMH) students take a few classes along with non–special education students."

5.   School principals are famously resistant to online surveys, indeed to electronic communications from strangers. They're busy—and in many districts they have been admonished not to participate in research activities without clearance from the central office. In just a few cases were we able to clear that path for them. (We did, however, provide a modest gift certificate to those who completed the survey.)

6.   Site visits, histories, and other information indicate that IQ tests were more widely used in the past for admission to schools of this kind but came under fire as possibly discriminatory, and their use was subsequently curtailed.

7.   There are limited data on students' LEP (limited English proficient) status. We did not include a survey question about bilingual or ELL (English language learners) programs in our schools but also encountered no evidence of any, though several schools that we visited remarked that many students come from homes in which English is not spoken and that many went through ELL programs in earlier grades. Some schools also emphasize intensive writing programs, especially for new students, because few of their pupils have had much earlier practice in this realm. (That, of course, can be a general comment on middle school curricula and isn't necessarily related to non-English-speaking status.)

8. We sought information about school budgets, but the responses proved impossible to tabulate. Readers will find some discussion of budgets and financial resources in the school profiles in part II.

9. One possible explanation is that many schools on our list do not operate full-fledged special-education programs—nor do they receive extra funds for such programs or for other "categorical" programs such as bilingual education and Title I. On the other hand, several that we visited do receive additional funds for class-size reduction and such, often because of their magnet status.

10. We queried survey respondents about the education and prior experience of their teaching staffs, as well as their demographics. Respondents from some state-sponsored residential and university-affiliated schools did not answer these questions because, they said, their teachers are actually employed by the university. Therefore, we have no data from these schools, which is apt to be significant when parsing several data points, such as teachers with doctorates.

11. In general, these schools are either exempted by state law or are affiliated with a college or university.

Chapter 4: Illinois Mathematics and Science Academy, Aurora, IL

1. Based on current figures, the maximum a family would pay over three years is $10,444.

2. Source: 2010–2011 IMSA Parent/Student Handbook, pp. 6–7, https://www3.imsa.edu/living/handbook. Teachers do track progress and enter student grades in an information system that both parents and students can monitor.

3. The number of students that IMSA can admit is limited by the number of available dorm rooms.

4. Youngsters who are not officially in 9th grade but have taken or are taking sufficiently advanced classes (e.g., algebra, high school science) may apply and be admitted as sophomores.

5. www.imsa.edu/admissions/apply/Admissions_Policy_JA_200605 .pdf.

6. Comparing IMSA's admissions policies before the audit and today shows the latter to be far more detailed and much better at clarifying terms.

7. IMSA's "admissions public policy" further specifies: "The Academy shall ensure adequate geographic, gender, and ethnic representation in

admission decisions by approximating the diversity of the applicant pool from among qualified applicants. Admission decisions will not be controlled by quotas nor will admission standards be compromised to achieve diversity."

8.   IMSA students may go home on weekends, but doing so isn't feasible for many who live more than an hour or two away. Every six weeks or so, however, all students are granted a four-day extended weekend when they are required to leave campus.

9.   This rate is consistent with those reported by other state-sponsored residential high schools, both in our survey data and reported elsewhere.

10.   By law, IMSA students are exempt from taking the Prairie State Achievement Examination (PSAE), the state's high school accountability test, which includes the ACT. But most IMSA students take the ACT itself for purposes of college admissions, which affords some basis for comparing their academic achievement with that of students attending other high schools in the state. The average composite score of the IMSA class of 2009 was 31.5. This is nearly three points higher than the next-highest-scoring Illinois high school, Northside College Prep (28.6 in 2009), one of the Chicago Public Schools' selective-enrollment high schools.

11.   The school does have evidence that a much higher percentage of its graduates earn undergraduate degrees in STEM fields than the national average. According to an alumni/ae fact sheet, "Using the 1,342 graduate records returned from the National Student Clearinghouse (from 3,768 IMSA graduates through 2008), 60% of undergraduate degrees earned by those alumni are in science, technology, engineering or mathematics (STEM), compared to the national average of 33%."

Chapter 5: School Without Walls, Washington, D.C.

1.   The District also operates a selective high school focused on the arts.

2.   The DCPS assessment regimen includes a "composition" test (along with reading and math) in 7th grade.

3.   Subsequent to our visit, DCPS announced plans to centralize the admissions process for its selective schools. http://dcps.dc.gov/DCPS/commonapp.

4.   Some jocularly dub it the "school without balls."

5.   There are, of course, many nonacademic reasons for leaving the school, including changing tastes, transportation hassles, families moving out of town.

6.   This may account in part for the underrepresentation of boys—but all of D.C.'s selective high schools are heavily female, even McKinley Technology High School, which may also have something to do with the educational challenges facing African-American boys, Washington being a city where 80+ percent of District pupils are black.

7.   George Washington University does not otherwise confer associates' degrees; getting this one approved by the faculty is said to have been a struggle.

8.   This kind of organizational angst is a downside to the education-reform goal of replacing "last in, first out" with decisions based more on individual teacher performance.

9.   The current facility is full—and there's concern among parents and staff about risking the school's family-like intimacy if it gets bigger.

Chapter 6: Central High School Magnet Career Academy, Louisville, KY

1.   John E. Kleber, *The Encyclopedia of Louisville* (Lexington: University Press of Kentucky, 2001).

2.   DuPont Manual also has the highest average ACT score in Kentucky.

3.   Students obviously don't graduate from high school prepared to head straight to work in the law or a related profession.

4.   These questions ask: "Is the student Hispanic/Latino? (Yes/No) Is the student from one or more of these races? (Check all that apply.) American Indian/Native Alaska, Asian, Black or African-American, Native Hawaiian or other Pacific Islander, White."

Chapter 7: Liberal Arts and Science Academy, Austin, TX

1.   This story is briefly told—and much else about the modern history of public education in Austin extensively told—by Stanford's Larry Cuban in *As Good As It Gets: What School Reform Brought to Austin* (Cambridge, MA: Harvard University Press, 2010).

2.   One still encounters references to "the LA" and "the SA," now melded into LASA, the former being the part of the school (and a few long-time teachers) who came from the English/history program, the latter being the part whose origins were in math and science.

3. It still seems not to have a federal ID number within the NCES Common Core of Data system (hereafter NCES CCD).

4. The high school that formerly housed the "liberal arts" magnet never produced satisfactory scores after that program moved out and has since been closed and reopened with a new name, instructional team, and academic plan.

5. Another factor in the decision to separate LASA from LBJ was a sizable Gates Foundation grant to redesign a number of Austin high schools. Evidently the LBJ makeover plan required its separation from the LASA magnet program. For additional information, see http://www.gatesfoundation.org/press-releases/Pages/austin-school-district-invest ment-061114.aspx.

6. This rubric is available online at http://www.lasaonline.org/our pages/auto/2010/10/13/60072046/LASA%20Admissions%20Rubric% 202011.pdf, and the application form can be viewed at http://www.lasa online.org/ourpages/auto/2010/10/13/60072046/LASA%20application% 202012-2013.pdf.

7. Other requirements for "probationary" entrants: They must submit final grades (from 8th grade) and their 8th-grade scores on the state achieve-ment tests, and must pass all their classes during their first semester at LASA.

8. We were told that employing and, especially, retaining talented black teachers is a problem for the whole AISD system because they are often recruited into higher-paying jobs in the city's thriving for-profit sec-tor as well as by suburban and private schools.

9. http://www.breakthroughaustin.org/.

10. About 10 percent of new entrants arrive from private schools.

11. High school students are famously reluctant to admit that their families are poor enough to qualify for the free or reduced-price lunches, and this may be especially so in an "elite" school. It should also be noted that Texas, overall, has the lowest rate of special-education pupils in the country.

12. One peculiarity is that LASA students are bused on the "middle school" schedule, meaning that the school starts and ends its day earlier than other district high schools—including the one downstairs.

13. Though LASA is located in the relatively poor northeastern part of Austin, many of its students hail from the more prosperous western and southwestern parts of town. Though the "mix" that this produces within the school is appealing, it also means that travel times can be long. (Austin has a full measure of traffic challenges.) Parents commented that just get-ting their kids together socially—or athletically—with school friends from the "other side of town" is a major hassle.

14. Texas's preferential college admissions for kids in the top tenth of their high school classes is a bit of a problem here because nearly all LASA students would be in the top 10 percent at ordinary schools. The youngsters we spoke with seemed, however, to view this as an acceptable trade-off for the education they're receiving.

15. In order of decision making, the district considers "program" (Is what this teacher does still needed by this school?), "performance," seniority, and then credentials such as graduate degrees and certification.

16. For additional descriptions of the "signature" courses see http://www.lasaonline.org/apps/pages/index.jsp?uREC_ID=104455&type=d&pREC_ID=208072. For a comprehensive description of all course offerings see http://www.lasaonline.org/ourpages/auto/2010/11/29/21695101/LASA%20Course%20Descriptions_%202011-12.pdf.

17. Although LASA is the only complete high school in AISD that is academically selective, the district runs several other magnet programs that appeal to different interests and priorities of students and families. These include a fine-arts academy, an all-girls school "for young women leaders," a high-tech program, a performing arts program, an International Baccalaureate program, and a "global studies" program.

Chapter 8: Jones College Prep, Chicago, IL

1. To apply to a selective-enrollment high school, students must have seventh-grade nationally normed test scores at a stanine 5 or higher in both reading and math. According to the Office of Academic Enhancement website, "Students who have Individualized Education Programs (IEPs) and 504 Plans, and those students in state-approved bilingual programs, are eligible with reading comprehension and mathematics total stanines that total 10, such as a 3 and 7, or 6 and 4."

2. Notably, these schools are located in predominantly black neighborhoods.

3. http://www.jonescollegeprep.org/mission_statement.jsp.

4. This description of AMPS was accurate as of the time of our visit to Jones College Prep. In August 2011, however, the recently arrived CEO of the Chicago Public Schools, Jean-Claude Brizard, announced a major restructuring of CPS that eliminated the separate AMPS office and school classification. http://www.chicagotribune.com/news/education/ct-met-cps-selective-20110801,0,6396148.story.

Chapter 9: Benjamin Franklin High School, New Orleans, LA

1. The New Orleans charter picture is complicated—and vast. Louisiana now boasts five different kinds of charter schools, distinguished primarily by what entity authorizes them. The best-known authorizer by far is the Recovery School District, which in May 2011 sponsored fifty-one charters in Orleans Parish and directly operated fifteen schools there. But what's left of the old Orleans Parish school system also sponsored a dozen charters—while directly operating only four schools.

2. BFHS currently admits all students within the applicant pool who meet its demanding cutoff criteria, though that means gradual growth in the school's total enrollment. Because it's not yet back to pre-Katrina size, however, this hasn't been a problem regarding school capacity.

3. There's been another recent interaction with OCR, unresolved as of this writing. See http://www.nola.com/education/index.ssf/2010/01/post_73.html.

4. Alternatively, one can take a "concurrent enrollment" course in a local college.

5. Its football team has not, however, been chalking up a lot of wins.

6. When we asked one African-American student what it's like returning each afternoon from Ben Franklin to his low-income neighborhood with a bulging backpack, he replied "They think I'm selling something!"

7. NOPS has about half a billion dollars in long-term debt, much of it reportedly accumulated in connection with past corruption, yet it now operates only a few schools from which revenues can be generated to pay it off.

8. It appeared from one direct observation of the board in action that the (African-American) board president is opposed to selectivity and the superintendent is no enthusiast.

Chapter 10: Townsend Harris High School, Queens, NY

1. There are mixed explanations for LaGuardia's decision, some citing budget pressures on the city during World War II, others asserting that the mayor found Townsend Harris too elitist, still others suggesting that one of hizzoner's close relatives failed to gain admission. This topic—and much more about the history of the original school—is treated extensively in Eileen F. Lebow, *The Bright Boys: A History of Townsend Harris High School* (Westport, CT: Greenwood Press, 2000).

2.   Saul Cohen, then president of Queens College, played a key role in this resurrection, helped by then-borough president Donald Manes. They prevailed upon the board of education, board of estimate, mayor, and others to start a new, selective high school on the college campus, and to construct a new building for it. Until then, the alumni had not been able to gain any political traction. Cohen and his faculty favored a "grades and interview" approach to admissions rather than test-based admissions. They planned for a small co-ed school with a "classical" curriculum, close ties to the college, and plenty of minority students. They navigated the politics of jealous high school principals in far northeastern Queens and a bit of minority agitation about "elitism." They also approved the first principal—and ensured that he got to choose the initial faculty. Cohen says he regards all this as one of his foremost career achievements.

3.   To be *eligible* for entrance, a youngster must display a 7th-grade GPA of at least 90 percent and be at the 90th percentile or above on the state's standardized reading and math assessments, as well as having a middle school "record of excellent attendance and punctuality."

4.   The citywide Education Department also superimposes some of its own priorities on the matching process, particularly when it comes to admitting disabled youngsters to "screened" schools and programs. In the case of schools like Townsend Harris, at least, it appears that the department is now placing such applicants there if they meet the school's "objective" criteria even if the school itself does not "rank" them. This, we were told, is meant to prevent schools from *not* "ranking" youngsters on account of their disabilities—a practice Townsend Harris officials say their school never engaged in.

5.   http://www.nytimes.com/2011/05/08/nyregion/in-applying-for-high-school-some-8th-graders-find-a-maze.html?_r=1&scp=1&sq=Lost%20in%20the%20admissions%20maze&st=cse.

6.   Nine of the city's Specialized High Schools have statutory protection—indeed, a legislative mandate—to admit pupils solely on the basis of a special test (though LaGuardia also requires auditions). The relevant amendment to the New York State Education Code dates to 1971, when there were demands to do away with these "elitist" institutions and their "culturally biased" entrance exam. Two Bronx legislators managed to get enacted a bill that says "Admission to [these schools] shall be solely and exclusively by taking a competitive, objective and scholastic achievement examination. . . . No candidate may be admitted to a special high school unless he [*sic*] has successfully achieved a score above the cut-off score for the openings in the school for which he has taken the examination." The political trade-off was creation of a "Discovery Program" to assist disadvantaged

and minority youngsters to prepare for the competitive exam, although that program seems to have fallen by the wayside. http://www.city-journal.org/html/9_2_how_gothams_elite.html.

7. The LaGuardia High School of the Arts relies on an audition process. Another well-known and highly selective New York public school, Hunter College High School, handles its own admissions via its own separate test—and takes in students only at 7th grade.

8. The "zones" across which Townsend Harris apportions its admittees are based on family address, not where the middle school is located.

9. Heading to the school from midtown Manhattan early one morning, the author hailed a taxi. Its driver was an immigrant from India, whose older child had just been admitted to Townsend Harris and whose explanation of why they had applied there was precisely the classic immigrant tale—with a safety factor added. The family lives in central Queens, not far from THHS, and the father explained that Townsend Harris is appealing both because of its academic strength and because—unlike some other nearby options—it doesn't have police officers routinely arriving to forestall gang violence when school lets out in the afternoon.

10. For individual teachers, "enrichment" duty occurs twice a week. The THHS faculty voted for this arrangement under terms of New York City's "school-based options."

11. It was pointed out, though, that since every senior takes courses—and gets transferable college credits—at Queens College, fewer take Advanced Placement exams at THHS than otherwise might.

12. Though the school ranks its applicants, it never actually "meets" them, and because a computer handles the match between student and school, the school has no real say over which candidates—separate and apart from their scores and other "credentials"—are most apt to thrive within its culture and norms.

13. See http://gothamschools.org/2011/05/16/regents-give-districts-choice-of-tougher-teacher-evaluation/ and http://www.huffingtonpost.com/2011/05/16/new-york-state-tests-scores-teacher-evaluations_n_862537.html.

Chapter 11: Pine View School for the Gifted, Osprey, FL

1. NCES CCD, 2009–10.
2. Some alumni/ae from Pine View's early classes recalled also being interviewed as part of the admissions process.

3. Source: "John Woolever, Pine View's first principal, dies" (April 13, 2010), retrieved on August 9, 2011, http://www.heraldtribune.com/article/20100413/article/4131076.

4. Only a few schools that responded to our survey use IQ scores in their admissions process (see table 3.9).

5. Four possibilities are listed on the gifted eligibility worksheet: "evidence of ability beyond the general curriculum," "evidence of social maturity above classmates," "interests far advanced for regular class work," and "needs stimulation of advanced program." A student's IQ score and rating-scale results can double as evidence for this section.

6. Woodcock-Johnson III or Wechsler Individual Achievement Test III.

7. "Weighting" refers to the widespread, if controversial, practice of giving students additional points toward their GPA for grades in courses that carry honors or Advanced Placement labels. Thus a B grade in honors English might count as 4.0 points toward one's GPA calculation.

8. http://www.redcounty.com/content/sarasotas-pine-view-school-comparing-apples-apples.

Chapter 12: Oxford Academy, Cypress, CA

1. http://www.avid.org/.

2. Whitney High School is the sole subject of the book *School of Dreams: Making the Grade at a Top American High School* by award-winning journalist Edward Humes (Boston: Houghton Mifflin Harcourt, 2003).

Chapter 13: Bergen County Academies, Hackensack, NJ

1. More than twenty of these districts don't actually operate any schools; they're taxing and administrative units that send their youngsters to school in neighboring districts.

2. That number has been reduced since Chris Christie became governor, and the positions may be abolished altogether as an economy measure.

3. http://www.njccvts.org/school-districts.aspx.

4. New Jersey has community colleges, too, mostly also county-specific. It's not easy to understand where their offerings and programs leave off and those of the adult-education programs of the voc-tech system begin. It appears, at least to the outsider, as if there's considerable overlap.

5.   A measure of institutional preservation was also at work, as the old vocational school's enrollment had declined to just a few hundred. Without something changing, the place would have withered away.

6.   Bergen County also operates another selective-admission "technical high school" in Teterboro, though its criteria for entrance are not as rigorous and its academic reputation is not as strong.

7.   Grieco died in 2004, aged sixty-three, and is still revered at BCA.

8.   This is separate and distinct from, and far older than, New Jersey's new program of interdistrict school choice, which is optional for districts. See http://www.nj.gov/education/choice/.

9.   For example, fourteen districts within Bergen County are "capped" at eleven BCA entrants each. In a recent admission cycle, the number of BCA applicants from those districts ranged from eight in North Arlington to almost ten times as many in Hackensack.

10.   A sample BCA admissions test in math can be glimpsed at http://bcts.bergen.org/images/stories/BCTS/Admissions/BCA/TEST/SAMHAK2.pdf. Keep in mind that these are taken by 8th graders. A sample forty-minute English essay test can be seen at http://bcts.bergen.org/images/stories/BCTS/pdf/eleven.pdf.

11.   The explanation we were given is complicated but has mostly to do with budgets and staffing arrangements based on "sections" of twenty pupils each. Allowing individual students to change academies willy-nilly would, apparently, throw off all these calculations.

12.   http://www.state.nj.us/education/news/2011/0520csg.htm.

13.   http://www.state.nj.us/cgi-bin/education/csg/11/csg.pl?string =dist_code0290&maxhits=650. The Bergen County Academies comprise about half of the Bergen County Vocational District, which also runs the aforementioned school in Teterboro and one in Paramus. It doesn't appear possible to extract separate—and comparable—data from state reports for BCA alone. When we asked the school about its per-pupil expenditures, staff there estimated $18,000–20,000.

14.   Parents and their association are also involved with the school in a host of other ways, including clerical help around the school, participating in "career days" for students, and organizing two enormous annual events—an "international dinner" and a picnic that typically draws 1,200 people.

Chapter 14: Thomas Jefferson High School for Science and Technology, Annandale, VA

1. http://education.usnews.rankingsandreviews.com/best-high-schools/listings/virginia/thomas-jefferson-high-school-for-science-and-technology.

2. The other two are Maggie Walker, located in Richmond, which has more of a humanities focus ("government and international studies"), and the Appomattox Regional School ("for the arts and technology") in Petersburg. In addition to school-year programs, Governor's Schools include a number of summer-only offerings and a virtual high school.

3. The most ambitious of these that we observed involves creation of a wheelchair for quadriplegics that will be steered via their brain waves.

4. As in the real world, sometimes those glitches are caused by external constraints. One girl's ambitious "vertical axis" wind-powered energy-generation experiment was set back when key elements took many months to be procured (from China). Another's effort to grow and then sort breast-cancer cells encountered a detour when it turned out that Fairfax County's ban on doing potentially hurtful experiments on "vertebrates" applied to the zebra fish that were to be the medium for this study.

5. http://www.fcps.edu/mediapub/pressrel/T.J.hsstadmissstats_class2015.pdf. (We found more current data at http://schoolprofiles.fcps.edu/schlprfl/f?p=108:13:283535994964042::::P0_CURRENT_SCHOOL_ID:300 and updated text accordingly. Note that the "missing" 2 percent of students [demographically] are "other" races.)

6. TJ students tend to stay through graduation. Fewer than 1 percent drop by the wayside because they fail to maintain the B average that the school requires. Another 7 or 8 percent leave because their families move, they weary of the commute, or they decide this isn't the right school for them. But more than nine in ten freshmen get TJ diplomas at the end of 12th grade.

7. This becomes an issue with overseas students whose parents are keen for them to attend TJ and for out-of-district youngsters. The school's admissions office takes considerable pains to verify their eligibility, demanding three separate documents to check the actual residency of both the applicant and his/her parent or guardian.

8. The application instructions can be found at http://www.tjhsst.edu/abouttj/admissions/apply_freshman_winter.html.

9. The test is described in detail at http://www.tjhsst.edu/abouttj/admissions/apply_freshman_winter_testing.htmlandathttp://www.tjhsst

.edu/abouttj/admissions/apply_freshman_winter_testing_getting%20 ready.html. The student handbook intended to acquaint applicants with the test, including sample tests, can be found at http://www.tjhsst.edu/ abouttj/admissions/forms/Fairfax_Stdnt_Hndbk_2011.pdf.

10. http://www.tjprep-va.com/tjhsstadmissstats_class2015.pdf.

11. See chapter 6 for additional background on the 2007 Supreme Court decision.

12. Six percent of TJ students are classified by Fairfax County as "other," meaning predominantly youngsters of mixed racial background.

13. Teachers said there was at least one instance of a group of Korean youngsters living, dorm-style, in an apartment of their own while attending TJ. One teacher also passed along the delicious rumor that there's a TJ prep program located *in* Seoul, though a *Washington Post* reporter who spent a recent year in Korea was unable to confirm that.

14. "Creaming" has been a big issue in some of the other school systems that are supposed to be served by TJ, and several of them have refused in some years to let their star pupils go there.

15. Fairfax County confers an extra GPA point for an AP course, meaning, for example, that an A-minus earned in an Advanced Placement course is scored at 4.7 instead of 3.7 in calculating a student's average. The county also adds an extra half point for many non-AP courses at TJ, in recognition of the fact that they are at least equivalent to "honors" classes at other schools and that some non-AP courses actually make the AP course in that subject a prerequisite.

16. English lit, government, U.S. history, and calculus.

17. For the course description, see http://www.tjhsst.edu/curriculum/ scitech/geo/geo.php. For the "defensive" portion, see the last page of that description. Note, though, that TJ students may also sit for the environmental sciences AP exam even without taking the course, and apparently many do.

18. A former principal remarked that the "de-staffing" challenges within FCPS were real and that, during his time at the school, he had the last word on no more than 80 percent of the teachers who came to work there.

19. The Partnership Fund's website shows an appeal for $10 million as part of the building renovation.

Chapter 15: Similarities and Differences

1. Subsequent to our visit, the District of Columbia announced plans to centralize and standardize admission to its several selective high schools, including SWW. New York and Chicago already do that, and Philadelphia—which we did not visit—reportedly does much the same thing.

Chapter 16: Dilemmas and Challenges

1.   James S. Coleman, "Some Points on Choice in Education," *Sociology of Education*, vol. 65, no. 4, October 1992.

2.   In many high schools today, parents play a role in determining—or at least influencing—their children's course-level placements.

3.   To our knowledge, such screening has not been promoted by the Advanced Placement or International Baccalaureate programs themselves but, rather, decided by individual schools, districts, and occasionally states.

4.   The 22,000 number includes combination schools that contain some lower grades as well as the traditional high school grades.

5.   Almost three-quarters of what we here term private "high schools" actually combine at least some of the earlier grades along with the high school grades. Education's private sector includes only about 3,000 "pure" high schools.

6.   "Stuyvesant High School 2010–2011 School Comprehensive Educational Plan (CEP) School Demographics and Accountability Snapshot," retrieved from http://schools.nyc.gov/SchoolPortals/02/M475/AboutUs/Statistics/default.htm.

7.   As best we can tell, only nine selective public high schools, all in New York City, use students' score rankings on a single exam as the sole criterion by which to determine whom among their many applicants to admit. Though that has been their practice for decades, it continues to raise concerns, as is evident in a recent move by New York State assemblyman Karim Camara to amend the law to make schools like Stuyvesant, Bronx Science, and Brooklyn Tech weigh applicants' grades and interviews as well as their test scores. Although other schools on our list take exam scores seriously (table 3.9), all the rest appear to incorporate some—occasionally many—other factors into their admission decisions.

8.   The schools' desire for alumni/ae contributions is beginning to make them more serious about keeping track of and in touch with their graduates.

9.   Atila Abdulkadiroglu, Joshua D. Angrist, and Parag A. Pathak, "The Elite Illusion: Achievement Effects at Boston and New York Exam Schools," working paper 17264, National Bureau of Economic Research, July 2011.

10.   Will Dobbie and Roland G. Fryer, Jr., "Exam High Schools and Academic Achievement: Evidence from New York City," working paper 17286, National Bureau of Economic Research, August 2011. A third study, this one by University of Houston economists, tracked the impact of attending academically rigorous "gifted and talented" middle schools in a southwest-

ern city (probably Houston) in which two such schools are oversubscribed by qualified applicants and use a lottery to determine who is admitted. The track records of those admitted could be compared with those of similarly qualified youngsters who enrolled elsewhere—though most likely in other gifted/talented programs offered by the same school system. The results are similar. See Sa Bui, Steven Craig, and Scott Imberman, "Poor Results for High Achievers," *Education Next*, vol. 12, no. 1, Winter 2012, available online at http://educationnext.org/poor-results-for-high-achievers/.

11. One study currently in progress focuses on the influence of STEM-focused high schools (several involved are on our list) on graduates' college studies and eventual professions. See R. Subotnik, R. H. Tai, R. Rickoff, and J. Almarode, "Specialized Public High Schools of Science, Mathematics, and Technology and the STEM Pipeline: What Do We Know Now and What Will We Know in 5 Years?" *Roeper Review*, vol. 32, 2010, 7–16.

12. Of the relatively small number that depart, the reason most often cited by school administrators is "not able to maintain academic standards." Others leave after deciding this isn't the school for them or that football matters more or the commute is too long or the family is relocating.

13. As many an education analyst knows from painful experience, any cross-school, cross-district, or cross-state comparison of budgets and expenditures is a nightmarish challenge throughout American public education.

14. We're mindful that earned degrees are no real gauge of teacher competence, but the doctorates, at least, hint at a measure of intellectual depth and seriousness on the part of instructors who, having earned them, choose the high school teaching route.

15. Of course, we've no idea what the principals are like in schools that didn't respond, or in the few schools that ignored or rebuffed our requests to visit.

16. Only a few schools on our list are charters, though several more enjoy a measure of freedom due to being state operated or university affiliated.

17. That's one reason why "congratulating" them for doing well on state tests and similar assessments is a bit circular. By and large, they don't admit kids who haven't already demonstrated their prowess on such metrics.

18. http://www.scarsdaleschools.k12.ny.us/cms/lib5/NY01001205/Centricity/Domain/89/ScarsdaleHSProfile.pdf.

19. http://www.usatoday.com/news/education/2010-02-04-1Aap scores04_ST_N.htm.

Chapter 17: Conclusions

1. See note 1 of the introduction.

2. See, for example, Steve Farkas, Ann Duffett, and Tom Loveless, "High-Achieving Students in the Era of No Child Left Behind," Thomas B. Fordham Institute, 2008, http://www.edexcellence.net/publications/high-achieving-students-in.html.

3. One among many overviews of "effective schools research" is by Marshall S. Smith and Stewart Purkey, "Too Soon to Cheer? Synthesis of Research on Effective Schools," which can be found at http://www.ascd.org/ASCD/pdf/journals/ed_lead/el_198212_purkey.pdf.

4. Also worthy of attention is the observation by Paul Hill and colleagues that "coherence" is central to the success of schools and that being tugged in multiple directions by diverse constituencies, incentives, funding streams, and such is damaging to school effectiveness. See, for example, Paul Hill and Mary Beth Celio, *Fixing Urban Schools* (Washington, DC: Brookings Institution Press, 1998).

5. James S. Coleman, "Some Points on Choice in Education," *Sociology of Education*, vol. 65, no. 4, October 1992.

Index

● ● ● ●